Enhancing Sexual Health, Self-Identity and
Wellbeing among Men who have Sex with Men

of related interest

Counselling Skills for Working with Shame
Christiane Sanderson
ISBN 978 1 84905 562 8
eISBN 978 1 78450 001 6
Part of the Essential Skills for Counselling *series*

Counselling Skills for Working with Gender Diversity and Identity
Michael Beattie and Penny Lenihan
ISBN 978 1 78592 741 6
eISBN 978 1 78450 481 6
Part of the Essential Skills for Counselling *series*

The A-Z of Gender and Sexuality
From Ace to Ze
Morgan Potts
ISBN 978 1 78592 342 5
eISBN 978 1 78450 663 6

Counseling Transgender and Non-Binary Youth
The Essential Guide
Irwin Krieger
ISBN 978 1 78592 743 0
eISBN 978 1 78450 482 3

Improving Mental Health through Social Support
Building Positive and Empowering Relationships
Jonathan Leach
ISBN 978 1 84905 518 5
eISBN 978 0 85700 932 6

Queer Sex
A Trans and Non-Binary Guide to Intimacy, Pleasure and Relationships
Juno Roche
ISBN 978 1 78592 406 4
eISBN 978 1 78450 770 1

Enhancing Sexual Health, Self-Identity and Wellbeing among Men who have Sex with Men

A GUIDE FOR PRACTITIONERS

RUSI JASPAL

Foreword by Professor Dame Glynis Breakwell
Foreword by Dr Laura Waters

Jessica Kingsley *Publishers*
London and Philadelphia

First published in 2018
by Jessica Kingsley Publishers
73 Collier Street
London N1 9BE, UK
and
400 Market Street, Suite 400
Philadelphia, PA 19106, USA

www.jkp.com

Copyright © Rusi Jaspal 2018
Foreword copyright © Glynis Breakwell 2018
Foreword copyright © Laura Waters 2018

All rights reserved. No part of this publication may be reproduced in any material form (including photocopying, storing in any medium by electronic means or transmitting) without the written permission of the copyright owner except in accordance with the provisions of the law or under terms of a licence issued in the UK by the Copyright Licensing Agency Ltd. www.cla.co.uk or in overseas territories by the relevant reproduction rights organisation, for details see www.ifrro.org. Applications for the copyright owner's written permission to reproduce any part of this publication should be addressed to the publisher.

Warning: The doing of an unauthorised act in relation to a copyright work may result in both a civil claim for damages and criminal prosecution.

Library of Congress Cataloging in Publication Data
A CIP catalog record for this book is available from the Library of Congress

British Library Cataloguing in Publication Data
A CIP catalogue record for this book is available from the British Library

ISBN 978 1 78592 322 7
eISBN 978 1 78450 636 0

Printed and bound in the United States

Contents

Foreword by Professor Dame Glynis Breakwell 7

Foreword by Dr Laura Waters 11

Acknowledgements 15

Part I: Introduction

1. Social Psychology for Practitioners in Sexual Health and Wellbeing 19

Part II: Theory and Research

2. Self-Identity, Psychological Wellbeing and Sexual Health among MSM. 35

3. Social Psychological Approaches to Promoting Health and Wellbeing. 61

4. Identity Process Theory: Social Representation, Identity and Action. 85

Part III: Practice

5. Promoting Psychological Wellbeing among MSM 117

6. Developing Effective Sexual Health Interventions for MSM 139

7. Integrating Tenets of Identity Theory into HIV Medicine 161

Part IV: Conclusion

8. Integrating Theory into Practice 185

References 197

Subject Index. 209

Author Index. 213

About the Author 215

Foreword
Professor Dame Glynis Breakwell

This book is about the role of identity processes in shaping the sexual health and wellbeing of men who have sex with men (MSM). It explores the complex reasons, rooted in culture and context, which underlie behaviours that might be misunderstood by observers or simplistically labelled reckless or self-harming. This is a book addressed to practitioners working to support the health and wellbeing of MSM. The book seeks to equip practitioners with methods derived from social psychological theories for explaining the behaviour of individuals, groups and communities who are at risk and who are asking for support. It argues that, used systematically and with common sense, these methods will enhance the effectiveness of the support that practitioners can offer and may result in enduring change for those in need of help.

Readers should be warned this is not a book that offers simple recipes for action by practitioners. It offers no 'one size fits all' mantras or solutions. It does not strip down the social psychological theories that it presents to their bare skeletons in order to make them palatable. The introductions it offers of these theories are accurate and cover what is necessary to make them really useful to an experienced practitioner. Getting the best out of this book requires readers to reflect on their own practice and think through how they would have intervened differently in some of their past cases if they had used the methods suggested by Jaspal.

The book does not restrict itself to solely discussing social psychological models for practitioner intervention, the succinct summaries of current biomedical methods are also useful. However Jaspal, not surprisingly given his eminence as a social psychological theorist, is particularly effective in describing the sources of stress experienced by MSM and the nature of the threats to identity that they generate. He uses identity process theory (IPT) extensively in this analysis. When I originally proposed the theory in the 1980s it was primarily as a way of understanding how people develop and deploy coping strategies when they are faced with a threat to their identity. Strangely, most researchers who have used IPT have been concerned with testing the model of identity structure and principles that it proposes. They have not focused on the analysis that it offers of the coping strategies that people use when threatened. In this book, Jaspal has used that analysis of coping strategies in a way that few other theorists attempted to do. For that I am personally grateful. It is about time that the emphasis turned to thinking about coping strategies. Without doubt, understanding and anticipating coping strategies is of prime importance to practitioners.

An essential ingredient in understanding coping strategies is to recognise that they can be very complex. They can reside in cognitive or emotional responses in the individual and they can be vested in the dynamic interactions between individuals and within and across groups in a community. This is probably why Jaspal argues that interventions to support people who face threats to identity should not always be individualised. His proposal that social representations theory can be used in concert with IPT to understand how sexual health and wellbeing among MSM might be enhanced is founded upon the argument that interventions can be better targeted if they take account of the communities in which the individual lives. Jaspal recognises the importance of communities in moderating the impact of practitioners' interventions. He encourages practitioners to understand how those communities can be brought to bear upon the enhancement of interventions. One interesting exemplar he uses is the role of virtual, internet-based communities in the creation and maintenance of identity for MSM. Identity in these cases is embedded in an extended community which is digital – a community which can be both a source of threat and of coping.

The approach towards the enhancement of sexual health and wellbeing suggested in this book is not only relevant to MSM. It is an approach which can inform any practitioner who is attempting to understand how to help any person facing identity threat. Threats to identity come in many, many forms - from physical injury to memory loss or from social stigmatisation to job loss. The lessons to be learned from this book are relevant to many contexts. A person's identity is a dynamic, evolving system – being created over a lifetime. Supporting and channelling that evolution is often a most valuable task of a practitioner.

Glynis Breakwell
January 2018

Foreword

Dr Laura Waters

As a clinician working in sexual health and HIV, the disproportionate impact of sexually transmitted infections (STIs) on MSM, particularly from Black and Minority Ethnic (BME) communities, is an issue I face daily. Public Health England's 2017 report highlighted that MSM and BME groups, along with young heterosexuals, experience the greatest impact of STIs. MSM form a small proportion of the UK population, yet account for the majority of syphilis and gonorrhoea cases. 2016 syphilis figures showed the highest rates of infection since 1949, and almost doubling since just 2012, mostly in MSM. This yielded many headlines. The same report illustrated the highest population STI rates amongst Black individuals, particularly those of Caribbean origin, and attributed this to a "complex interplay of cultural, socio-economic and behavioural factors". Recent years have seen outbreaks of other STIs in MSM including the enteric infections Shigella and hepatitis A, the latter compounded by shortages of hepatitis A vaccine. Yet there was also some good news. The "undetectable =untransmissible" or "U=U" message, that is, individuals taking HIV drugs that render the virus undetectable on a sustained basis cannot transmit HIV to their sexual partners, really gained hold with even the Centres for Disease Control and Prevention (CDC) in the US supporting the message. Additionally, dramatic declines in new HIV diagnoses in MSM in England highlighted that better testing, earlier HIV treatment and targeted prevention (including PrEP) provide us with the tools to ultimately stop new HIV infections. However, eradication of HIV can be achieved only by diagnosing the 13% of people currently living with undiagnosed HIV in the UK. Barriers to testing related to ethnicity and self-identified sexuality are significant.

Having admired the work of Professor Jaspal on sexual risk-taking and the experiences of people living with HIV, and his awareness-raising related to the issues faced by BME MSM, it was an honour to be asked to write a foreword for this book! His publication on polarised press reporting related to HIV pre-exposure prophylaxis (PrEP) was particularly pertinent to someone who spent many months contributing to a subsequently abandoned NHS England policy – an unfortunate triumph of fear of risk (and spending) over hope. I hope the PrEP Impact trial, borne of the original policy, will answer some of the ongoing questions related to PrEP use in BME communities.

This book describes, in an eloquent and approachable manner, the relationships between identity, sexual risk and wellbeing. The three cases summarised in Part 1 will be all too familiar to professionals engaged in sexual health care and STI prevention. As a doctor well versed in biomedical aspects of our specialty, this book was a sobering reminder that my knowledge and use of psychosocial questioning is limited. Part 2 highlights the psychological impact of social stressors, particularly the section on homonegativity, and, in the same chapter, a description of potential benefits of geospatial apps (so often associated with negative STI and drug use connotations) related to sexual identity and negotiation of condom use. The summary of counselling psychology was highly informative and the author's linking of different approaches back to the Chapter 1 cases particularly helpful. Similarly, the linkage of the section on theories of behaviour change to the same three cases puts the three models in a context that, for me, rendered the descriptions far more meaningful. Having established the importance of psychosocial factors with regards to MSM sexual health outcomes, identity and wellbeing, Chapter 4 describes social and identity theories and, crucially, the relevance to sexual health practitioners; I was inspired by the benefits of intergroup strategies, particularly as my local service uses a group work model for sexual dysfunction, coping with an HIV diagnosis and risk-reduction for people with hepatitis C. Finally, Part 3 describes practice. In Chapter 5 we learn about promotion of psychological wellbeing through two case studies: self-identity in British Pakistani Muslim MSM (I found 'religious representations of sexuality' particularly enlightening) and the psychosocial challenges surrounding a new HIV diagnosis (especially the evidence-based reminder about stigma). Chapter 6 uses more case studies to describe the development of effective sexual health interventions including a sauna project in Leicester and the 'Selfie' project, part of Public Health England's BME MSM project. Finally, Chapter 7 outlines how HIV practice can be enhanced by identity theory, focusing on PrEP and HIV medication adherence; the latter topic was a real wake-up for me that the advances in HIV drugs do not necessarily negate the barriers patients experience when expected to take the medication daily. Each chapter in Part 3 ends with a must-read section on 'implications for practitioners', with important lessons that I intend to incorporate in my teaching and my practice.

As we struggle with rising rates of some STIs, it is our duty to ensure our increasingly limited resources are utilised effectively, and herein lies that evidence and how we can use this to best optimise our interventions. This book summarises a wealth of evidence and examples into a highly informative, even essential, read for all working with MSM.

In England, recent years have seen marked reductions in public health spending with a direct impact on sexual health services including clinic closures. 2018 sees the launch of online STI services and it remains to be seen how well these address not just disease detection and management, but also tailored sexual health promotion and risk reduction advice. However, despite the challenges we face, I am proud to be part of a committed and multi-disciplinary specialty and will be recommending this book to the doctors, nurses, support staff, psychologists, health advisors, outreach workers, epidemiologists and researchers who do so much to improve the sexual wellbeing of MSM. I will end by suggesting that this book is also an essential read for the commissioners who have to decide how best to spend their constrained sexual health funds. Cutting psychosocial support and access to interventions may seem a quick-win from a spending regard but without understanding, and addressing, the drivers of poor sexual health this may ultimately prove the falsest of economies.

Laura Waters
January 2018

Acknowledgements

This book is the culmination of numerous research projects exploring self-identity, wellbeing and sexual health among men who have sex with men (MSM). I am grateful to my co-workers and PhD students over the years who have contributed to these projects and without whom the research described in this book would never have come to fruition. I thank my PhD students Zaqia Rehman and Sebastian Cordoba for their insightful comments on my original musings in relation to this book. I am particularly thankful to Periklis Papaloukas who worked as a research assistant on the Public Health England-funded projects outlined in Chapter 6, to Dr Joann Griffith who has been a constant source of valuable insight into the counselling psychology models described in Chapter 3, and to Dr Barbara Lopes whose clinical psychological expertise has been invaluable. This book has benefitted enormously from Dr Jake Bayley's meticulous and constructive feedback, especially on Chapter 2, as well as his rigorous critical evaluation of the role that social sciences research can play in HIV medicine. I acknowledge the input of Professor Julie Fish and Dr Iain Williamson, both of De Montfort University, who collaborated with me on the Black and Minority Ethnic MSM Project, which is discussed in Chapter 6. This book has indirectly benefitted from discussions with fellow members of the Medical Board of NAZ Project London. I should like to acknowledge the input of Tanya Edwards, my former personal assistant, who provided impeccable administrative support during the composition of this book and indeed the research projects that preceded it. I am very grateful to De Montfort University (UK) and Åbo Akademi University (Finland), my two academic homes, for providing stimulating research environments for my scholarly activities. Finally, I would like to thank Babak Hessamian, not only for his love, encouragement and unwavering support in everything that I do, but also for his unremitting patience with me during the writing of this and other books.

Part I

INTRODUCTION

Chapter 1

Social Psychology for Practitioners in Sexual Health and Wellbeing

Gay, bisexual and other men who have sex with men (MSM) can face a series of psychosocial challenges during the life course. Some of these challenges are transient and short-lived, while others persist over time. Some are societal in nature, while others are psychological in origin. Individuals may encounter homophobia, stigma, and rejection from others. They may perceive aspects of identity (such as their sexual orientation) to be problematic, internalise stigma, and experience feelings of low self-worth, guilt and shame. The antecedents of these social and psychological challenges are multifarious and include the presence of particular stereotypes, images and representations in our social context, as well as specific past experiences that shape our perspectives on our identities and the world around us. The consequences of these social and psychological challenges can be similarly far-reaching and impinge on various dimensions of our lives, not least on sexual health and psychological wellbeing. Some individuals may come to experience shame, anxiety and depression, and engage in behaviours that can put their sexual health at risk.

The tripartite relationship between sexual health, self-identity and wellbeing constitutes the focus of this volume. The inter-relations between these three components will be outlined and discussed in the chapters that follow. The following three cases illustrate and exemplify the social and psychological challenges faced by MSM, as well as the ways in which wellbeing and sexual health may be affected:

Case 1: Mark, an HIV-negative gay man

Mark is a 27-year-old gay man who has recently moved from a small town in Derbyshire to London, having completed his studies. When he arrived in London six months ago, Mark immediately took full advantage of his new life in the capital and was keen to make new friends, to socialise and to explore the gay scene in London. He rented a flat with three other gay friends in an area with a large gay population. Given that his hometown in Derbyshire did not have any gay bars or clubs, he was particularly excited about exploring the gay scene in London and was sure that he would enjoy it. Mark downloaded Grindr[1] on his phone and was delighted to see that there were so many gay men in his neighbourhood. He compared this to his experience of being gay in Derbyshire, which had felt very lonely, and now felt elated to be in such a gay-friendly city. Each time he opened Grindr on his phone, he was propositioned by attractive gay men and ended up meeting two or three new guys a week. He liked the fact that there were so many guys on the application and he felt that he was making up for the disappointing sex life he had had in his home town. Mark also discovered that there were two gay saunas in his area, which he began to frequent in order to meet sexual partners. He had never had so much sex before. Mark knew about HIV and that people could catch it from not using a condom. However, given that the guys he was meeting did not 'appear' to have HIV, he did not see himself as being at risk. Although he had condoms at home, sometimes he did not bother using them, especially if condom use was not suggested by his sexual partners. On one occasion, he was invited to a chemsex[2] party in his neighbourhood. Although slightly nervous at first, Mark went along to see what it was like. Most of the guys at the party were taking drugs and eventually Mark was offered drugs too and accepted. Suddenly, he felt an enormous bout of confidence and felt able to approach

---

1   Grindr is a gay geospatial mobile social networking application (see detailed overview in Chapter 2).
2   The term 'chemsex' refers to the use of psychoactive drugs in sexualised settings (see detailed overview in Chapter 2).

guys that he found attractive. He greatly enjoyed the sex he had that night. Since that night, Mark has regularly attended chemsex parties, and no longer enjoys sober sex as much. These days Mark goes to parties almost every weekend and, while it was just a bit of fun at the beginning, now it feels as if it is taking over his life. He no longer feels as able to concentrate on other things in his life, like his friends, his job and his new boyfriend. Many of the people who matter to Mark seem to be distancing themselves from him and he feels increasingly lonely. Recently, Mark noticed a white sore around his anus and booked an appointment with his doctor who diagnosed him with both syphilis and rectal gonorrhoea. Though he tested negative for HIV, the doctor informed him that he was at high risk of infection. This has made Mark reflect on his life in London. He realises that he does not really enjoy the casual sexual encounters he has been having and that he often regrets them afterwards. He feels fearful of getting HIV as he now realises that he is at significant risk. Mark wants to make some changes in his life but does not know where to begin. It feels as if a lot of things need to change but Mark wonders what his life will be like if he makes these changes.

Case 2: Ahmed, a British Muslim gay man

Ahmed is a 25-year-old British Pakistani Muslim gay man. He grew up in a conservative Muslim family in a large Pakistani community in inner-city Bradford. Most of his neighbours, family friends and school friends were, like him, of Pakistani background, and he had almost no friends of other ethnic backgrounds. From a very early age, Ahmed realised that he was attracted to men but did not understand why he felt this way and what this meant. He felt abnormal and ashamed of himself and initially tried to fight his same-sex attraction. When Ahmed went to the mosque and began to read the Koran, he came to believe that his feelings were sinful and that he must attempt to change them. As a teenager, he convinced himself that his feelings were transient and that he would eventually change and become heterosexual. At school, other boys would tease Ahmed and call him gay because he did not like to play football and because most of his friends were girls. These early experiences of teasing and bullying caused Ahmed immense psychological distress and made him feel inadequate. He became withdrawn at school and in other contexts. After a while, rumours began to circulate about Ahmed's sexual orientation and soon several of his classmates joined in and bullied him. Some even threatened him with physical violence. These experiences, coupled with his early belief that homosexuality was sinful, led Ahmed to believe that he was right all along – that being gay was a terrible thing and that the bullies were in fact right to treat him as they did. Ahmed tried to immerse himself in religion as a means of distancing himself from his sexual orientation but, as he got older, he found it increasingly difficult to resist sexual urges. He watched gay porn online but always felt awful about himself afterwards – this made him feel confused, guilty and dirty. He downloaded Grindr on his smart phone and began to meet up with guys for sex. These experiences too contributed to his sense of low self-worth and perceived immorality. One of the men he met on Grindr invited him to a gay club in London. Ahmed felt uneasy about going to a club where he might be recognised and 'outed' to other people, but decided to take the risk and accepted the invitation. In the club he felt immensely uncomfortable and at times even feared that God would deliver some form of divine punishment to him for being in that environment. Now that Ahmed has completed his degree at the University of Bradford, his parents have begun to discuss arranged marriage and to introduce him to potential spouses – the daughters of relatives and family friends. This has made him feel very anxious and conflicted. On the one hand, he knows he feels no attraction to women but, on the other hand, he believes that an arranged marriage could be an effective 'distraction' from his gay lifestyle. Sometimes Ahmed refuses to discuss marriage with his parents, which has caused them to become suspicious. Ahmed in turn is fearful of the consequences – both for himself and for his family's reputation – if people in his community find out that he is gay. Ahmed is feeling increasingly depressed, anxious and helpless. He cannot imagine having a relationship with another man, even though deep down he would like to. The idea of a relationship scares him so he just meets other guys for sex. Ahmed's use of Grindr has increased significantly and he is now meeting more and more guys for casual sex. He does not really understand why he is doing this.

Case 3: Juan, a gay man living with HIV

Juan is a 33-year-old gay man from Spain. He was diagnosed with HIV at a gay men's health charity in his hometown during the summer of 2014. As he did not view his sexual behaviour as risky, Juan expected to receive a negative test result and was thus shocked to learn that he was in fact HIV-positive. The gay men's health charity referred Juan to the local hospital to confirm the reactive test result. Although his CD4 count was still relatively high, Juan requested to initiate antiretroviral therapy (ART) immediately. Still shocked at his diagnosis, Juan viewed his medication as an unfortunate daily reminder of his HIV infection. Moreover, days after initiating treatment, Juan began to experience negative physical side effects. He discussed his side effects with one of the doctors at the clinic, who was dismissive and unhelpful. The doctor appeared to be suggesting that this is what life with HIV is like and that Juan should simply get used to it. Juan felt that the doctor was unsympathetic towards him because he was gay and living with HIV. This situation was further complicated by the fact that Juan had a very difficult relationship with his family. As a child, he suffered sexual abuse, and he felt let-down by his parents who never acknowledged this. He felt unable to disclose his HIV status to his family, with whom he was living at the time of his diagnosis. In fact, given his strict Catholic upbringing, he also felt unable to come out as gay and, thus, he felt that he had to conceal both his sexual identity and his HIV status from significant others. This made him resent his parents. Although Juan did have a small group of HIV-positive friends from whom he derived some social support, he viewed himself as different from them and implicitly stigmatised his own friends, whom he regarded as responsible for their infection. A year after his diagnosis, Juan decided to move to London to distance himself from his family and in order to 'be himself'. However, he felt lonely in London. Concerned about his declining health, Juan registered as a patient at his local sexual health clinic. His HIV consultant advised him to initiate ART immediately, reassuring him that he would be well looked after and that any side effects would be dealt with. However, Juan, still distrustful of medical professionals following his experience in Spain, initially refused treatment. This posed a dilemma for him because, on the one hand, he was well aware of his poor disease prognosis in the absence of medication but, on the other hand, he did not wish to think about his HIV infection and feared further side effects and indifference from his medical team. In view of a significant drop in his CD4 count, Juan reluctantly began ART. With his new drug regimen, he experienced no physical side effects but did continue to experience psychological adversity, including loneliness, depression and shame. Juan decided not to attend support groups, partly because he did not wish to disclose his HIV status to others and because he did not think he would have anything in common with other support group attendees. Indeed, he continued to deny that he had engaged in sexual risk behaviours in an attempt to differentiate himself from others living with HIV. As Juan's mental health has begun to deteriorate, he is missing doses of his medication, which has increased the risk of drug resistance and of onward HIV transmission to his sexual partners. He finds it difficult to discuss these issues with his doctor and has also started to miss appointments. To deal with his feelings of loneliness, Juan is meeting sexual partners online and in gay bars. After facing rejection from potential sexual partners to whom he has disclosed his HIV status, he feels more ashamed and distressed about being HIV-positive. He has started to attend chemsex parties in London because nobody asks him his status there, allowing him to forget about HIV and to experience a sense of connection and intimacy with other men. Juan now has a detectable viral load but is not consistently using condoms with sexual partners of unknown HIV status.

This is not a book about chemsex in London, difficulties in adjusting to an HIV diagnosis among Spanish gay men, or the potential incompatibilities between religion and homosexuality among British Muslim gay men *per se*. Rather, this book is about the things that these cases have in common, namely the role of identity in determining sexual health and wellbeing outcomes among MSM. The cases allude to changes in personal and social circumstances, the desire to gain and maintain a sense of control and competence in complex situations, and the impact that events and circumstances can have on one's sense of self-worth. They demonstrate that the reasons underlying behaviours that some observers may perceive to be reckless and irresponsible actually have more complex underpinnings that are rooted in culture, context and identity. They emphasise the impact that self-identity and sexual health can have for psychological wellbeing.

The cases also raise a series of challenging questions among practitioners who may work with the individuals described in them. How can HIV risk and HIV prevention be communicated to Mark in a way that will lead to effective and enduring behaviour change? How can he be supported to disengage from chemsex in a way that does not stigmatise him and that does not disrupt his life narrative? Why is Ahmed experiencing such distress in relation to being Muslim and gay? Why does he not just distance himself from his religion if this is deemed to be incompatible with his sexual orientation? Why does he appear to be taking more sexual risks now that he has problems at home? Despite his knowledge of HIV and of the effectiveness of ART, why is Juan so reluctant to initiate and to adhere to ART? Why does he actively avoid other people living with HIV? How can he be retained in HIV care? More generally, how can practitioners be better equipped to support Mark, Ahmed and Juan with their sexual health and wellbeing needs? The overarching aim of this volume is to draw attention to these challenging questions and to equip practitioners with the social psychological tools for understanding the tripartite relationship between self-identity, sexual health and wellbeing; for developing effective clinical practice cognisant of this tripartite relationship; and for constructing theory-driven public health interventions. A central thesis of this volume is that a combination of both individual and public health interventions is required in order to address the aforementioned questions and to enact effective and enduring change in patients.

In view of the multi-level nature of this project – focusing on both individual health and public health – social psychology seems the ideal starting-point. Social psychology is essentially the study of how the individual interacts with the social world — the individual's cognition, emotion and behaviour is understood to be shaped by the social world (Jaspal and Breakwell 2014). Social psychology thus focuses on individual cognition, social influence processes, relationships with others and how people think, feel and behave as group members. Social psychologists have a long-standing interest in solving problems. They tend to favour methodological approaches, such as experiments and interviews, to understand the ways in which people think and behave and, crucially, to try to *predict* how people will think and behave in particular contexts. Description is important because it enables us to understand the past and present, but prediction is equally as important because it enables us to foresee, with varying degrees of accuracy, future events. While some social psychological theories describe, others predict.

Given that the description and prediction of attitudes and behaviour have constituted the principal focus of social psychology, it is easy to see why social psychologists have made such important contributions to the field of sexual health, self-identity and wellbeing among MSM. After all, if one can understand how and why people have engaged in risk behaviours in the past, one is better positioned to develop individual and public health interventions for preventing these behaviours in the future. For instance, Juan (Case 3) is clearly experiencing significant psychosocial challenges in relation to his HIV diagnosis, due in part to social stigma in Spain, his religious background which he perceives to be homonegative, and fears of rejection from sexual partners. These issues appear to be associated with his decreased self-care and increased engagement in sexual risk-taking behaviours. Furthermore, his poor experience of HIV care seems to be related to his current disengagement from services. In short, by understanding some of these psychosocial issues, practitioners may be able to tailor HIV care in ways that acknowledge them and, thus, maximise the likelihood of access to and retention in care. It may be possible to predict engagement and retention in care and to focus efforts on those less likely to be engaged and retained in care. Moreover, this can provide scope for enhancing among practitioners cultural competence in relation to patients.

Much social psychological research is grounded in robust theory that has been tested and validated in other empirical contexts. It therefore gives us a head start in terms of understanding what has worked and indeed failed in analogous contexts. In Part 2 of this volume, relevant theory and research from social psychology in relation to MSM is presented. Overall, this volume constitutes an attempt to highlight and discuss how social psychological theory and research can empower practitioners in sexual health and wellbeing among MSM.

Some definitions

From the outset it is useful to provide some definitions. The title of this volume refers to 'men who have sex with men'; it points to three concepts – sexual health, self-identity and wellbeing – each with long-standing traditions of research, theory and commentary from a multitude of disciplinary approaches; and it identifies a community of beneficiaries, namely 'practitioners'. Each requires commentary.

Identity is a complex construct. It is especially complex in the context of sexuality due in part to the stigma that is often appended to some sexual identity categories. Most same-sex attracted men in Western, industrialised societies, such as the UK, self-identify as gay and they may express great pride in their gay identity. A smaller minority self-identifies as bisexual. However, it must be noted that some same-sex attracted men reject these categories as inaccurate descriptors of their sexual identity. They may attempt to eschew the social stigma appended to gay and bisexual identities, which may be particularly acute in some social and cultural contexts, as exemplified in Cases 2 and 3 above. Some same-sex attracted men may in fact self-identify as heterosexual and cite various reasons for doing so, such as 'I only have sex with men but feel no emotional attachment to them' or 'I am only top[3] when I have sex with men and so I'm not really gay'. Some may self-identify as 'queer', claiming that the categories 'gay' and 'bisexual' are restrictive. It is also noteworthy that (sexual) identity categories only really become available to people in particular social and cultural contexts. In some Middle Eastern societies, sex between men has always occurred but there has never been a category like 'gay' in public discourse, so same-sex attracted men have never self-identified in those terms.

---

3 The terms 'top' and 'bottom' refer to insertive and receptive sexual partners, respectively.

While debates around identity politics are acknowledged, in this book the more inclusive category 'men who have sex with men' is employed. The category deliberately eschews the construct of sexual identity and includes all of the groups of same-sex attracted men described above. The term focuses on sexual behaviour, rather than identity.

The concept of sexual health is to be understood in the broadest sense, encompassing aspects of both physical and psychosocial health in relation to sexuality. It concerns not only the absence of disease but also the promotion of sexual wellbeing. The World Health Organisation (2006, p.5) describes it aptly as 'a state of physical, emotional, mental and social wellbeing in relation to sexuality'. It is thus essential to consider the factors that may lead to the incidence of sexual transmitted infections (STIs), such as HIV, but also their emotional, mental and social consequences. More generally, it is important to explore how individuals think, feel and behave in relation to their sexuality and the implications for wellbeing. This can include sexual orientation (such as being gay, bisexual, heterosexual or something else) and sexual practices and preferences (such as the desire to engage in group sex or to use drugs in sexualised settings) which may impact on psychological wellbeing.

As elaborated in Chapter 4, 'self-identity' refers to the psychological image that the individual has of himself.[4] It is essentially the answer the individual provides to the question, 'Who am I?' The answer is subjective but it is certainly informed by external sources, such as social images, norms and representations. Self-identity will encompass aspects that are derived from the individual's experience, including their group memberships, relationships with others, individual traits and so on. The unique constellation of these various aspects is what makes each individual's self-identity unique and distinctive. The concept is useful for explaining and predicting human attitudes and behaviour, as self-identity often provides a lens for attitude formation and for the adoption of particular behaviours.

The concept of wellbeing is nebulous and can refer to a multitude of distinct but inter-related phenomena. Here it is defined as the state of psychological equilibrium between the challenges one faces and the

---

4 The pronoun 'he' is used throughout the book, as this is the pronoun most commonly used by cisgender men.

resources one possesses for dealing with these challenges (Dodge et al. 2012). As outlined in Chapter 4, the individual will regularly face challenges (also thought of in terms of threats to identity), some of which will be relatively trivial and transient and others which will be more serious and chronic. In any case, these challenges undermine one's state of wellbeing. This may be described in terms of 'feeling down' or 'sad' or 'anxious' and so on. However, the individual will have a series of coping strategies available to him. As indicated in Chapter 4, there are many factors – both social and psychological – that determine which coping strategies are available to the individual. These factors can either extend or limit the individual's capacity to cope with adversity. The ability to select strategies for coping effectively with challenges will in turn determine the extent to which the individual experiences wellbeing. Conversely, the inability to cope effectively, due, for instance, to the absence of coping strategies, will shift the equilibrium in favour of the life challenge, thereby undermining wellbeing.

The primary beneficiaries of this volume are practitioners who work with MSM. The term 'practitioner' is employed to refer to medical, nursing, mental health and other health practitioners, as well as those involved in the design and implementation of public health interventions to enhance sexual health, self-identity and wellbeing among MSM. Essentially, this can include any professional who practises in the field of health. In particular, this volume is intended to enhance clinical practice among sexual health and HIV physicians and other professionals who seek to prevent and to treat HIV infection among MSM, among psychologists working with MSM, and public health specialists who design and implement interventions for sexual health, self-identity and wellbeing.

The benefits of social psychology for practice

An important objective of sexual health and HIV physicians is the medical treatment of HIV and other STIs. The biomedical model of treatment is understandably prevalent in the medical profession. There is variation in the extent to which medical professionals enquire about aspects of self-identity, wellbeing and the psychosocial aspects of sexual health among their patients. This variation can be attributed to cultural factors, individual differences, constraints on the practitioner's time and resources, and the practitioner's level of cultural competence around issues relevant to MSM (Daramilas and Jaspal 2017). Physicians may not necessarily ask their HIV patients about their personal lives, such as whether or not they are currently in a romantic relationship, whether or not they have disclosed their HIV status to family and friends, and how they feel about their HIV status. In some cases, the sole aim may be to monitor the viral load of the patient, to ensure that their CD4 count is satisfactorily high, and to ensure that HIV-related diseases and complications are managed effectively. The physician may feel more comfortable discussing with their patients the physiological, rather than psychological, aspects of living with HIV and the principal concern may be the biomedical treatment of the condition, rather than psychological support. The biomedical approach is consistent with the training, knowledge and expertise of most physicians. Psychological health may be viewed only as the domain of psychologists, psychiatrists or counsellors. It is acknowledged that most physicians do utilise screening questions to tap into psychopathology, such as depression and anxiety, and refer their patients to relevant members of the interdisciplinary team, such as psychologists. However, a key argument in this volume is that an understanding of the psychosocial aspects of both sexual health and HIV, more specifically, could greatly enhance clinical practice in this field.

Similarly, the area of sexual health promotion and HIV prevention could benefit from greater insight into psychosocial underpinnings. For instance, MSM who are diagnosed with a bacterial rectal STI and, more generally, those who report unprotected anal intercourse with partners of unknown HIV status are at high risk of HIV infection. Medical professionals seek to inform patients about the risks associated with particular sexual behaviours in order to promote behaviour change and to encourage the adoption of preventative behaviours. Condom use is advocated, although it must be acknowledged that condom use is inconsistent among many MSM. Indeed, as discussed in Chapter 2, MSM may use condoms inconsistently, not necessarily because of a lack of awareness or understanding of HIV risk, but rather due to various social and psychological factors that may impede it. The information deficit model approach assumes that the more information one provides, the more likely it is that patients will internalise this information and behave in accordance with it. However, there is now considerable evidence that psychosocial factors, and especially identity concerns, can override awareness, understanding and reason as determinants of particular behaviours (see Jaspal, Nerlich and Cinnirella 2014). This volume therefore provides an overview and analysis of several of the psychosocial issues that can impede the adoption of sexual health promotion and HIV prevention behaviours, such as condom use and the uptake of pre-exposure prophylaxis (PrEP), among MSM.

Counselling psychologists and other mental health practitioners who work with MSM are familiar with issues concerning sexual health, self-identity and wellbeing. These dimensions of MSM's lives may constitute sources of low self-esteem, shame, anxiety and depression. They may be the principal reason for seeking psychological support. Indeed, many practitioners in this field specialise in the psychosocial aspects of HIV diagnosis, sexual risk-taking, poor self-image, and general wellbeing problems. As outlined in Chapter 3, there are several therapeutic approaches to counselling psychology – each with its own theoretical and epistemological underpinnings. These approaches all have a high level of effectiveness in promoting wellbeing in MSM, although each is better suited to some areas of psychological distress than to others. A key tenet of this volume is that holistic, integrative approaches are likely to be more effective in psychotherapy around complex, interconnected issues, such as sexual health, self-identity and wellbeing. This volume provides an overview of these interconnected issues and places particular emphasis on the construct of identity in practice with MSM.

It has been demonstrated that the most successful public health interventions are those that are grounded in robust empirical research and underpinned by theories of behaviour change (Fish *et al.* 2016). Unfortunately, some public health interventions, including those that aim to reduce the risk of acquiring HIV and other STIs and to enhance wellbeing in MSM, are not actually guided by any particular theoretical approach. The effectiveness of such interventions is likely to be limited. There are several possible theories of behaviour change that can be drawn upon in the design and implementation of behavioural interventions. However, these theories are often multi-faceted, complex and difficult to operationalise. This can increase the temptation of utilising aspects of one model, rather than appreciating the opportunities afforded by the integration of various models. Furthermore, identity concerns are often overlooked in public health interventions, partly because such a focus is deemed to be incompatible with the dominant theoretical approach favoured by the practitioner. This volume provides insight into how behavioural interventions for enhancing sexual health, self-identity and wellbeing may be optimised.

Overview

The second part of this volume focuses on theory and research relevant to sexual health, self-identity and wellbeing among MSM. In Chapter 2, epidemiological and social psychological data are outlined and discussed. There is a focus on sexual health and HIV epidemiological data, the psychological impact of social stressors that can lead to identity concerns and poor sexual health and wellbeing, and various sexual health and HIV risk practices. Chapter 3 provides an overview of dominant models and approaches that may guide the work of practitioners working with MSM. The chapter presents a review of the key therapeutic frameworks from counselling psychology, which can be utilised in order to address sexual health, self-identity and wellbeing issues among MSM, and on the social psychological models that can inform social, behavioural and public health interventions in this population. A key focus of this volume is self-identity and the processes that guide its construction and protection. Accordingly, Chapter 4 outlines the major tenets of social representations theory, which is a descriptive theory of how people make sense of the world, and identity process theory, which is a model of identity construction, threat and coping. It is suggested that these social psychological theories ought to inform the design and implementation of both therapeutic approaches and public health interventions for enhancing sexual health, self-identity and wellbeing among MSM. The third part of this volume focuses on three areas of practice, namely promoting psychological wellbeing, developing effective sexual health interventions, and integrating tenets of identity theory in HIV medicine. In all three chapters, the focus is on promoting health and wellbeing among MSM. The chapters present relevant case studies and data from previous research in these areas, an overview of possible therapeutic and behavioural interventions and, most importantly, recommendations for enhancing practice in these areas. The final part and chapter of this volume attempts to integrate theories from social psychology and public health in future work with MSM. A 'toolkit' for practitioners is presented.

Part II

THEORY AND RESEARCH

Chapter 2

Self-Identity, Psychological Wellbeing and Sexual Health among MSM

This chapter focuses on aspects of self-identity, psychological wellbeing and sexual health among MSM. Epidemiological data concerning STI and HIV incidence, and social psychological research data concerning various social, psychological and health outcomes in MSM are provided. These data demonstrate the significant sexual health inequalities faced by MSM and highlight the need to develop effective strategies for addressing them. Some of the emerging challenges in relation to sexual health, identity and wellbeing are discussed. These are regarded as possible antecedents to psychological adversity and sexual risk-taking behaviour. These challenges include adverse experiences in childhood, external and internal homonegativity, chemsex or drug use in sexualised settings, condomless sex, sex-seeking on geospatial gay social networking applications, and sexual compulsivity. Throughout this chapter, there is a focus on the various socio-structural factors that can impinge on MSM's health and wellbeing, such as homonegativity, stigma and exclusion. The chapter concludes with an overview of the challenges and possible means of counteracting adverse health and wellbeing outcomes in MSM.

The epidemiology of STIs and HIV among MSM

Although MSM are estimated to represent just 2 per cent of the London population, a recent epidemiological report by Public Health England (2015b) showed that MSM constituted 28 per cent of the STI diagnoses recorded in the city in 2014, which demonstrates the significant sexual health inequalities faced by individuals in this population. The incidence of syphilis and gonorrhoea is particularly high – indeed, 90 per cent of all syphilis cases and 69 per cent of gonorrhoea cases were all among MSM. There was a 14 per cent increase in syphilis diagnoses between 2015 and 2016, and 23 per cent of chlamydia infections were among MSM (Public Health England 2017b). The incidence of Shigella (a bacterial infection spread through oral-faecal contact) has seen a three-fold increase in MSM since 2012. Some of the possible reasons underlying the high STI incidence include the higher number of sexual partners reported by MSM, the increasing practice of condomless sex in this group, the growing prevalence of chemsex and low levels of awareness of some STIs, such as Shigella. The high STI incidence in MSM is concerning particularly in view of reports of antibiotic resistance – some strains of gonorrhoea are no longer responding to antibiotics and, although less common, antibiotic resistance has also been detected in syphilis and chlamydia.

MSM also face significant inequalities in relation to HIV infection. HIV is a virus which attacks CD4 lymphocytes, an important type of white blood cell which is central to healthy immune functioning. The virus hijacks CD4 cells and replicates within them, ultimately destroying the original cells. This process continues until the infected individual's CD4 cells are entirely depleted, leading to the onset of opportunistic diseases and infections which can be fatal. HIV is the virus that causes autoimmune deficiency syndrome (AIDS). A non-infected individual will have between 500–1500 CD4 cells/mm^3. An HIV-positive individual is clinically defined as having AIDS when their CD4 cell count has dropped below 200 cells/mm^3 or when they have one or more AIDS-defining illnesses, such as Kaposi Sarcoma or Pneumocystis jiroveci Pneumonia. Since the first clinical observations of AIDS in 1981, 78 million people have been infected with HIV and 35 million have died of AIDS (UNAIDS 2017). There is no known vaccine or cure for HIV/AIDS. However, the illness is now treatable with ART, which can inhibit disease progression by interfering with the ability of HIV to replicate. Therefore, in countries in which ART is widely available, HIV is now considered to be a life-altering, rather than life-limiting, chronic condition. It has been found that patients who are diagnosed early (defined as CD4 count >500 cells/mm^3) and who initiate ART soon after diagnosis have a good prognosis, although it must also be acknowledged that HIV patients tend to experience more health problems and earlier ageing than uninfected individuals (Smith *et al.* 2012).

HIV remains a pressing public health concern, which disproportionately affects MSM in Western industrialised societies, such as the UK. HIV prevalence in the UK is approximately 0.18 per cent of the population aged between 15 and 59 – according to the 2015 HIV epidemiology report (Public Health England 2015b), some 103,700 people are currently living with the chronic condition in the UK. However, approximately 45,000 MSM were living with HIV in 2014, and in London it is estimated that one in 11 MSM is HIV-positive. In 2014, there were 5850 new diagnosed cases of (sexually transmitted) HIV, of which 57 per cent were among MSM. There are a number of reasons for the continued incidence of HIV in MSM, several of which are discussed below. In addition to the biological risk factors, such as the fact that receptive anal intercourse is a high-risk transmission route, there are several psychosocial factors that increase HIV vulnerability, such as social stigma, shame and denial.

Given the high prevalence and incidence of HIV in MSM, it is essential that MSM be encouraged to test for HIV on a regular basis. The current recommendation is that sexually active MSM be tested every six to twelve months and that those who report inconsistent condom use test every three months. Although national campaigns for HIV testing (such as the 'It Starts With Me' campaign and National HIV Testing Week) have certainly increased rates of testing in MSM, there is also evidence that many are testing infrequently or not at all. It was estimated that, in 2015 13 per cent of people living with HIV were unaware of their infection. HIV-diagnosed individuals are able to access ART and are able to modify their sexual behaviour to reduce the risk of onward HIV transmission. According to HIV testing data collected by Public Health England (Ogaz *et al.* 2016), in 2015, 90 per cent of MSM attending sexual health clinics were offered an HIV test. Moreover, between November 2015 and September 2016 13,722 home-sampling kits from MSM were tested, yielding a 1.1 per cent positivity rate. In a qualitative study of testing preference among MSM in London and the English Midlands, Jaspal (2017c) identified a series of barriers to testing in genito-urinary (GUM) clinics, the most important of which was perceived social stigma from health professionals. Moreover, some MSM felt uneasy about testing for HIV in community settings due to fears of being involuntarily 'outed' as gay. Clearly, interventions are needed to increase patterns of HIV testing.

Although it is clear that MSM continue to face significant inequalities in relation to HIV infection, some sexual health clinics in London have recently reported significant decreases in HIV incidence in MSM (Brown *et al.* 2017). This fall in HIV incidence has been attributed to two principal factors: namely, treatment as prevention (TasP) and PrEP. TasP has been effective in reducing the risk of onward HIV transmission, because successful ART reduces the individual's viral load to 'undetectable' levels, which in turn reduces infectiousness. Evidence from the PARTNERS Study (Rodger *et al.* 2016) suggests that the risk of onward HIV transmission – with or without a condom – is effectively zero, provided that the individual has been virally suppressed for at least six months, is adhering to their medication, and does not have other STIs. There were no within-couple HIV transmissions in the 548 heterosexual and 340 MSM couples who participated in the PARTNERS study, despite their engagement in acts of condomless sex.

Moreover, given the significant increases in rates of HIV testing among MSM, HIV-infected individuals are increasingly diagnosed and linked into HIV care soon after infection, that is, they are offered the opportunity to initiate ART. It is also noteworthy that data presented by the INSIGHT START Study Group (2015) clearly demonstrate the physical health benefits of early initiation of ART regardless of the individual's CD4 count or viral load.[1] In the START Study, there was a 53 per cent reduction in the onset of serious illness or death in the group that received ART early (that is, with a CD4 count >500 cells/mm^3). Furthermore, there was a 72 per cent reduction in the onset of AIDS-related illnesses, namely tuberculosis, Kaposi Sarcoma, and malignant lymphomas in the clinical intervention group. In view of this evidence, BHIVA guidelines recommend initiation of ART regardless of the patient's CD4 cell count (BHIVA 2012).

PrEP is a biomedical HIV prevention option for individuals at high risk of HIV exposure. The drug Truvada®, consisting of the two reverse transcriptase inhibitors emtricitabine and tenofovir, is currently

---

[1] CD4 count and viral load are clinical indicators of HIV disease progression, which can be used to determine the need to initiate ART.

approved for use as PrEP in the US. Clinical trials in a number of countries and contexts and in distinct populations converge in evidencing the high effectiveness of PrEP as a means of preventing HIV infection (Anderson *et al.* 2012). A series of clinical trial studies, including iPrEx (Grant *et al.* 2010), Partners PrEP (Baeten *et al.* 2010), IPERGAY (Molina *et al.* 2015), and PROUD (McCormack *et al.* 2016), have demonstrated the effectiveness of orally administered PrEP, on both daily and intermittent event-driven bases. Moreover, a mathematical modelling study of the effect of PrEP on HIV incidence among MSM in the UK suggested that rolling-out PrEP to just 25 per cent of high-activity MSM could greatly reduce HIV incidence in this population (Punyacharoensin *et al.* 2016).

In 2012, the Food and Drug Administration approved PrEP for use in the US. However, in the UK and in other Western countries, PrEP has caused controversy, particularly in relation to its funding. Critics argue that the National Health Service (NHS) should not fund an expensive biomedical approach to preventing HIV given that condoms are also very effective. At the time of writing, there were varying levels of access to PrEP in the UK. In the absence of full provision on the NHS, some MSM obtain generic versions of PrEP (e.g. Tenvir-EM) online, given that generic PrEP is considerably cheaper than Truvada. Evidence collected by 56 Dean Street, a sexual health clinic in Central London, suggests that there have thus far been no cases of counterfeit drug preparations in MSM purchasing PrEP online and that it is thus protective against HIV (Wang *et al.* 2017).

As indicated in Chapter 1, MSM are increasingly well informed about the risk of HIV and other STIs and about the protectiveness of condoms and other prevention options. However, the incidence of HIV and other STIs persists. The remainder of this chapter focuses on various psychosocial factors that can increase the risk of low wellbeing and poor sexual health in MSM.

The psychological impact of social stressors

MSM face several significant social stressors, which can in turn undermine identity, psychological wellbeing and sexual health outcomes. Possible social stressors include childhood sexual abuse and its enduring impact in adulthood; homonegativity across the life course; internalised homophobia; and, in the case of those living with HIV, HIV stigma.

Childhood sexual abuse

Adverse childhood experiences – both physical and emotional – have been identified as a significant predictor of morbidity and mortality in later adulthood (e.g. Brown *et al.* 2009). Childhood sexual abuse, in particular, is an important risk factor for both psychological adversity and poor sexual health in MSM. Childhood sexual abuse is a form of early psychological adversity that appears to be more prevalent in MSM than in heterosexuals, with one study suggesting that prevalence is almost four times greater in MSM than among men in the general population (Friedman *et al.* 2011). Moreover, some studies suggest that MSM of ethnic minority background are more likely to report childhood sexual abuse than White MSM (e.g. Welles *et al.* 2009), which may be attributed to the taboo nature of discussing sex in general and of disclosing sexual abuse in particular. It has also been observed that childhood sexual abuse is more prevalent in MSM living with HIV than among uninfected MSM (Lloyd and Operario 2012), which raises questions about the status of childhood sexual abuse as a risk factor for HIV infection. The available evidence converges in demonstrating the negative psychosocial ramifications of childhood sexual abuse.

Research indicates that self-reported history of childhood sexual abuse is associated with an elevated risk of mental health problems (Boroughs *et al.* 2015) and HIV infection and other STIs (Lloyd and Operario 2012). The reasons for the link between childhood sexual abuse, mental health problems and HIV risk are multifarious. It is also noteworthy that different forms of childhood sexual abuse appear to be related to distinct wellbeing outcomes and maladaptive behaviours in adulthood. For instance, Boroughs *et al.* (2015) found that MSM with a history of childhood sexual abuse with penetration were more likely to manifest post-traumatic stress disorder symptoms and HIV risk behaviours, while those facing childhood sexual abuse from a family member were most likely to report substance use disorder. It is thus difficult to generalise the long-term impacts of this form of childhood adversity.

Some studies suggest that the psychological sequelae of childhood sexual abuse compromise the individual's ability to make adequate risk appraisals in relation to their sexual behaviour (Arreola, Neilands and Diaz 2009). Research among HIV-positive MSM has found a correlation between history of childhood sexual abuse and unprotected anal intercourse with partners of negative or unknown HIV status (O'Leary *et al.* 2003). Moreover, one study found that HIV-positive MSM with a history of childhood sexual abuse engaged in more acts of unprotected anal intercourse than those reporting no abuse (Welles *et al.* 2009). A systematic review of relevant studies indicated that MSM with a history of childhood sexual abuse were significantly more likely to have casual sexual partners, to misuse substances and to engage in sexual behaviour while under the influence of either drugs or alcohol (Lloyd and Operario 2012). These behaviours can collectively reduce the individual's ability to make optimal sexual health decisions. Moreover, there is evidence that HIV-negative MSM with a history of childhood sexual abuse may derive fewer benefits from HIV prevention interventions than those with no prior history of abuse. Indeed, the EXPLORE Study noted that there was no effect on HIV prevention rates in MSM participants with a history of childhood sexual abuse (Mimiaga *et al.* 2009).

As noted above, childhood sexual abuse appears to constitute a serious psychological stressor that is more prevalent in HIV-positive MSM than in HIV-negative MSM. In a study of HIV-positive MSM in six US cities (Welles *et al.* 2009), it was found that individuals with a history of childhood sexual abuse manifested significantly higher levels of depression, anxiety and internalised homophobia, and that they reported higher levels of compulsive sexual behaviours than those reporting no abuse. Several of these sequelae of childhood sexual abuse are associated with decreased engagement in HIV care and with poor adherence to ART, both of which can undermine disease prognosis in patients. In Welles *et al.*'s (2009) study, MSM reporting abuse were less likely to self-identify as gay and more likely to be behaviourally bisexual than those reporting no abuse. Furthermore, in their study of Black and Minority Ethnic (BME) MSM in the UK, Jaspal *et al.* (2018) found that sexual abuse was associated with sexual risk-taking behaviours and that this relationship was mediated by the maladaptive coping strategy of substance misuse.

O'Leary et al. (2003) found that childhood sexual abuse was associated with anxiety, hostility and suicidality, which reflects poor wellbeing, on the one hand, and with increased HIV risk, on the other. Qualitative research with male victims of childhood sexual abuse suggests that shame, a key correlate of previous abuse, is experienced and manifested in a variety of ways with negative outcomes for self-identity, and that deflection and disassociation tend to characterise coping responses in adulthood (Dorahy and Clearwater 2012). Similarly, in a study of the impact of shame on health-related quality of life among HIV patients with a history of childhood sexual abuse (Persons et al. 2010), it was found that shame was inversely related to all dimensions of health-related quality of life, including physical wellbeing, functional and global wellbeing, emotional and social wellbeing and cognitive functioning.

It is noteworthy that childhood sexual abuse remains highly stigmatised and that there is perhaps greater stigma appended to being a *male* victim. This can lead MSM with a childhood sexual abuse history to remain silent about their experiences for years or even decades (Easton 2012), which can in turn make it difficult to address the psychological and behavioural sequelae of these early childhood experiences. The silence surrounding their adverse childhood experiences can also aggravate existing feelings of shame and other negative affective states, and inhibit access to positive coping strategies, such as self-disclosure and the derivation of social support (see Chapter 4). In their study of barriers to disclosure among male victims, Easton, Saltzman and Willis (2014) identify three clusters of barriers, namely sociopolitical (e.g. masculinity norms, lack of societal awareness), interpersonal (e.g. mistrust of other people, fear of being labelled by others) and personal (e.g. negative emotions, sexual identity issues). Addressing some of these barriers to disclosure could improve interventions for promoting wellbeing and sexual health among MSM with a history of childhood sexual abuse.

Homonegavitity across the life course

Experiences of homonegativity, that is, perceived stigmatisation of one's sexual minority identity, can pose significant social and psychological challenges for MSM. Such experiences may begin early in the life course and be manifested in the form of bullying at school, which can have lasting negative impacts in adulthood. Homonegative bullying in schools is unfortunately a frequent occurrence, which is often underreported by victims. In a recent report on lesbian, gay, bisexual and transgender (LGBT) bullying in British schools (Stonewall 2017), it was found that 45 per cent of the 3713 LGBT pupils surveyed had experienced bullying, that 52 per cent 'frequently' or 'often' heard homophobic language and that 45 per cent had never disclosed their bullying experience to anybody else. Bullying is much more prevalent among sexual minority individuals than heterosexual individuals. In thinking about the consequences of homonegative bullying, it seems appropriate to quote Meyer's (1995, p.38) observation that 'gay people, like members of other minority groups, are subjected to chronic stress related to this stigmatization'.

Actual experiences of stigma and/or bullying can give rise to the expectation that one will continue to face stigma, that is, an anticipation of stigma, which can undermine the quality of encounters and relationships with others and induce avoidant behaviours in MSM (Meyer 2003). Bullying against sexual minority individuals may be implicitly justified by the presence of heteronormative, and sometimes overtly homonegative, imagery in dominant culture, including stigmatisation from the media, religious authorities, parents and so on. In other words, it may come to appear 'normal' and expected. As noted, homonegative bullying is severely underreported – indeed, the aforementioned Stonewall report on homonegative bullying in schools found that 45 per cent of victims of bullying never reported their experience to anyone else and that 53 per cent felt that there was no adult at school with whom they could discuss LGBT issues. The lack of disclosure can be attributed, at least in part, to the shame that often accompanies victimisation, fear that one might be involuntarily 'outed' as gay if one speaks out and the perception that action will not be taken against the bullies. Many young gay people report witnessing inertia from school authorities and parents, which can reinforce the belief that complaining would be futile. Furthermore, some individuals face homonegativity from their parents who may implicitly or explicitly express disdain for homosexuality or be dismissive of their child's sexual orientation when it is disclosed. This can be distressing for the sexual minority individual and sometimes induce internalised homophobia (see below).

Much bullying is verbal in nature, which school authorities may perceive to be less severe than physical bullying. However, the psychosocial and physical effects of verbal bullying can be equally as negative as those associated with physical bullying (e.g. Nishina et al. 2005). Lacking any sources of support in the face of bullying can lead to feelings of vulnerability and helplessness, sometimes with dangerous consequences. Indeed, sexual minority youths who are bullied are at increased risk of developing psychological problems, such as anxiety or depression (Gini and Pozzoli 2009). Former victims of homonegative bullying report higher rates of alcohol and substance misuse, post-traumatic stress disorder, depression and suicidal ideation in adulthood (Rivers 2000, 2001, 2004). It has also been found that former bullying victims who exhibit post-traumatic stress disorder are also more likely to suffer from depression and to have more casual sexual partners than their peers, increasing the risk of HIV and other STIs (Rivers 2004). Victims of bullying may also develop problems in forming close relationships with others in adulthood (Carlisle and Rofes 2007), which may in turn be associated with sexually compulsive behaviours. Bullying can also lead to the internalisation of stigma, and to 'revictimisation' behaviours, that is, engagement in behaviours that can put one at risk of further victimisation (see also Jaspal et al. 2018). Vulnerability in adulthood can be attributed to one's inability to come to terms with childhood trauma, such as homonegative bullying. Given the low levels of disclosure and, thus, decreased social support, vulnerability in adulthood may be frequent.

Unfortunately, it seems that homonegative bullying takes place at various stages in the life course – at primary school, secondary school and university or in the workplace. The high prevalence of homonegativity across time and space, that is, at distinct temporal points in the life course and in a wide range of social contexts, can lead to the entrenched belief that one's sexual identity is indeed flawed but also to the anticipation of stigma from others. One may come to accept uncritically the homonegative assertions of society and of one's bullies. That is what is often referred to as internalised homophobia.

MSM may refrain from 'coming out' as sexual minorities due to fears of stigma and discrimination and may thus be deprived of the social support necessary for coping with stressors associated with their sexual minority identity (Jaspal and Siraj 2011). They may feign heterosexuality and some may even partake in homonegativity as a means of distancing themselves psychologically and socially from their own sexual minority identity. Furthermore, it is easy to see how psychological problems, such as paranoia and the sinister attribution error, may arise from the anticipation of homonegativity. More specifically, the victimised individual may misattribute innocent remarks, looks or behaviours from others to homonegativity, and erroneously view the actions of others as sinister, harmful and malevolent. This may begin to disrupt relationships with other people.

Some MSM report homonegative stigma in healthcare settings which can in turn lead to avoidance or disengagement from healthcare. Furthermore, the anticipation of stigma from heterosexual people can sometimes encourage the development of intergroup boundaries between 'us' and 'them', which in turn impedes positive forms of contact with the outgroup. Indeed, some MSM may immerse themselves in their sexual ingroup, distancing themselves from heterosexuals. They may develop negative perceptions of the outgroup, which is generally conducive to discordant intergroup relations. In some cases, individuals may themselves come to believe that the stigmatising behaviour they face is justified and warranted, which can give rise to long-term exposure to stigma and to 'revictimisation' behaviours (Jaspal et al. 2018). The loss of self-esteem is particularly prevalent among victims of homonegative bullying (Blais, Gervais and Hébert 2014), which, as indicated above, is associated with engagement in risk behaviours that can undermine both psychological and physical wellbeing. This may consist of drug use, alcohol use and sexual risk-taking.

Internalised homophobia

An unfortunate psychological correlate of socialisation in a homonegative environment is internalised homophobia, which can be defined as 'the gay person's direction of negative social attitudes toward the self, leading to a devaluation of the self and resultant internal conflicts and poor self-regard' (Meyer and Dean 1998, p.161).

It is important to distinguish between degree of 'outness' (that is, the extent to which one is open about one's sexual identity) and internalised homophobia. While it is true that MSM with internalised homophobia are less likely to disclose their sexual identity to others, it is also plausible that some MSM refrain from disclosing their identity to others without themselves harbouring negative feelings and emotions about it. In such cases, situational factors may be causal in that the principal objective is to avoid negative social repercussions of coming out as gay. Non-disclosure may thus be self-protective.

Individuals who are immersed in a social context characterised by homonegative tropes, images and stereotypes may come to internalise them and to accept uncritically their veracity. This can be especially acute for those MSM who have faced homophobic bullying in childhood which has persisted in adulthood. Moreover, internalised homophobia is often the outcome of negative experiences of disclosing one's sexual identity to others, particularly to significant others, such as one's parents or close friends, from whom one might normally anticipate acceptance and validation. This may serve to crystallise and reinforce in one's cognitive framework the notion that one's homosexuality is of negative valence. The internalisation of homophobia can of course decrease the individual's evaluation of himself and he may come to perceive himself as flawed and inferior to heterosexuals. Unfortunately, individuals with internalised homophobia tend to experience negative emotions, such as self-disgust, self-hatred, shame and guilt, which can greatly undermine psychological wellbeing.

It is easy to see how, at an intrapsychic level, internalised homophobia can challenge self-identity among MSM who may struggle to construct a positive sexual identity and lack authenticity in their sense of self. It has been found that MSM with internalised homophobia generally have a 'weaker' gay identity and that they are more likely to experience low self-esteem, emotional instability and guilt in relation to sex (Rowen and Malcolm 2002). It has, for instance, been observed that MSM who are diagnosed with HIV may experience a resurgence of internalised homophobia given that their sexual orientation may be perceived as the causal factor in their HIV infection (Ross and Rosser 1996). In such cases, one may attribute one's HIV infection to one's sexual orientation, which is unlikely to be conducive to a positive sexual identity. Furthermore, there is evidence that MSM with a history of childhood sexual abuse are more likely to manifest internalised homophobia than those without a history of sexual abuse (Gold, Feinstein, Skidmore and Marx 2011). Some individuals may establish a causal relationship between their abuse experience and their sexual orientation and, thus, come to view their sexual orientation negatively. Others may internalise feelings of self-blame, guilt and shame in relation to their abuse experience given the psychological link between that experience and their sexual orientation.

At a group identity level, internalised homophobia may be similarly challenging. Many MSM with internalised homophobia strive to conceal their sexual orientation from others and, in the process of doing so, may isolate themselves from particular groups and individuals. For instance, some MSM with internalised homophobia may actively avoid or themselves stigmatise other gay men because of the activation of negative cognitions about the self. Some may even isolate themselves from people who they believe might suspect that they are gay. In short, internalised homophobia can adversely impact social relations and lead to isolation.

Internalised homophobia can undermine sexual health outcomes among MSM for a number of reasons. First, MSM with internalised homophobia are less likely to be affiliated to the gay community and may therefore have decreased access to sexual health information and knowledge. They may not have the same level of exposure to safer sex messages and to HIV prevention campaigns that other gay men tend to have. Second, a significant correlate of internalised homophobia is decreased self-esteem, which may preclude the desire to engage in safer sex behaviours. Third, internalised homophobia is often associated with maladaptive coping strategies, such as alcohol and substance misuse and engagement in chemsex, which can contribute to the incidence of sexual risk-taking behaviours. Fourth, mental health problems, such as depression, anxiety, self-harm and suicidal ideation, are correlates of internalised homophobia across several empirical studies. Mental health issues are a significant risk factor for poor sexual health (Jaspal and Dhairyawan 2018). Fifth, internalised homophobia can have negative effects for the individual's ability to establish intimacy, commitment and satisfaction in romantic relationships. Research shows that MSM with internalised homophobia tend to report more relationship problems than those with no internalised homophobia (Frost and Meyer 2009). Given that romantic relationships can serve as a reminder of one's (devalued) sexual orientation, some individuals may avoid deep and lasting romantic relationships and instead seek pathways for sexual expression without intimacy, closeness or commitment. Thus, internalised homophobia can increase one's risk of acquiring HIV. In the next section, HIV is discussed in terms of a psychosocial stressor.

HIV stigma

In their overview of stigma, Crocker, Major and Steele (1998, p.505) note that '[s]tigmatized individuals possess (or are believed to possess) some attribute, or characteristic, that conveys a social identity that is devalued in a particular social context'. HIV carries social stigma due partly to its public association with taboo issues, such as sexual promiscuity, sex work and drug use, and the beliefs that HIV is synonymous with AIDS and invariably life-limiting. Furthermore, for MSM living with HIV, sexuality may constitute an additional layer of stigma. In view of the prevalent culture of heteronormativity and, in some cases, overt homonegativity in society, MSM with HIV may also face stigma due to their sexual minority identity.

Individuals living with HIV may fear that they will be judged or mistreated if they disclose their HIV status to others, rendering them targets for discrimination and depriving them of the social support often needed to cope effectively with an HIV diagnosis. Given the negative stereotypes frequently appended to HIV-positive people concerning 'promiscuity' and 'abnormal' sexual behaviour, individuals living with HIV may come to feel marginalised from society. While some people are overtly discriminated against and judged for being HIV-positive, others may feel that they are pitied and that their future prospects are overshadowed by widespread perceptions of sickness and mortality. Moreover, fear, which often results from the silencing of HIV, constitutes a component of HIV stigma. Some people may associate HIV with contagion and believe that even casual interpersonal contact with HIV-positive individuals will put them at risk of infection. This can lead people living with HIV to feel lonely and isolated.

Stigma is of course context-dependent – some social contexts will be construed as more or less stigmatising than others and indeed some may be perceived to be entirely free of stigma, such as support group settings. Stigma is related to non-disclosure of one's HIV status to family and friends, which can inhibit access to social support, and to sexual partners which may facilitate onward HIV transmission (Overstreet, Earnshaw, Kalichman and Quinn 2013). Many MSM living with HIV decide not to disclose their positive serostatus to family members, due at least in part to the anticipation of stigma. There is also evidence of HIV stigma in the gay community, which has led to divisions between people on the basis of their serostatus (Smit *et al.* 2012). For instance, men living with HIV may be positioned as being less socially and sexually desirable due to their positive serostatus. Fear of infection is a concern in the gay community. Individuals may be judged as having ignored the prevalent norm of condom use. There has also been discussion of the notion of 'slut shaming' in the gay community which refers to the moral denigration of individuals due to their perceived or actual sexual behaviours (McDavitt and Mutchler 2014). HIV may also be 'weaponised' in that it may be used as a means of controlling, coercing or even silencing the infected individual. For instance, others may involuntarily disclose an individual's HIV status in order to undermine, discredit or punish him.

HIV stigma is a significant stressor for people living with HIV and contributes to psychological distress (Earnshaw and Chaudoir 2009). It is easy to see how one's sense of self-esteem may be adversely impacted by HIV stigma. Stigma can be experienced, anticipated and/or internalised. Greater levels of stigma are associated with poor mental health, including depression (Emlet 2007). HIV-related shame, a byproduct of stigma, is a significant predictor of reduced health-related quality of life among patients (Persons *et al.* 2010).

Like homophobia, HIV stigma may also be internalised by the individual living with HIV. Indeed, in their qualitative interview study of HIV-positive MSM, Jeffries *et al.* (2015) found that stigma could result in the internalisation of stigma, to non-disclosure of HIV status to others and to the avoidance of HIV-related matters. Individuals may come to accept uncritically the stigmatising images, tropes and stereotypes concerning HIV and, in some cases, to believe that they are deserving of their infection and that this is indicative of their moral standing in society. This may be attributed, in part, to attitudes that the HIV-positive individual may have held prior to their own infection, and to negative attitudes and stereotypes of HIV that may be pervasive in one's social context. It has been found that internalised HIV stigma can lead to feelings of guilt and shame, and to reduced disclosure of one's HIV status to others (Cloete *et al.* 2008). In a correlational survey study of HIV patients in the US (Fekete, Williams and Skinta 2017), it was found that internalised HIV stigma was related to poorer sleep quality and to daytime sleep dysfunction through loneliness and depression. Indeed, social isolation and depression are likely outcomes of encountering HIV stigma. Loneliness is in turn associated with decreased condom use with partners of unknown HIV status, which could give rise to onward transmission (Hubach *et al.* 2015).

Sexual health risk behaviours

Psychological stressors, such as childhood adversity, homonegativity and HIV stigma, are associated with a series of sexual health risk behaviours, most notably inconsistent condom use.

Condomless sex

Despite their generally high levels of awareness and understanding concerning the risks associated with condomless sex, many MSM do not use condoms consistently. A recent large-scale survey of MSM in 20 US cities conducted by the Centres for Disease Control and Prevention (2016) revealed that almost two thirds of respondents reported condomless anal sex in the last 12 months. It is unclear how growing availability of PrEP has affected condom use among MSM. Much research has been conducted to facilitate understanding of the possible reasons underlying condomless sex. In this chapter, there is a focus on the various psychosocial challenges that may be faced by MSM, several of which correlate with condomless sex. In this section, some possible reasons for this are outlined.

At a basic level, negative attitudes towards condoms can lead some individuals to refrain from using them. Some MSM find condoms physically uncomfortable and may feel that they decrease the physical sensation of sexual intercourse, which, in some cases, is associated with erectile dysfunction (the inability to get and sustain an erection during sex) or delayed ejaculation. There is a perception among some individuals that condom use can interrupt sexual intercourse and decrease sexual pleasure. Furthermore, condom self-efficacy has been cited as a common cause of inconsistent condom use – some people feel unable to negotiate condom use with their partners who may not wish to use them, for instance. More specifically, individuals may feel uncomfortable or embarrassed about raising the topic of condom use and may therefore refrain from doing so. Some people may deem condomless sex to be risk-free if they believe they share their partner's HIV status, which has been referred to as 'serosorting'. This may be perceived as removing one's risk of acquiring HIV if both partners believe themselves to be HIV-negative, or as removing the risk of onward transmission in the case of HIV-positive individuals. This strategy is not always effective, however, given that one may not know, or accurately disclose, one's HIV status.

Encouraging condom use in MSM is a long-standing challenge for practitioners. Although there are mixed results about the effectiveness of fear as a motivator for behaviour change (e.g. Sherr 1990), it has been argued that fear of AIDS was a key factor in promoting large-scale behaviour change in MSM in the pre-ART era when HIV was a fatal disease (e.g. Shernoff and Palacios-Jiminez 1988). There is evidence that some MSM feel that it is inevitable that they will eventually acquire HIV, given its association with sex between men, and thus view attempts to prevent HIV (such as condom use) as futile. In this case, fear of HIV evokes paralysis in relation to prevention. On the other hand, in the era of ART, fear may no longer be effective in promoting safer sex behaviours, especially as some younger MSM associate HIV/AIDS with a past era that is no longer relevant to the present. HIV may be trivialised as a condition that is easily treated and, thus, less of a hazard than it was. The very many potential physical and psychosocial challenges associated with HIV infection may not be acknowledged.

Furthermore, it is noteworthy that some people attenuate their risk of acquiring HIV, despite engaging in what can objectively be construed as high-risk behaviours, such as condomless sex. They may associate HIV with outgroups and simply not see themselves as the 'kind of people that get HIV'. In other words, they view their own behaviour as low-risk. Human beings engage in interpersonal comparisons and may regard the behaviour of others as inherently more risky than their own. For instance, some MSM regard chemsex as the prototypical HIV risk behaviour, which can lead them to believe that they are therefore not at risk of HIV. This can in turn perpetuate engagement in other high-risk behaviours, such as condomless sex. In these cases, there is a need for greater awareness and understanding of sexual risk. On the one hand, some MSM do appear to have low levels of knowledge and understanding of sexual risk and HIV, possibly because they have had limited exposure to such information. This indicates the need to engage some groups and communities around sexual health and HIV through outreach work and other initiatives (see Jaspal et al. 2016). On the other hand, some report that safer sex messages appear to lack relevance to them and to their lives which highlights the importance of a more tailored, culturally sensitive approach to sexual health communication.

In addition to these psychosocial factors, personality plays an important role in risk-taking – some personality traits may predispose individuals to sexual risk-taking behaviours, such as condomless sex. Various studies have found that sensation-seeking, hedonism and neuroticism are significant predictors of condomless sex (e.g. Halkitis *et al.* 2005). Among MSM with these personality traits, the derivation of physical and psychological pleasure may override awareness of risk. Furthermore, there is some evidence that condomless sex may be viewed as more 'butch' and thus as a marker of masculinity (Halkitis *et al.* 2003).

Relationship type can play a role in determining condom use. Individuals may initially use condoms with a sexual partner but later decide to engage in condomless sex in order to demonstrate 'trust' and 'commitment'. Indeed, in one study of gay men's reasons for engaging in condomless sex (Flowers *et al.* 1997), it was found that love, trust and commitment (of which condomless sex could be an expression) were perceived to be more important than one's own health. More generally, some MSM may regard condomless sex as facilitating feelings of intimacy.

Geospatial gay social networking applications

The nature of intimacy among MSM has been greatly affected by novel methods of connecting with others socially, sexually and psychologically, such as on geospatial gay social networking applications. These applications (henceforth 'location-aware applications') play a significant role in the lives of many MSM (Goedel and Duncan 2015). Grindr, which was launched in 2009, has emerged as one of the most important location-aware applications with over two million daily users in 192 countries.[2] Individuals use Grindr and similar location-aware applications for a variety of purposes – to meet new friends, to establish relationships and, in many cases, to arrange casual sexual encounters. Location-aware applications allow users to identify other MSM (often an 'invisible' identity) in their geographical vicinity. Moreover, MSM (and particularly those who are less open about their sexual identities) may prefer to use location-aware applications to connect with other men discreetly.

Prior to the advent of the internet, MSM used particular social and physical contexts to meet other men, such as saunas, bathhouses, bars and clubs (Bérubé 2003). In the 1970s, for example, some

---

2 Grindr. Accessed 4 January 2018 at www.grindr.com

MSM employed subtle signifiers (e.g. the 'hankie code' of coloured handkerchiefs worn in back pockets) to communicate their sexual preferences to each other. When the internet became widely available in the 1990s, it revolutionised the ways in which MSM could connect with one another. The internet has enabled users *inter alia* (1) to identify other men much more easily than in many offline social settings where MSM may constitute an invisible minority, and (2) to derive a sense of community and to meet potential sexual partners in a manner that safeguards anonymity. This community can be accessed online in the privacy of one's own home. Moreover, some MSM feel safer meeting others online, rather than in cruising grounds, for instance, where there may be an elevated risk of being mugged or assaulted (Hennelly 2010).

Although MSM use location-aware applications for various purposes, the search for casual sex constitutes a priority for many Grindr users. One survey revealed that 38 per cent of their respondents reported using Grindr to find new sexual partners and that, on average, individuals reported opening the application over eight times and spending 1.3 hours on it per day (Goedel and Duncan 2015). These data suggest that Grindr constitutes an important aspect of some users' daily lives, and support the hypothesis that users of location-aware applications are generally more sexually active than non-users. Indeed, in their empirical study of online/offline partner-seeking among MSM, Grov *et al.* (2014) found that those individuals who sought partners offline generally had fewer sexual partners than those seeking partners online, largely due to ease of access.

The proliferation of location-aware applications has facilitated social and sexual contact between MSM, with implications for self-identity. In a study of Grindr users, Blackwell and Birnholtz (2015, p.17) note that Grindr enables people to connect with one another in ways that transcend geographical boundaries, itself 'often blurring the boundaries around physical places and communities defined by shared interests in particular activities'. This transcendence of physical space and 'communities' can offer new ways of constructing identity. For instance, a sexual preference that is habitually concealed due to social stigma can be manifested more openly when one feels affiliated to a community of like-minded others. Yet, herein lies a potential problem: modes of self-definition and self-presentation are visible to other users whose responses may not be affirmative. Indeed, in their study, Blackwell and Birnholtz describe Grindr users' competing desires to appear attractive to other users, on the one hand, and to maintain an appropriate level of 'identifiability' on the application, on the other. Online identities can become 'visible' in offline settings.

In a qualitative study of identity processes among MSM who use Grindr, Jaspal (2017b) found that users felt more able to construct and revise their sexual identities in psychologically satisfactory ways than in offline settings, although they did acknowledge a potent and coercive norm of seeking casual sex on the application. Furthermore, study participants perceived greater agency and self-efficacy in relation to their sexuality. More specifically, some described an increased ability to discuss sexual preferences and to negotiate condom use prior to meeting with potential partners. Although this study suggests that location-aware applications can provide opportunities for negotiating sexual risk and self-identity, they can of course also facilitate sexual compulsivity in users.

Sexual compulsivity

Sexual compulsivity refers to the frequent occurrence of sexual fantasies, urges and behaviours which are difficult to control and which can disrupt one's daily functioning. This can adversely impact sexual health and public health due to the elevated risk of exposure to HIV and other STIs among individuals with a high number of sexual partners. Being in a state of elevated sexual arousal can impair one's ability to take rational decisions regarding risk and behaviour, which could in turn increase the risk of engaging in unsafe sexual practices (Bancroft *et al.* 2003). MSM with sexual compulsivity are likely to have more sexual partners, to have more instances of unprotected anal sex (including with HIV serodiscordant partners), to engage in chemsex (Grov, Parsons and Bimbi 2010), and, in the case of HIV-positive MSM with sexual compulsivity, to fail to disclose their HIV status to sexual partners (Rosser *et al.* 2008). Sexual compulsivity is more prevalent among MSM than among heterosexual men, which could partly be attributed to the greater availability of sexual outlets for MSM. Moreover, it is more prevalent in MSM living with HIV than among HIV-negative MSM (Coleman *et al.* 2010).

Sexual compulsivity generally correlates negatively with self-esteem and positively with sensation-seeking (Chaney and Burns-Wortham 2015). Other correlates include a history of childhood sexual abuse, depression and substance use (Parsons, Grov and Golub 2012). There is emerging evidence that proximal minority stressors (e.g. internalised homophobia) and emotion dysregulation (that is, difficulties in experiencing, processing and expressing emotions) predict sexual compulsivity in MSM (Pachankis et al. 2015). Both internalised homophobia and emotion dysregulation are potential outcomes of socialisation within a rejecting environment in which individuals may have felt obliged to conceal their identities and the emotions associated with them. It is easy to see how an individual rejected on the basis of his sexual orientation and/or HIV status might be especially susceptible to emotion dysregulation. Furthermore, rejection on the basis of identity elements, such as one's sexual orientation or one's HIV status, can challenge the individual's sense of belonging and connectedness, which in turn may induce feelings of loneliness.

Sexual compulsivity may ultimately constitute an attempt to buffer the negative psychosocial effects of rejection, proximal minority stressors and emotion dysregulation – it may constitute a coping strategy. Some MSM may engage in sexually compulsive behaviour in an attempt to establish feelings of intimacy and connectedness with others, despite the transient nature of their sexual encounters. To this extent, it can come to constitute a short-term strategy for coping with rejection. Furthermore, sex may be utilised as a means of alleviating anxiety, shame, guilt and other negative emotional experiences associated with minority stress, for instance. Yet, some individuals with sexual compulsivity do develop maladaptive cognitions about sex; that is, they may come to associate it with few benefits and with harm to the self, though they may continue to pursue it (Pachankis et al. 2014). This can lead individuals to believe that they simply have no control over their sexual behaviour and that it is best attributed to external circumstances beyond their control. Despite their maladaptive cognitions about sex, individuals may nevertheless construe it as essential to their daily functioning.

Chemsex

An increasingly important correlate of sexual compulsivity in MSM is engagement in chemsex – the use of psychoactive drugs in sexualised settings. In the last few years, chemsex has emerged as a significant public health concern among MSM. Chemsex often involves the use of psychoactive drugs such as mephedrone, γ-hydroxybutyrate (GHB), γ-butyrolactone (GBL), and crystallised methamphetamine, which are used to facilitate and enhance sexual encounters – often in group settings – that can last for hours or days and with multiple partners. Physiologically, the drugs have varying effects on the individual – while mephedrone raises one's heart rate and blood pressure, resulting in increased sexual arousal, GHB and GBL function as potent psychological disinhibitors. Chemsex users tend to report better sexual experiences given that some of the substances reduce inhibitions and increase sexual pleasure. Moreover, engagement in chemsex can reduce the presence of negative affect associated with stressors such as internalised homophobia and HIV stigma and, thus, protect feelings of self-esteem (Bourne *et al.* 2014). In addition to the addictive nature of the substances involved, which can lead to physiological dependence, the positive affect experienced in chemsex sessions can lead to a form of *psychological* dependence as some individuals may become immersed in this environment and, thus, lose the ability to enjoy sex outside of it. Indeed, some research has shown that chemsex users find 'sober' sex unsatisfactory (Bourne *et al.* 2014).

There is limited data on the prevalence of chemsex among MSM in the UK. The Chemsex Study (Bourne *et al.* 2014) found that a fifth of MSM survey respondents living in Lambeth, Southwark and Lewisham reported having engaged in chemsex in the last five years and that a tenth had done so in the last four weeks. Self-report survey data from 1484 HIV-negative or undiagnosed MSM recruited from 20 sexual health clinics in the UK demonstrated a 21.8 per cent prevalence of chemsex in the last three months (Sewell *et al.* 2017). An analysis of baseline data from the PROUD study revealed that 44 per cent of the 525 study participants reported having engaged in chemsex in the last three months (Dolling *et al.* 2016). However, it is noteworthy that the eligibility criteria for participating in the PROUD study included engagement in previous or likely engagement in high-risk sexual behaviour. In a retrospective case notes review study in two London sexual health clinics, Lee *et al.* (2015) found that 59 per cent of MSM who used the clinic in the latter half of 2014 reported chemsex. Chemsex participants were more likely to be HIV-positive than non-participants. Crucially, the prevalence of chemsex appears to be higher in MSM living with HIV. In a study of HIV patients recruited from 30 UK HIV clinics in 2014 (Pufall *et al.* 2016), it was found that 29 per cent of sexually active MSM had engaged in chemsex and that 10 per cent had engaged in 'slamsex' (injected drug use) in the previous year.

There has been considerable research into the correlates of chemsex and the social and psychological factors that appear to drive the practice among MSM. In looking at the possible drivers of chemsex, Pollard, Nadarzynski and Llewellyn (2017) suggest that multiple levels of stigma, minority stress and maladaptive coping strategies may be contributing factors. In their qualitative research with chemsex participants, Weatherburn *et al.* (2016) describe two distinct sets of motivations underlying the practice. On the one hand, chemsex can enable individuals to have the type of sex that they desire by increasing their sexual stamina and confidence and by decreasing inhibitions while, on the other hand, the drugs can enhance the quality of the sexual encounter by increasing attraction and facilitating greater interpersonal rapport (see also Bourne *et al.* 2014).

The practice of chemsex is associated with other sexual risk-taking behaviours, such as transactional sex, group sex, fisting, sharing sex toys and HIV serodiscordant sexual relations (Lee *et al.* 2015). In their study of HIV-positive MSM, Pufall *et al.* (2016) found that the practice was associated *inter alia* with diagnosed depression/anxiety and with higher odds of engaging in condomless anal sex. Among MSM living with HIV, there appears to be an association between participation in chemsex and non-adherence to ART (Perera, Bourne and Thomas 2017), which can result in virological failure and onward HIV transmission.

There is some debate about the extent to which chemsex is harmful. In many cases, individuals engage transiently in chemsex and are able to limit its impact on other dimensions of their lives, such as their sexual health, work life and their ability to enjoy positive interpersonal relations in sober settings. However, for some MSM who engage in chemsex, the practice can cause significant harm, such as addiction, exposure to HIV and other STIs, mental health problems and the inability to develop social relationships. A significant public health challenge associated with chemsex is of course its role in the transmission of HIV and, increasingly, hepatitis C infection and as a barrier to good health outcomes among MSM living with HIV. Evidence concerning the role of chemsex in HIV transmission is inconclusive. Condom use and HIV status disclosure in these settings may be inconsistent and adherence to ART may be poor among some participants. All of these factors can drive HIV transmission and undermine health outcomes among MSM living with HIV.

Overview

The epidemiological data offered in this chapter demonstrate the high prevalence of HIV and STIs in MSM, but provide room for optimism about the combined role of condom use, HIV testing, TasP and PrEP for reducing the incidence of HIV in this population. However, there are some challenges. Condom use appears to be inconsistent. HIV testing needs to be further encouraged among those at risk. People living with HIV must be linked into and retained in care. Those at highest risk of HIV should be able to access PrEP. There are many obstacles to effective HIV prevention and sexual health promotion in this group. One challenge concerns the lack of sexual health awareness and understanding among some individuals, which can be addressed partly through awareness-raising campaigns that are culturally and socially relevant to the target group. However, there are also a series of psychosocial challenges to sexual health, self-identity and wellbeing, some of which have been described in this chapter. The overview of psychosocial challenges is not intended to be exhaustive and there are many others that could have been included. Social stressors, such as childhood sexual abuse, homonegativity across the life course, internalised homophobia and HIV stigma, are disproportionately prevalent in MSM and can collectively challenge self-identity and undermine psychological wellbeing. These stressors are also associated with engagement in risk-taking behaviours. Practices, such as condomless sex, the use of geospatial gay social networking applications, sexual compulsivity and chemsex, also highly prevalent among MSM, can shape, in one way or another, self-identity, sexual health outcomes and wellbeing in this population. While this chapter summarises key research concerning the aforementioned social stressors and risk behaviours and provides insight into debates concerning their role in shaping health and wellbeing outcomes in MSM, it falls short of explicating the psychosocial 'mechanisms' underpinning them. Furthermore, the nature of the relationship between these stressors/ practices and health and wellbeing outcomes in MSM is similarly underexplored. This chapter leaves us with some important questions. Why are these stressors and practices challenging for social and psychological functioning? Are some of the practices actually (maladaptive) strategies for coping with the psychological stressors? More fundamentally, are all of the stressors described in this chapter necessarily experienced by all MSM as psychologically distressing? How can MSM who present with psychological distress and/or are at risk of poor wellbeing and sexual health be adequately supported by practitioners? These questions constitute the foci of the next two chapters.

Chapter 3

Social Psychological Approaches to Promoting Health and Wellbeing

Social psychology has formed the basis for the development of theories, frameworks and models that have subsequently informed therapeutic practice and behaviour change interventions to enhance health and wellbeing. This chapter provides an overview of key therapeutic frameworks from counselling psychology, which have been utilised in therapeutic work with MSM. The chapter also outlines significant models of behaviour change, which have underpinned public health interventions that aim to enhance sexual health, self-identity and psychological wellbeing among MSM. The potential advantages associated with these frameworks and models are considered in view of the psychosocial stressors and health inequalities outlined in Chapter 2. In order to illustrate the potential utility of these frameworks for enhancing health and wellbeing in MSM, tenets of them are applied to the three cases of psychological distress and sexual health risk that were described in the first chapter of this volume.

Therapeutic frameworks from counselling psychology

Counselling psychology draws extensively on psychology and psychotherapy. Counselling psychologists attempt to help their patient cope with psychological distress and to establish a sense of psychological wellbeing in collaboration with their patient. In other words, the process is generally intended to be facilitative, rather than prescriptive and directive. As outlined in Chapter 1 of this volume, this is one of the factors that differentiate counselling psychology approaches from the dominant model in medicine. Counselling psychology approaches tend to take a holistic and developmental perspective on the patient's life and acknowledge the biological, cultural, socio-structural, economic and political contexts in which the patient resides.

Several chapters in this volume highlight possible cases in which counselling psychology interventions may be required. For instance, MSM are at heightened risk of experiencing a range of mental health issues (such as poor self-image, anxiety, depression, stress, guilt, shame, hypersexuality); traumatic past experiences (such as bullying, childhood sexual abuse, an HIV diagnosis); and problematic interpersonal relations (such as intimate relationship problems, family problems, homophobia, racism and others). It has already been shown how problems of this nature can escalate and severely undermine the identity, sexual health and wellbeing of the individual and become associated with maladaptive behaviours.

The counselling psychologist will initially seek to provide an 'assessment' of the patient and their presenting issues. Although the initial assessment is intended to provide a safe, supportive and empathic space in which the patient can recount their story and disclose sensitive information about themselves, this process does inevitably involve an element of clinical judgement on the part of the psychologist, who will utilise this as an opportunity to assess risk, patient motivation, and the suitability and form of psychological intervention that may be most appropriate (Bager-Charleson and van Rijn 2013). The assessment enables the psychologist to take note of information that is relevant to the patient's presenting issues and, thus, worthy of exploration in the therapeutic process. For instance, a therapist working with MSM with sexual identity concerns will plausibly attempt to capture information relating to sexual identity, self-categorisation, sexual identity disclosure, feelings about others' reactions to this, sexual behaviour and so on. Furthermore, the practitioner must conduct a risk assessment, the content of which will depend largely upon the patient and their circumstances. This may include the risk of suicide or self-harm, the risk that the patient may pose to others, and ethical and legal issues. For instance, some individuals newly diagnosed with HIV experience suicidal ideation and some may not disclose their HIV status to intimate partners due to fears of rejection, which poses an ethical dilemma.

Furthermore, it is increasingly recognised that the psychological experiences of guilt and shame can be debilitating for patients and that they ought to be acknowledged and addressed in order to facilitate optimal therapeutic outcomes (Clark 2012). Ideally, the detection of adverse psychological experiences, such as guilt and shame, should form part of the assessment stage. In short, the assessment stage is of vital importance and indeed the success of the counselling psychology intervention will in part depend on the way in which the assessment has been conducted.

The information gathered as part of the patient assessment is used to create a case formulation. The case formulation summarises the salient features of the case and integrates often disparate and fragmented issues, events and experiences, sometimes occurring across the life course, into a coherent, inter-connected synopsis. The case formulation can be greatly illuminating and informative for the patient when it is offered to them, but it also constitutes an essential step in the counselling psychology intervention, as it informs the process and goals of therapy (Henderson and Martin 2014). The case formulation must be framed in sensitive and empathic language that is accessible to the patient and devoid of stigma on the basis of sexuality, HIV status and other relevant characteristics. Both the assessment and the case formulation – but particularly the latter – will be informed by psychological theory. Indeed, an objective of the case formulation is to link theory to practice (Johnstone 2011).

In the remainder of this section, three therapeutic frameworks from counselling psychology are presented, namely (1) psychodynamic approaches, (2) humanistic person-centred approaches and (3) cognitive-behavioural approaches. It is not possible to refer to a single, unified therapeutic model in each domain, given the diversity that characterises these approaches theoretically, philosophically and in practice. It is noteworthy that there have been schisms in these and other counselling psychology approaches, leading to further diversity in them. The aim of this section is to highlight some of the overarching tenets of these frameworks and to focus on more prevalent practice models within them. In short, they should be regarded as broad therapeutic frameworks. The three cases outlined in Chapter 1 of this volume are evoked as a means of illustrating how tenets of the frameworks could be fruitfully deployed in the therapeutic setting.

Psychodynamic approaches

A principal aim of the psychodynamic practitioner is to investigate and to shed light on unconscious processes, given the view in psychodynamic approaches that these processes determine the nature of human functioning, interactions with others and with one's environment, and the experience of psychological distress. By understanding psychological symptoms, one is better positioned to understand the psychological processes underlying distress. Psychodynamic approaches propose that, in response to distressing thoughts, desires and wishes in relation to ourselves or others, we use a series of defence mechanisms, either consciously or unconsciously. These defence mechanisms are designed to keep distressing thoughts, desires and wishes out of consciousness. In this section, relational psychoanalysis, an approach that is grounded in the psychodynamic tradition, will be outlined. In order to contextualise this approach, principles of the psychodynamic paradigm are also discussed.

In his psychoanalysis, Freud (1949) provided a physiological perspective on psychology in that he highlighted the primacy of underlying sexual instincts to human psychological functioning, including our motivations, cognitions, feelings, and to human behaviour. Freud argued that human beings have a psychobiological need to satisfy innate sexual impulses but that constraints in our external reality, such as the presence of societal norms, values and ideologies, impede the satisfaction of these needs. The frustration of these needs in turn gives rise to new personality structures and ensuing behaviours, which Freud referred to as the 'Ego'. Crucially, the 'Superego', that is, internalised societal norms and values and hence our conscience and sense of guilt, may also be in conflict with the sexual instincts that we wish to satisfy. According to Freudian psychoanalysis, it is the Ego that protects human beings from the debilitating psychological 'Angst', guilt and shame that they would experience if aware of the conflicts between their innate sexual impulses and the Superego. Indeed, as demonstrated earlier in this volume, guilt and shame are two aversive psychological experiences that many MSM face due principally to self-identity concerns. The Ego employs several psychological defence mechanisms to keep conflicts out of human awareness (that is, in our unconscious) and, thus, to shield us from our threatening reality. However, in his theory, Freud highlights the limited effectiveness of our psychological defence mechanisms, which in turn causes psychological distress in various forms, such as depression, anxiety and phobias. These negative feelings are essentially manifestations of 'intrapsychic conflicts'. It is important to stress that, while we remain unaware of our intrapsychic conflicts, they may continue to have an insidious impact on our thoughts, feelings and behaviours.

Psychodynamic approaches based on Freudian psychoanalysis aim to sensitise the patient to these conflicts and their origins, thereby providing the patient with access to the unconscious, and to work through the conflicts in an attempt to resolve them. The psychodynamic therapist adopts a 'neutral' stance to avoid 'contaminating' the patient's psyche and listens attentively to all aspects of the patient's account, essentially becoming a 'neutral screen' onto which the patient transfers their conflicting desires. The therapist aims to interpret the patient's attempts to project onto them his desires and experiences from the past, the psychological defence mechanisms that appear to be deployed and the psychological symptoms manifested by the patient. The therapist seeks to provide the patient with some insight into the meanings and underpinnings of his intrapsychic conflicts, and the links between them and the patient's experience of the world, relationships with others and life decisions. The patient is thus better positioned to seek more effective ways of resolving his intrapsychic conflicts and to limit the impact of these conflicts on his life.

Relational psychoanalysis is an important psychodynamic approach, which acknowledges that our 'embeddedness in a matrix of relationships, past and present, continually shape the development of personality' (Wachtel 2008, p.viii). This area of psychoanalysis is broad and fragmented but the common thread between all relational psychoanalytic approaches is the centrality of interpersonal relations to how we think, feel and behave. Human beings have an innate need for relatedness and communication with others, and satisfaction of this need is said to be central to human development. It is our early relationships in life that come to shape our cognitions, emotions and personalities and that become 'relational configurations', which are guiding principles or schemata for our subsequent relationships in adulthood. We use these principles or schemata to develop perceptions, interpretations and expectations about later relationships. It is noteworthy that we do not perceive our relational configurations purely from the synchronic perspective of adulthood but rather these configurations are imbued with our early perceptions as children.

Psychological distress can occur as a result of relational configurations that encourage the formation and development of painful or abusive relationships, low levels of authenticity and mutual intimacy in relationships, and other forms of relationship impairment (Perlman and Frankel 2009). Relational configurations are neither static nor immutable, and the role of relational psychoanalytic therapy is to raise awareness of problematic relational configurations and to enable the patient to replace them with more flexible and adaptive ones.

In Chapter 1, the case of Juan, a Spanish gay man living with HIV, was described. The case is complex and multi-faceted and outlines several psychosocial issues that are worthy of psychotherapeutic attention. Key areas of concern include his non-adherence to ART, his engagement in chemsex and his self-isolation. Juan himself recognises that these actions are potentially harmful to his health and wellbeing. He is aware that non-adherence to ART could lead to poor disease prognosis, that his engagement in chemsex could cause drug dependence, drug overdose and exposure to other STIs, and that his self-isolation makes him feel lonely and depressed, sometimes reinforcing the other two maladaptive behaviours. From a relational psychoanalytic perspective, the therapist might hypothesise that, due to his difficult and often uncommunicative relationship with his parents, to whom he felt unable to confide his traumatic childhood experience of sexual abuse, Juan has developed and internalised a relational configuration where other people are regarded with suspicion, as uncaring and unsupportive. Moreover, the relational configuration has led him to feel unworthy of care, affection and love. This is of course also consistent with attachment theory which postulates that insecure and avoidant forms of attachment lead to poor interpersonal relations, an unstable sense of self and feelings of decreased self-worth in adulthood (Cassidy and Shaver 1999).

It could be hypothesised that this relational configuration has served as a psychological template for making subsequent decisions in adulthood, including his choice of romantic partners. Seeing himself as unworthy of care, affection and love, Juan has preferred to engage in transient casual sexual encounters, rather than developing intimate, long-term relationships, often allowing his sexual partners to coax him into high-risk behaviours, such as condomless sex. Juan tends to disengage from romantic relationships that appear to be more intimate, affectionate and respectful – given the inconsistency of these relationships with his relational configuration, he does not quite know how to respond to – and to sustain – them. Juan's disengagement from HIV care, his refusal to adhere to ART and his engagement in chemsex could be regarded as acts of self-harm, especially in view of his own construal of these behaviours as harmful. His feelings of guilt and shame in relation to his childhood sexual abuse experiences and HIV infection, coupled with his anger at his parents whom he perceives as having been emotionally absent when he needed them, give rise to a desire to punish – the anger against his parents is unconsciously displaced towards himself, which could explain his self-destructive behaviours. The aim of the relational therapist would be to raise awareness of the role of the problematic relational configuration in the patient's current relationships, feelings and behaviours and, dyadically, to seek alternative methods for expressing the negative emotions associated with early experiences.

The humanistic person–centred approach

The humanistic person-centred approach draws upon tenets of phenomenology, which enables the practitioner to provide a comprehensive and sensitive analysis of the phenomenon under investigation without being overly influenced by their prior assumptions about that phenomenon, and humanism, which emphasises the individual's agency and competence in self-reflection, decision-making and action. Maslow was a key theorist of humanism and, accordingly, his work on self-actualisation and the hierarchy of needs (Maslow 1943) merits attention. It is argued that human beings possess basic needs, some of which are physiological in nature (such as food, water and rest) and others which relate to safety and security. We also have psychological needs relating to belonging and love (such as intimate relationships and friends) and to esteem, namely the need to feel valued and accomplished. Upon successful achievement of these needs, the individual is said to be able to realise self-actualisation, that is, to achieve his full potential.

In his reflections on therapeutic personality change, that is, constructive changes in the patient, Carl Rogers (1957) specified the necessary tenets of a successful therapeutic relationship with patients. More specifically, it is argued that during the therapy session the therapist must have a sense of self-integration and congruence in the face of the patient's possible sense of incongruence, vulnerability and anxiety. In other words, the therapist must remain authentic in the therapeutic encounter. Critical aspects of the therapeutic relationship include unconditional positive regard on the part of the therapist, whereby the therapist places no expectations or conditions upon the patient, and empathy, which allows the therapist to attempt to enter the emotional and psychological world of the patient. It is important that the therapist remains unconditionally positive and empathic towards the patient, despite the possibility of becoming personally displeased with thoughts and behaviours that they may disclose during the therapeutic encounter.

Issues around selfhood are of central importance in the person-centred approach. The self-concept is said to consist of self-worth, self-image and one's ideal self. According to the theory, the individual will seek feelings, experiences and behaviours which are consistent with their self-image and which reflect the ideal self. Greater synergy between the self-image and the ideal self will result in increased self-worth as the individual will experience a sense of congruence. Conversely, it is the feeling of *incongruence* that tends to lead the patient to seek therapy. During childhood and in later life, individuals are exposed to 'conditions of worth' which essentially reflect norms and expectations specified by significant others, such as parents, siblings, family, friends and institutions. These conditions of worth may be expectations that we think or behave in particular ways in order to achieve psychological needs such as belonging and esteem. Non-adherence to these conditions of worth can deprive us of these important needs. In person-centred therapy, it is essential to identify and label externally imposed conditions of worth in order to facilitate a better understanding of incongruence and to offer unconditional positive regard of the patient. The aim is to enable the patient to feel accepted and valued for who he is and who he aims to become. This greatly increases the potential for self-actualisation. In short, the principal objective of the therapist is to promote feelings of self-worth in the patient, to reduce incongruence between his ideal and actual selves, and to facilitate self-actualisation, that is, self-healing and self-growth.

In Case 2, outlined in the first chapter of this volume, Ahmed, a British Pakistani Muslim (BPM) gay man, is experiencing feelings of helplessness, anxiety and depression due to perceived conflict between his sexual orientation and religious identity. A humanistic person-centred approach to therapy could be fruitful. Ahmed perceives a conflict between his ideal self – a heterosexual Muslim man – and his actual self – a gay Muslim man. Since childhood, he has been exposed to coercive norms about what it means to be a 'good' Muslim and how he should behave as a 'real' man. These expectations or 'conditions of worth', coupled with his actual experiences of marginalisation and bullying, have led to the internalisation of stigma, low self-worth, guilt and shame. Ahmed's basic needs of belonging, love, intimate relationships and self-esteem are severely jeopardised. The therapist would need to provide consistent positive regard for Ahmed, reassuring him through their interactions that he is a valued and esteemed individual, and to remain empathic, though not sympathetic, about his experiences. Promoting acceptance, self-forgiveness and self-compassion in the patient is essential for working with guilt and shame in the therapeutic encounter (Clark 2012).

Furthermore, it would be necessary to work with Ahmed to raise awareness of the role of externally imposed conditions of worth in the way he is feeling about his self-identity and for him to recognise what these conditions might be in his context. Ahmed would need to take a stance on these conditions of worth and the significance that he himself wishes to append to them. Is he able to consider himself a person of worth despite these externally imposed conditions? According to the humanistic person-centred approach, self-actualisation is possible and the therapist would work with Ahmed to achieve this. This may include exploring the possibility of expanding his social circle to include exposure to other social norms and values, which challenge these previous conditions of worth, while also acknowledging that these conditions should not be central to his self-worth. In a similar vein, expansion of his social circle may enable him to derive feelings of belonging, love, intimacy and so on. The overarching aim of the therapeutic relationship would be to minimise the gulf between Ahmed's ideal and actual selves, in order to facilitate self-actualisation. This would most likely involve rethinking the consequences for Ahmed of attempting to live his life as a heterosexual man and of accepting his gay identity, while exploring the possibility of being gay *and* Muslim. While the humanistic person-centred therapist does not attempt to be directive in the therapeutic encounter, it is important that they work with the patient to explore the potential consequences of his decisions, while acknowledging the patient's agency, autonomy and potential for self-actualisation.

Cognitive-behavioural approaches

Put simply, the principal aim of cognitive-behavioural therapy (CBT) is to change aspects of the patient's thinking and behaviour. Its success depends on the patient's active participation in the process of change and his level of motivation to achieve such change. CBT owes a debt to behavioural theory (Skinner 1938; Eysenck 1960). Building on behavioural theory, CBT (Beck 1976) was developed to account for the role of cognitive processes, such as thinking, belief formation, interpretation and understanding, in affect and behaviour.

CBT can be defined as a psychological therapy which seeks to resolve psychological distress by altering dysfunctional cognitions, affective states and behaviours through a systematic, goal-oriented procedure. A fundamental premise of CBT is that most emotional problems are the product of particular patterns of thought and behaviour. Thus, the approach proposes that changes to thought and behaviour can in turn alleviate these persistent emotional problems. During childhood and in later life, the individual will form core beliefs about himself, others and the environment through engagement with the social world, most notably, with significant others, such as family, friends and social ingroup members.

Negative core beliefs about the self can include 'I am worthless', 'I am ugly', 'I am unworthy of other people's affection'. Core beliefs, whether negative or positive, will guide cognitions and behaviours in everyday life. They lead to elaborations in particular social contexts and in response to specific situations. For instance, the individual may come to believe the following: 'I am ugly. So if I do not use lots of make-up everyone will realise that I am ugly', or 'I am worthless. So if I speak to anyone, everyone will realise that I am worthless and reject me'. These assumptions or elaborations that emanate from one's core beliefs can lead to the activation of negative automatic thoughts. These are essentially negative causal attributions that one makes in order to make sense of one's surroundings. For instance, the belief 'I am worthless' could, in the context of a gay bar, lead to the negative automatic thought that 'people are looking at me and smiling because they find me ugly'. These thoughts are automatic because they occur outside of the individual's control and volition. They can induce feelings of anxiety, low mood and fear. Consequently, the individual will behave protectively in order to avoid realisation of the anticipated negative events. He may seek excuses to avoid frequenting a context in which the feared events may occur (e.g. being looked at). The protective behaviour (e.g. avoidance) may alleviate the feelings of anxiety and fear associated with the negative outcome, but it can also be maladaptive in that it may lead the individual to isolate himself and to avoid any form of contact with potential partners and friends. Crucially, unless the core belief that 'I am worthless' does not change, the individual will continue to experience the negative automatic thoughts, which will in turn lead to (maladaptive) patterns of action.

CBT seeks to challenge negative automatic thoughts, which are associated with undesirable patterns of action. The key is to identify negative automatic thoughts in the patient's everyday life, as well as links between particular thoughts, emotions and behaviours as a first step towards disrupting this interdependent system. These thoughts can be easily identified given that they are essentially elaborations of core beliefs in specific contexts. As the patient discusses his concerns in the workplace or in his relationship, etc., negative automatic thoughts will surface and they can be discussed. An important objective of CBT is to develop a formulation, which is a dyadically designed intervention for identifying the origins of the problem at hand, how it has developed over time and the factors that currently maintain it. More specifically, there is a focus on the potential vulnerability factors (e.g. early childhood experiences), beliefs about oneself (e.g. 'I am worthless'), rules and assumptions (e.g. 'If I speak, people will realise I am worthless'), possible triggers (e.g. an event at which one has been invited to speak publicly), cognitions (e.g. 'I will make a fool of myself at the event'), and behaviours (e.g. 'I must avoid attending this event'). Moreover, the associated feelings (e.g. anxiety) and physical symptoms (e.g. sleeplessness) surrounding cognitions and behaviours are considered.

Once the patient's core beliefs and negative automatic thoughts have been identified, the patient is invited to find 'evidence' that contradict them so that they are better positioned to elicit an alternative thought. This act of eliciting a more positive alternative thought is likely to reduce anxiety and mitigate the risk of maladaptive coping strategies designed to facilitate exit from the threatening position.

The patient and therapist proceed to design a behavioural intervention, which consists of a series of pleasurable and meaningful activities for the patient to feel more positive and to build greater confidence. An additional behavioural approach may be to allow gradual and controlled exposure to stimuli that have provoked anxiety in the past, as a means of reducing these negative feelings and detaching the stimuli from negative automatic thoughts.

In Case 3, Juan's difficulties with his identity, wellbeing and sexual health were described. Principles of CBT could be useful. Juan had felt unattractive and undesirable as he never seemed to be noticed by people that he liked. This, coupled with the stigma of homosexuality in his social context, led him to internalise a core belief that he was unworthy and undesirable, which in turn developed into negative automatic thoughts that he should remain silent and invisible – out of public view – lest others discover his lack of worth. Moreover, Juan came of age feeling that he was unworthy of a romantic relationship and preferred to limit his relations with potential boyfriends to casual sexual encounters. His recent HIV infection and early experiences of rejection reinforced his core beliefs around unworthiness. An additional negative thought that plagued him was that, if others discovered that he was HIV-positive, they would realise that he is not a person of worth. These negative automatic thoughts have led Juan to behave protectively in ways that inhibit the possibility of romantic relationships with others – he attends chemsex parties, makes clear on his Grindr profile that he is looking for sex only and actively distances himself from people who exhibit interest in a romantic relationship with him. Moreover, his core belief of unworthiness makes Juan question the point of ART – why should he want to live at all, if he thinks he is unworthy?

The therapist would work with Juan to identify possible vulnerability factors, such as his problematic relationship with his parents and his traumatic childhood abuse experience, considering their potential impact for his core belief formation. In addition to identifying the patient's core beliefs and the related rules and assumptions, the therapist would encourage the patient to think about evidence (e.g. events, encounters) that contradict these negative core beliefs. Are there occasions where Juan has felt worthy? Are there significant others who have said things that suggest that he is a person of worth? Have other men shown a romantic interest in Juan and, if so, why does he think this may be? Such instances would be explored with the patient. However, it must be acknowledged that, in some cases, the patient will be unable to identify such occasions. Indeed, patients with a history of significant trauma, such as childhood sexual abuse, tend to manifest intense feelings of shame and, thus, experience difficulties in identifying past experiences of self-worth. While it is important for the therapist to attempt to elicit positive past experiences, in some cases, there may be a need to recognise that this is simply impossible but also to reassure the patient that this in and of itself is not a reason to feel ashamed. As highlighted in all of the therapeutic approaches, acceptance from the practitioner is key. Self-acceptance on the part of the patient is a goal. Although it is not unusual for the patient to be unable to identify past experiences of self-worth, an important objective is for him to accept that experiences of trauma and low self-worth do not define him.

It would be necessary to explore with Juan the possible triggers for the activation of negative automatic thoughts. It appears that romantic scenarios are a key context in which Juan's negative automatic thoughts are activated, making him feel anxious, nervous and fearful. Therefore, he avoids these contexts. Having considered alternative thoughts and explanations, the patient and therapist would work to develop a behavioural intervention for alleviating Juan's negative affect and maladaptive behaviours. This may consist of encouraging Juan to increase his involvement in spaces and groups designed to support people living with HIV, to focus his attention on the things that he thinks he does well, and to spend time with people who make him feel like a worthy and esteemed person. In short, the pathways to better psychological outcomes are both social and psychological in nature.

The three therapeutic frameworks aim to address psychological distress experienced at an individual level. A multi-faceted approach to enhancing sexual health, self-identity and wellbeing in MSM would also include a public health intervention, focusing on positive behaviour change.

Social psychological models of behaviour change

In Chapter 2, attitudes and behaviours which may undermine sexual health, self-identity and wellbeing among MSM were outlined. Interventions may be developed in order to challenge problematic or maladaptive behaviours in specific populations. There is sometimes a temptation to accept uncritically the causal relationship between attitudes and behaviour. In other words, practitioners may view attitude change as leading naturally and coherently to behaviour change. For instance, it may be assumed that, provided that MSM can be encouraged to develop a positive attitude towards condoms, they will use them consistently. There is an element of truth in this, and attitudes and behaviours are indeed related. However, there are many other factors that can intervene in the link between attitudes and behaviours, rendering this a complex, if uneasy, relationship. Some of these factors are considered in this section and in Chapter 4. Indeed, it is quite possible to hold a given attitude and to engage in a behaviour that appears to be completely inconsistent with this attitude due, for instance, to peer pressure or to identity concerns.

In this section, three social psychological models of behaviour change are briefly outlined and their relevance to the areas of sexual health, self-identity and wellbeing in MSM are explored. These models include (1) social cognitive theory, (2) theory of planned behaviour, and (3) transtheoretical stages of change model. As in the previous section of this chapter, the three cases outlined in Chapter 1 are evoked as a means of illustrating how theories of behaviour change could productively inform public health interventions for the central foci of this book.

Social cognitive theory

Social cognitive theory (Bandura 1986) was developed in order to understand how people acquire and maintain particular behaviours and indeed how these behavioural patterns might be modified. It owes a debt to social learning theory in that it proposes that individuals acquire their behaviours through social learning, including through individual experiences, by observing others and through interactions with their social environment. The theory proposes dynamic, reciprocal interactions between personal factors, environmental factors and behaviour (see Figure 1). A key tenet of the theory is that social influence processes are central to behaviour, which highlights the need to consider external social reinforcements of particular behaviours.

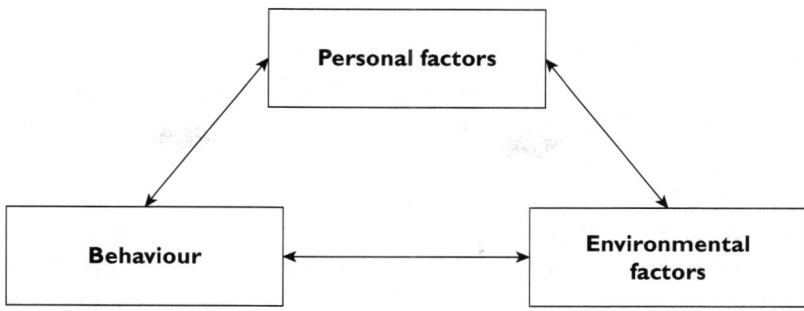

Figure 1: Social cognitive theory

Personal factors include the individual's ability to perform a given behaviour, their expectations regarding the outcomes of adopting or performing that behaviour, and feelings of competence and control (self-efficacy) in relation to that behaviour. A key difference between social cognitive theory and other models is the importance attributed to self-efficacy, that is, *perceived* control and competence. This may be different from one's actual ability to perform a behaviour in that the individual may erroneously overestimate or underestimate their ability. Self-efficacy will in turn be informed by environmental factors, such as feedback from other people or social norms. Environmental factors can include the presence of other people, such as family and friends, social norms that are prevalent in one's context, and physical aspects of one's environment, such as the physical availability of things. A central prediction of the theory is that the individual observes behaviours in other people in their social context and will in turn come to reproduce these behaviours themselves. This can be referred to as 'modelling' the behaviour. Furthermore, the model highlights the importance of social reinforcements in the external environment, which can perpetuate a particular behaviour. These reinforcements may include positive feedback from significant others or the existence of a context or environment that facilitates a given behaviour. Collectively, personal and environmental factors are said to drive the individual's adoption of particular behaviours.

Aspects of social cognitive theory can be usefully applied to behaviour change among MSM at risk of decreased psychological wellbeing. Case 2, which was presented in Chapter 1, described Ahmed's strategy of self-isolation from other gay men due to internalised homophobia and fear of involuntary disclosure of his sexual orientation, which in turn led to intense feelings of fear, anxiety and depression. Ahmed recognises that he would ideally like to meet someone for an intimate relationship but avoids engaging in behaviours that might facilitate this. An aim of the behaviour change intervention may be to facilitate a change in his social behaviour to develop more intimate relationships with other men. There may be various personal factors that encourage emotional self-distancing from other gay men, such as the belief that this could lead to a concurrent self-distancing from one's homosexuality, and the belief that self-association with other gay men could lead to involuntary disclosure of one's sexual orientation. Ahmed may perceive low levels of self-efficacy in relation to the gay community due to his lack of experience, and he may feel unable to be more involved and to relate positively to other gay men. This could render the prospect of frequenting gay spaces challenging. Furthermore, dominant social norms in his primarily heterosexual ethnic ingroup may stigmatise gay romantic relationships and there may be no positive reinforcements for such relationships. Alternatively, in the context of the gay community, this may be construed as more socially acceptable and, thus, feasible for the individual. Social cognitive theory provides useful insights into the interaction between key personal and environmental factors that either facilitate or inhibit any given behaviour – in this case, changing the nature of one's relationships with other gay men. Yet, there are other psychosocial factors, some of which were outlined in Chapter 2, that could impinge on behaviour. In current formulations of social cognitive theory, these additional, intervening factors are not captured.

Theory of planned behaviour

The theory of planned behaviour (Ajzen 1985) suggests that people decide to behave in particular ways as a result of rational thought processes (see Figure 2). The individual considers a series of behavioural options and the potential direct outcomes and consequences of performing this behaviour. This cognitive process is influenced by the individual's attitudes towards that particular behaviour (i.e. whether the behaviour and its consequences are evaluated positively or negatively), subjective norms (i.e. the individual's belief about what significant others will think about the behaviour) and perceived behavioural control (i.e. the individual's belief regarding his ability to perform the behaviour). Following evaluation of these options, the individual takes the decision to perform a given behaviour. This cognitive process consisting of these three important factors, collectively, gives rise to a *behavioural intention*, which, according to the theory, constitutes a key predictor of whether or not the behaviour actually materialises. All three factors contribute to the formation of a behavioural intention. If one of them (e.g. the subjective norm concerning the new behaviour) is weak, then the overall behavioural intention decreases. Perceived behavioural control is likely to be an especially important factor given that the individual must believe that behaviour change is actually possible. However, there are also inter-relations between the factors in that a positive attitude towards the new behaviour may motivate the individual to avoid particular social contexts or people who reinforce an undesirable behaviour, which in turn may increase perceived behavioural control.

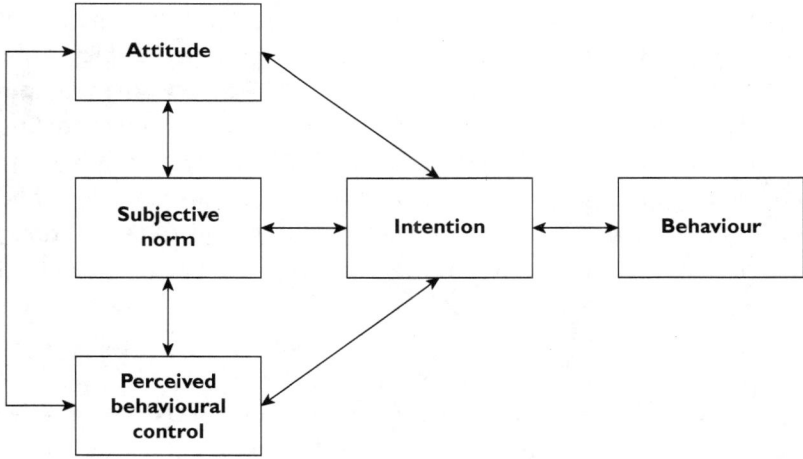

Figure 2: Theory of planned behaviour

The theory of planned behaviour can be fruitfully applied to behaviour change among MSM at risk of poor sexual health. In Chapter 1, Case 1 described Mark's desire to change various behaviours that put him at elevated risk of acquiring HIV. One of these behaviours included Mark's frequent use of Grindr in order to meet multiple sexual partners with whom he was not consistently using condoms. It is possible to apply tenets of the theory of planned behaviour to facilitate changes to this specific behaviour – condomless sex with multiple casual partners.

First, Mark would need to formulate an evaluation of this particular behaviour, that is, his attitude towards it. Following his diagnosis with two STIs and his discovery that he was at high risk of HIV, Mark came to the realisation that he did not hold a positive attitude towards this behaviour. He concluded that he was not enjoying himself and questioned why he was doing it. Mark would also need to develop an attitude towards the alternative behaviour, such as sex with condoms with a smaller number of partners. This attitude could be positive in that it would put him at lower risk of HIV and other STIs, but it could also be negative given the potential for decreased sensation and pleasure as a result of the behaviour change. It is noteworthy that attitudes concern not only the specific behaviours but also their outcomes and consequences. The intervention may focus on challenging attitudes that inhibit behaviour change and on promoting those that are conducive to the change. This may involve exposure to particular attitudes and group-based discussions regarding relevant topics.

Second, Mark would draw upon the perceived views and attitudes of other people who matter to him in order to detect an overarching 'norm'. This will depend on social context. While gay friends who are not in monogamous relationships and his sexual partners might find his desire to limit his number of sexual partners and to use condoms all the time as conservative and heteronormative, his gay friends in monogamous relationships, heterosexual friends and family members might conversely find this new behaviour more socially desirable. In short, norms vary in accordance with social context. Mark may decide to focus on the views of the latter groups and, thus, arrive at a positive subjective norm concerning his proposed behaviour. The intervention may seek to increase the availability of a wide range of social groups to facilitate greater exposure to a more favourable subjective norm, on the one hand, and to challenge coercive norms and attitudes in specific groups that can lead to an unfavourable subjective norm, on the other hand.

Third, Mark would consider his ability to perform the new behaviour. Given his sensation-seeking and hedonistic personality traits and the ease with which sexual partners can be found using geospatial gay social networking applications, Mark may initially believe that he has little behavioural control. He may believe that, despite the merits of performing the new behaviour, he is unable to do so and that attempting behaviour change is thus futile. Perceived behavioural control is an important factor. Despite his own positive attitude and the positive subjective norm concerning the new behaviour, it may not be possible for him to sustain, or even to enact, this change in his behaviour. A key focus of the intervention might be to build feelings of self-efficacy in participants in order to empower them to enact behaviour change. This may focus on providing exposure to narratives of success from others in a similar situation or of developing individualised pathways to success that can be followed by the participant.

Transtheoretical stages of change model

The transtheoretical stages of change model integrates tenets and principles from other health behaviour models and has a focus on the following theoretical constructs: (1) stage of change, (2) decisional balance, (3) self-efficacy and (4) the processes of change (see Figure 3).

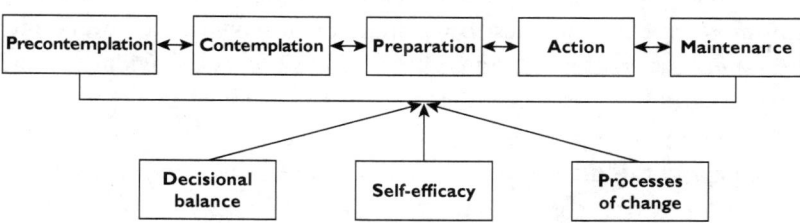

Figure 3: Transtheoretical stages of change model

The most important aspect of the theory is the stage of change, which refers to the individual's progression through a series of developmental stages in their journey towards behaviour change. These include: (1) precontemplation, which is when the individual does not intend to take action in the near future; (2) contemplation, which refers to the desire to take action within the next six months; (3) preparation, that is, the intention to take action in the next 30 days; (4) action, which refers to sustained behaviour change for up to six months; and (5) maintenance, that is, behaviour change that has been sustained for more than six months. The goal of practitioners is not only to promote behaviour change but also to sustain these changes in people so that they do not revert to previous behaviours. The model provides a heuristic lens for understanding the developmental journey towards behaviour change and specifies potential 'goals', such as aspiring to reach stages 3, 4 and then 5. It is noteworthy that individuals do not always move through these stages in the way suggested by the model and that there may be 'regression' to earlier stages before the achievement of long-term behaviour change.

As highlighted in the other two behaviour change models, self-efficacy is an important component of interventions for promoting behaviour change. In the transtheoretical stages of change model, the definition of self-efficacy emphasises the individual's belief in their ability to overcome potential obstacles that may impede sustained behaviour change. Decisional balance is a cognitive process whereby the individual considers the potential advantages and disadvantages of making a change to their behaviour. This is analogous to the process of considering the outcomes of a behaviour, which is described in other models. Decisional balance is a complex process. While dominant social norms, values and feedback from one's environment may emphasise the advantages of enacting a particular behaviour, the reality of that behaviour may present other kinds of (unforeseen) disadvantages to the individual. However, it should also be noted that, as the individual enacts and sustains behaviour change, they begin to adjust their lives in order to accommodate the change. Changes in social context or circumstances can also flag up new advantages or disadvantages that had not previously been considered. The processes of change refer to actions and activities that people engage in and the experiences and emotions that they experience as they try to progress through the aforementioned stages. For instance, the individual might develop relationships with people who enable him to sustain a particular behaviour. Decisional balance, self-efficacy and the processes of change, collectively, affect his ability to progress through the stages of change.

In thinking about Juan who was described in Case 3 in Chapter 1, it is easy to see how tenets of the transtheoretical stages of change model can help inform an intervention to promote positive engagement with HIV care and specifically Juan's adherence to ART. The decision to initiate ART is an important one because it is a life-long commitment and non-adherence to ART can result in viral resistance, poor disease progression and onward HIV transmission. As highlighted in Case 3, Juan experienced trepidation about initiating ART because he preferred to forget about his infection and, when he did begin, his adherence decreased until finally he disengaged from care. An intervention drawing upon the transtheoretical stages of change model would aim to facilitate Juan's progression through each stage, equipping him with the social, psychological and emotional resources to progress from preparation to action and finally to maintenance. This may involve providing information regarding the potential impact of ART on other aspects of his life, such as possible self-effects, memories about his HIV diagnosis and his relationships with others, while also exploring potential strategies for coping effectively with these impacts. Juan may be encouraged to consider how he might limit these negative impacts in order to gain confidence about adhering to ART.

A key objective of an ART adherence intervention informed by this model would be to enhance self-efficacy in participants like Juan, so that they feel empowered to cope effectively with the stressors and obstacles that could impede adherence. Peer support from other HIV-positive people who are adherent to their medication could enable participants in such an intervention to focus on the advantages of ART adherence, such as better disease prognosis, better health-related quality of life, decreased risk of onward HIV transmission, while considering and dealing effectively with the potential disadvantages. The intervention would seek to shift decisional balance in favour of adopting the desired behaviour, namely to initiate and adhere to ART. Finally, the processes of change need to be captured in the intervention. It is necessary to know what the participants are actually doing as they progress through the stages of change. Clearly, there are some behaviours like engaging in chemsex, which can be protective against other social stressors, such as HIV stigma, but potentially obstructive for ART adherence. It is vital that behavioural interventions capture, acknowledge and address the processes of change, that is, the accompanying behaviours and experiences that can either facilitate or inhibit the desired behaviour. Crucially, these behaviours may not always be readily disclosed by participants who anticipate stigma from others. Thus, gauging the processes of change requires sensitivity.

Overview

In this chapter, three counselling psychology frameworks and three models of behaviour change have been explored. Each has its merits.

Psychodynamic approaches focus on the unconscious and work to sensitise the patient to suppressed aspects of their past and present in order to promote positive psychological change. The acknowledgement of interpersonal relationships – both past and present – as determinants of wellbeing is valuable, especially in view of the interpersonal nature of the common stressors presented in Chapter 2. The humanistic person-centred approach specifies a series of human needs and the challenges to wellbeing that arise when they are, for whatever reason, curtailed. The theoretical acknowledgement of 'conditions of worth', which amount to societal expectations and prescriptions, rightly embeds the individual within their social context. The framework emphasises the human capacity for self-actualisation, which occurs when the ideal self and actual self are more closely aligned. The cognitive-behavioural approaches tend to focus on how individuals attempt to cope with psychological stress and, more specifically, to evade situations likely to cause or accentuate stress. The focus is on encouraging the patient to elect more productive, rather than maladaptive, coping strategies.

It is argued that therapeutic approaches aimed at the individual should be coupled with larger-scale interventions for enhancing self-identity, wellbeing and sexual health at a group level. These interventions should be guided by theories of behaviour change. Social cognitive theory attempts to reconcile the personal and environmental factors that shape behaviour, thereby acknowledging the importance of both cognition and society. Similarly, the theory of planned behaviour and the transtheoretical stages of change model both emphasise the role of individual attitudes and subjective norms, which arise from awareness of what significant others think, in shaping behaviour. All of the theories share a focus on self-efficacy, which is presented as a key principle guiding behaviour and indeed behaviour change.

These frameworks and models collectively allude to the importance of considering human identity in order for the practitioner to understand how human beings think, feel and behave. Identity is populated by one's past experiences, one's interpersonal relationships, cognitive frameworks for evaluating the present and the conditions of worth internalised over time. Personality traits and social factors contribute to identity. Furthermore, the frameworks and models demonstrate a need to understand how the individual's identity relates to the strategies they select in order to cope with adversity.

Each therapeutic framework specifies a limited number of strategies deployed by the individual but it is not always clear why a particular strategy will be chosen or whether it will be successful in promoting better psychological and physical health outcomes in the long-term. While the behaviour change models emphasise the importance of self-efficacy, other principles are known to be central to identity functioning. Understanding these principles could help practitioners develop more robust interventions for promoting sustained behaviour change in MSM. It is argued that the theoretical frameworks and models presented in this chapter could be enhanced by greater acknowledgement of how identity is constructed and indeed how it is protected. Accordingly, in the next chapter, social representations theory and identity process theory from social psychology are outlined and discussed.

Chapter 4

Identity Process Theory: Social Representation, Identity and Action

On the basis of the evidence presented in this volume, it is clear that both social and psychological factors contribute to self-identity, wellbeing and sexual health outcomes among MSM. It has been demonstrated that some personality traits, such as impulsivity, sensation-seeking and hedonism, may predispose an individual to engage in sexual risk-taking behaviours, which can undermine sexual health outcomes. In addition to these individual traits, there are clearly social and structural antecedents to sexual risk-taking behaviours, such as poverty, discrimination and social norms that facilitate and perhaps encourage particular practices. Moreover, social and psychological factors interact in producing wellbeing outcomes. People come to understand their identities and their experiences partly on the basis of the images, ideas and stereotypes that are prevalent within their socio-cultural milieu. In some cases, these images, ideas and stereotypes are negative and, thus, propel the individual towards feelings of self-disgust, shame and guilt vis-à-vis their identities and experiences. Accounts of sexual health, self-identity and wellbeing tend to focus on either the social or psychological levels, rather than integrating them. As highlighted in the previous chapter, in which therapeutic frameworks from counselling psychology and social psychological models of behaviour change were considered, this often results in a partial explanation of the issues that drive particular health and wellbeing outcomes. It is therefore necessary to utilise a theoretical framework that adequately captures both levels of analysis, as well as the inter-relations between them. Practitioners must consider how the social world impinges on the individual's meaning-making. In this chapter, it is proposed that tenets of social representations theory and identity process theory can facilitate a more holistic and nuanced understanding of how identity is constructed and defended in the face of threat. These theories are outlined and their relevance for practitioners working in the areas of self-identity, wellbeing and sexual health among MSM is considered.

Social representations

Social representations theory (Moscovici 1988, 2000) was designed to describe how abstract and unfamiliar ideas are diffused in society and how these ideas come to form part of our everyday thinking. These ideas eventually become 'common sense' and may be uncritically accepted by individuals. A social representation is defined as a system of values, ideas and practices regarding a given phenomenon (such as homosexuality, HIV or mental health), as well as the elaboration of that phenomenon so that people can understand, and think and communicate about it. Moreover, a social representation implicitly specifies 'appropriate' patterns of action, that is, how we ought to behave in relation to that phenomenon. For instance, some MSM themselves hold a negative social representation of homosexuality and associate it with stigmatised behaviours, which can reflect and perpetuate internalised homophobia. Some may feel ashamed of their homosexuality and, thus, conceal it and behave in ways that do not rouse suspicion about it.

In his analysis of how representations are formed, Moscovici (1988) outlines two fundamental processes, namely anchoring and objectification.

- Anchoring refers to the process of making something unfamiliar understandable by linking it to something familiar. Essentially, we link the unknown to the known. For instance, for individuals to develop an understanding of homosexuality, it must first be named and then imbued with familiar characteristics, which enable people to begin to understand, and think and communicate about it. Indeed, in reflecting on their sexual identity development, many MSM report not understanding their same-sex feelings and attractions and, particularly, not having the appropriate vocabulary to name it. Unfortunately, most MSM grow up in societies that are heteronormative and, in some cases, homonegative. They may be immersed in negative imagery about homosexuality, which draws upon discourses of sin, immorality and illness. Some may themselves come to link homosexuality to other stigmatised behaviours, such as promiscuity, and to stigmatised characteristics, such as disease or mental illness. It is easy to see how the anchoring of homosexuality to negative characteristics can encourage the perception that one must attempt to hide or even change one's sexual orientation. The difficulties associated with hiding one's sexuality and the impossibility of changing it can in turn induce feelings of despair among some MSM, leading to poor psychological wellbeing outcomes.

- Objectification is the process whereby unfamiliar and abstract phenomena are transformed into concrete and 'objective' common-sense realities. A common means of 'objectifying' an unfamiliar and abstract phenomenon is through the use of metaphors. Metaphors encourage us to view something in terms of something else. For instance, Jaspal and Nerlich (2017) describe how, in debates around PrEP, some journalists have referred to it metaphorically as a 'wonder drug', which raises expectations of the biomedical approach as a miraculous and invariably successful method for preventing HIV. Conversely, journalists who are less sympathetic towards PrEP have described it metaphorically in terms of a 'party drug' that leads to increased sexual risk-taking behaviours. This particular metaphorical construction of PrEP generalises the stigmatising characteristics of blithe, hedonistic partying to the use of PrEP, thereby stigmatising the prevention drug as well. Clearly, the metaphors that are used in relation to MSM, their health and practices can greatly shape the perceptions that MSM in turn formulate regarding themselves, their practices and their health.

The processes of anchoring and objectification perform both descriptive and evaluative functions by shedding light on what something is and how it should be evaluated. Together, these processes contribute to the formation of what we might call 'social representations'.

However, social representations are by no means independent entities over which individuals have no control. On the contrary, people themselves contribute to the formation of social representations and, as we will see below, can have considerable influence over their development. Thus, while the media, social institutions and other channels of societal information will clearly influence the genesis and development of social representations, people themselves also contribute to these processes through interpersonal communication, engagement with social institutions and, importantly, their own individual experiences.

It must be noted that 'expert' voices, such as the discourses of doctors, nurses and other healthcare practitioners, play an important role in the development of social representations, as their views are generally perceived to be grounded in specialist training and in empirical evidence. The discourses of healthcare professionals are especially important in the context of sexual health, self-identity and wellbeing because patients may actively seek the advice and expertise of such professionals. On the whole, patients attend consultations quite willing to be influenced. For instance, a MSM who has recently been diagnosed with HIV and knows little about the condition will be reliant on his medical team to explain HIV, his prognosis and the experience of living with the condition. It is therefore vital that healthcare professionals consider their use of anchoring and objectification in consultations with patients and that they are aware of their influential role in shaping patients' social representations.

On the other hand, it is also important to consider the social representations that may be prevalent in any given social context. These social representations also inform MSM's perceptions of their sexual health, self-identity and wellbeing. For instance, there is now a growing body of research into the lives of young ethnic minority MSM in Britain, which suggests that cultural and religious norms and values can make it difficult to come out as a sexual minority (e.g. Jaspal 2012). Thus, social representations that are prevalent in cultural and religious contexts constitute the backdrop against which many young ethnic minority MSM come to understand their sexual identities and, by extension, sexual health issues. Some may accept and internalise the negative religious social representation that homosexuality constitutes a sin and that HIV is divine punishment for engaging in sinful behaviour. Furthermore, MSM's lived experiences of their sexual orientation (as something that is long-standing, rather than chosen) can serve to challenge the social representation that homosexuality is sinful, because individuals may come to accept that they were simply born this way. Thus, individual experience too can contribute to their understanding of their sexuality.

Social representations are complex – on the one hand, they constitute the backdrop against which people develop a sense of who they are, that is, their identities, but, on the other hand, people respond to social representations in personalised ways. It is important therefore to consider the role of identity processes.

Identity process theory

Identity process theory (IPT) was founded by social psychologist Glynis Breakwell (Breakwell 1983, 1986, 1988, 1992, 2001, 2014) and later developed by others in research into a wide range of topics, including sexuality, politics and environmental behaviour (Jaspal 2014b; Jaspal and Breakwell 2014; Jaspal and Cinnirella 2010; Timotijevic and Breakwell 2000; Vignoles, Chryssochoou and Breakwell 2000). IPT essentially provides an integrative model of identity construction, threat and coping. It discusses the construct of identity in terms of its content and value dimensions. The content dimension of identity consists of a unique constellation of multiple elements (Linville 1985, 1987). Identity elements can be defined as categories derived from social experience but manifested in thought and action and include *inter alia* group memberships (e.g. being gay, Christian, middle class), individual traits (e.g. being shy, hardworking, untidy), and physical aspects (e.g. being tall, blue-eyed, of dark complexion). Identity consists of multiple elements, some of them seemingly unconnected and irrelevant, such as being tall and hardworking, and others directly related to one another, such as being gay and of religious faith, in the eyes of the individual at least. Identity elements differ in terms of their relative importance – some elements will be viewed as more important than others. Social representations play a role in determining the extent to which identity elements are related to one another, as well as their relative importance in specific contexts. Figure 4 outlines the relations between the processes, principles, experiences, outcomes and actions described in the theory.

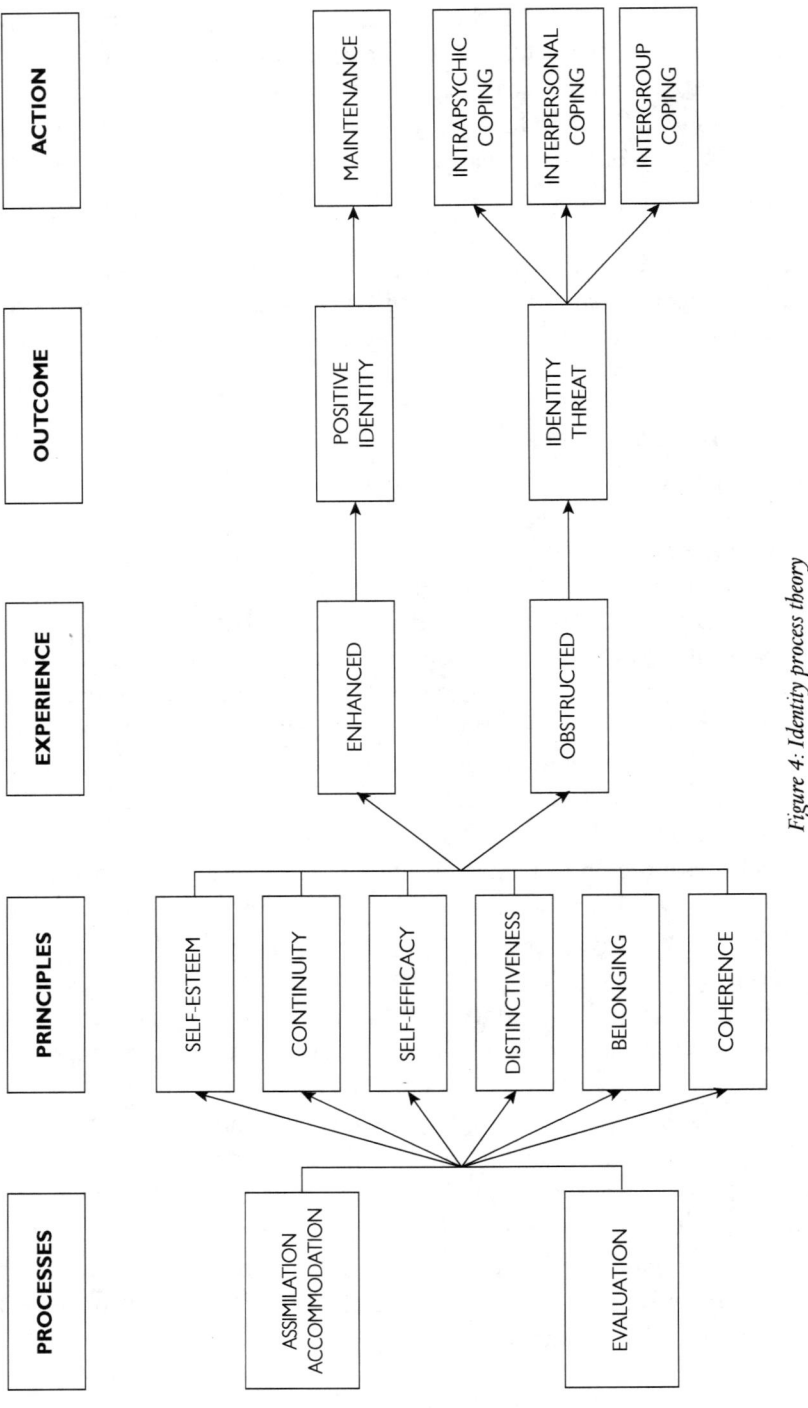

Figure 4: Identity process theory

The identity processes

According to the Breakwell's (1986) original formulation of IPT, individuals construct their identity by engaging in two psychological processes: *assimilation-accommodation* and *evaluation*.

Assimilation-accommodation refers to the process of absorbing and creating space for new information in identity. For instance, a same-sex attracted man may eventually come to view himself as gay, thereby assimilating this element to his identity. At this stage, being gay comes to form part of the content dimension of identity. However, in assimilating this new element, the individual may need to make modifications to the existing identity structure. For instance, he may re-think the importance or nature of his religious identity in order to accommodate his gay identity. It is noteworthy, however, that same-sex attracted men in some cultures may never view themselves as gay, perhaps because this category is not part of the cultural repertoire, that is, it is not a social representation in their society (see Murray and Roscoe 1997 for a discussion of sexual identity in Middle Eastern cultures). The assimilation-accommodation process is regarded as a single process with two components because when novel identity elements are assimilated to identity, they also need to be accommodated. This identity process is related principally to the content dimension of identity because the assimilation and accommodation of new elements to identity result in changes to identity content, such as their relevance and centrality, and can even result in the loss of other identity elements.

Evaluation refers to the process of attributing meaning and value to identity elements. The meanings and values appended to identity elements are dependent, at least in part, on social representations that are dominant in one's social context. For example, the same-sex attracted individual who comes out as gay may construe this new identity element as a group membership, which may lead him to modify his existing social relationships and friendship circles. He may wish to make gay friends and begin to distance himself from his heterosexual friends. However, as indicated above, in some societies, the dominant social representation of homosexuality is that this is an individual trait, rather than a group membership, which can lead some individuals to perceive it in precisely those terms and, thus, to refrain from seeking friends who share their sexual orientation. Furthermore, socialisation in a heteronormative environment may initially lead the same-sex attracted individual to append negative valence to being gay. He may feel ashamed of his sexual orientation and, thus, view it as something to be concealed or even changed. However, by associating with other gay people, the individual may be exposed to positive social representations of his sexual orientation and, thus, come to append positive valence to it. The evaluation process is related to the value dimension of identity.

The identity principles

In her statement of the theory, Breakwell (1986) states that the two identity processes do not function in a random manner but rather that they function to satisfy various motivational principles. On the basis of current IPT research, the following identity principles can be identified: self-esteem, self-efficacy, distinctiveness, continuity, belonging and coherence. These principles specify the desirable end-states for identity. They are states that individuals strive to be in. Consequently, the processes of assimilation-accommodation and evaluation function in ways that provide the individual with appropriate levels of these principles. It is unlikely that the individual will readily assimilate and accommodate an identity element that undermines the identity principles.

- Self-esteem refers to the subjective emotional evaluation that one has of oneself. The individual derives a subjective emotional evaluation of himself at least partly on the basis of how he believes himself to be evaluated by others. For instance, some MSM living with HIV report decreased self-esteem due to sexual problems that can arise a result of living with the condition, such as damage to sexual selfhood and the perception that is one is 'sexually hazardous' to others (Rohleder, McDermott and Cook 2017). It has also been observed that homophobic remarks from significant others (such as one's parents) can lead to a poor self-image among individuals who identify as gay as they may believe that they are devalued by others (Jaspal and Siraj 2011). Typically, self-esteem is damaged as a result of exposure to social stigma.

- Self-efficacy can be defined as one's belief that one can succeed in specific situations and accomplish desired tasks. As indicated in Chapter 3, it is central to models of behaviour change. While gay men generally manifest high levels of awareness and understanding of the effectiveness of condoms for the prevention of HIV and other STIs, many do not feel able to negotiate the use of condoms with their sexual partners and, thus, fail to use them. This is referred to as low condom self-efficacy. Furthermore, MSM with internalised homophobia may strive to change their sexual orientation but feel unable to do so, which can undermine feelings of competence and control, leading to decreased self-efficacy.

- Distinctiveness refers to the desire to establish and maintain a sense of differentiation from other individuals. The motive for distinctiveness must be managed alongside the competing motive for a sense of belonging within relevant social groups. For instance, although a gay man may perceive affinity and solidarity with other gay men, he may resist gay-related stereotypes and even criticise other gay men who appear to behave in accordance with these stereotypes in an attempt to establish and maintain a sense of (positive) differentiation. It is noteworthy that this drive is likely to be especially significant for MSM with internalised homophobia.

- Continuity constitutes the psychological thread that connects past, present and future. This allows the individual to perceive himself as the same despite the presence of social and individual change. Coming out as gay can jeopardise the continuity principle because this experience often entails changes to the nature of one's relationships – parents and friends may begin to treat one differently as a result of disclosing one's sexual identity. Furthermore, as indicated in Case 3 of Chapter 1, some MSM at risk of HIV are not actually aware of their risk-taking behaviour and may therefore experience shock and bewilderment upon receipt of a positive HIV diagnosis. An HIV diagnosis can precipitate not only negative cognitions about the self but also negative reactions from others, which can in turn induce negative projections of the future. Some patients may worry about their future health or their ability to establish and maintain close relationships with others. The experience of an HIV diagnosis can therefore be detrimental to one's sense of continuity.

- Belonging refers to the need for acceptance and inclusion in groups that are of social and psychological significance to the individual. Individuals who are newly diagnosed with HIV may experience isolation in the immediate aftermath of their diagnosis, which can result from rejection from others or the desire to conceal their positive serostatus from others. Individuals may anticipate rejection and opt for isolation, which of course inhibits feelings of acceptance and inclusion. Conversely, HIV-positive individuals may derive psychosocial benefits from joining HIV support groups and by meeting other people living with the condition. They may perceive feelings of acceptance and inclusion from other people sharing their experiences, which can enhance the belonging principle of identity.

- Coherence can be defined as the subjective perception of compatibility between identity elements that are construed as being relevant to one another. As indicated above, social representations play a fundamental role in determining the extent to which identity elements are relevant to one another and also whether or not they are compatible. As indicated in Case 2 in Chapter 1, some gay men of religious faith experience challenges in reconciling their sexual and religious identities, particularly if the norms, values and images associated with each identity are viewed as being in conflict with one another (Jaspal and Cinnirella 2010). They may experience psychological tensions when thinking about this conflict in identity, particularly if the identity elements are both valued by the individual. Research with gay Muslims suggests that, while Muslim identity is valued more favourably than being gay, homosexuality may be perceived as inescapable. Individuals may therefore struggle to come to terms with the perceived incompatibilities between these identity elements.

Identity enhancement and threat

We construct our identities in ways that provide us with appropriate levels of these principles. We generally view as more central to identity those elements that satisfy these principles. For instance, some gay men derive self-esteem, continuity and distinctiveness on the basis of their gay identity and may therefore view this identity element as particularly central to who they are. As depicted in Figure 4, those actions or identity elements that enhance the identity principles result in a positive identity and, thus, they are maintained. Conversely, those identity elements that jeopardise the identity principles lead to identity threat and may never be assimilated and accommodated in identity. For instance, some MSM living with HIV never come to view HIV as an identity element and continue to think of themselves as HIV-negative. This could be attributed to the negative impact of an HIV diagnosis for self-esteem, continuity, self-efficacy and so on. Yet, the consequences for physical health may be detrimental.

The identity principles are important predictors of behaviour. In fact, identity concerns can often override other factors that are thought to underlie behaviour, such as risk awareness. Although individuals may be aware of the risks associated with particular sexual practices, they may continue to engage in these practices if they are construed as enhancing the identity principles (Breakwell and Millward 1997). For instance, if engagement in condomless anal intercourse provides feelings of self-esteem, the individual may be more inclined to continue to engage in that behaviour despite the risks involved. Similarly, it has been observed that chemsex can provide some MSM with increased self-esteem due to the nature of sexual relations within this context, which can motivate individuals to engage in this practice despite their awareness of the associated health risks. In short, identity concerns can override risk awareness.

A key tenet of IPT is that if the principles are somehow jeopardised, for instance by changes in one's social context, identity is threatened. Challenges to a single principle can result in identity threat, but the threat is likely to be more acute if more than one principle is affected. Recent research suggests that individuals append more or less importance to particular identity principles in accordance with their personal values (Bardi, Jaspal, Schwartz and Polek 2014). Those individuals who value conservation and tradition tend to append greater importance to continuity than to distinctiveness, for instance. It is therefore likely that individuals who value conservation will experience challenges to the continuity principle as more threatening than those to the distinctiveness principle. It can be hypothesised that those MSM who themselves value conservation and tradition might experience greater threats to continuity and, thus, more serious challenges in disclosing their sexual identity to others.

It is noteworthy that the experience of threat is personal and subjective in that it is the individual who perceives it. It is quite possible that what is construed by one individual as a threat to their self-esteem may be dismissed as insignificant by others. It is also possible that what the practitioner believes to be a 'threatening position' is not experienced as such as by the individual himself. Two examples illustrate the subjectivity of identity threat. A passing remark about masculinity could ignite long-standing, latent threats to self-esteem in an MSM who has suffered homophobic bullying in the past, especially if the focus of the bullying was their gender non-normativity. Conversely, an MSM who has faced no past stigma on the basis of his gender non-normativity may not experience a threat to identity and may simply laugh off the remark. Furthermore, people living with HIV differ in the extent to which they come to terms with their diagnosis. While some individuals living with HIV experience severe challenges to their sense of continuity when they think of their diagnosis, others re-construe their HIV diagnosis as a catalyst for positive change in their lives and do not perceive it as a significant threat. Of course, it is possible that a coping strategy has already been deployed, leading to early termination of the threat. However, it appears that personality traits, past experiences, group memberships and indeed the social representation that one holds will collectively determine the ways in which an individual will construe any given event or experience and, thus, the extent to which it is threatening for identity. It is easy to see how other people (e.g. friends, family, practitioners) may overlook or miss a threat to identity, which can plausibly limit the social support that the threatened individual receives, particularly if the individual does not seek social support himself.

Action: coping with threats to identity

A crucial component of IPT concerns coping. Identity threat is aversive for psychological wellbeing and, thus, individuals attempt to cope with threat, that is, to minimise its effects or to eradicate it altogether. Coping strategies function primarily at three distinct levels of human interdependence: intrapsychic, interpersonal and intergroup. Some of the original coping strategies articulated in Breakwell's (1986) original formulation of IPT are described below. The aim is not to provide an exhaustive list of coping strategies but rather to discuss some of those strategies that may be deployed by the MSM who experiences threats to identity.

Intrapsychic coping strategies

Intrapsychic strategies function at the cognitive and emotional levels. Most of them seek to deflect the threat to identity and a small number facilitate acceptance of the threat. Intrapsychic strategies are almost always deployed in the first instance and later supplemented or replaced by interpersonal and/or intergroup strategies (see below). Most intrapsychic strategies are effective only in the short-term insofar as they minimise the effects of identity threat, and have limited value in the long-term. It is important to note that the individual hardly operates within a hermetic environment and, thus, social circumstances can disrupt the operation and effectiveness of most intrapsychic strategies – especially those that deflect threat.

Denial

Denial constitutes a common response to threat. By denying the existence of a threatening reality, one is able to protect one's sense of identity, albeit temporarily. For instance, a MSM newly diagnosed with HIV may face considerable threats to various identity principles – self-esteem, continuity, self-efficacy and coherence – all at the same time. These threats to identity may be further accentuated by threats associated with other stigmatised identity elements, such as his sexual orientation. The sheer magnitude of the threat to identity associated with his HIV diagnosis may lead him to shield himself from this threatening reality by denying it, its relevance, its urgency and its implications. Indeed, Juan, whose case was described in the first chapter of this volume, appeared to rely on denial as his principal coping strategy. The individual who denies his positive serostatus may initially appear to understand the information communicated to him but later disengage from sexual health services. This may enable him – temporarily at least – to return psychologically to his pre-diagnosis state, and to suppress distressing thoughts of his HIV diagnosis. He may engage in activities that enable him to forget his diagnosis, such as drug and alcohol misuse, and he may not disclose his HIV status to other people due to his own inability to accept this reality. He may avoid contact or relations with other HIV-positive individuals. In order to deny his HIV status effectively (the source of identity threat), he is highly unlikely to engage with sexual health services or to initiate ART, because such actions would serve as a reminder of his diagnosis and, of course, require some acceptance of his threatening reality.

Denial is rarely effective in the long term because the source of the threat is unlikely to disappear but may in fact grow in severity. In the case of HIV infection, the denial strategy can be detrimental to both physical and psychological wellbeing. In denying one's HIV status, one is unlikely to take steps to improve health outcomes, such as ART initiation, which in turn will undermine disease prognosis and lead to poor physical health outcomes, such as a compromised immune system, the onset of opportunistic infections or even death. On a psychological level, the newly diagnosed MSM will not assimilate or accommodate his HIV status in his identity and may therefore become avoidant and withdrawn, leading to a lack of social support. Though in denial, he may be reminded of his reality and face exposure to stigmatising images of HIV, which could further accentuate the threatening nature of his predicament. It is noteworthy that denial can sometimes be effective as a short-term coping strategy because it can allow the individual the time and space to develop potential cognitive and social resources for eventually engaging with the threat. However, denial generally impedes productive action against the source of the threat.

Transient depersonalisation

Transient depersonalisation could be described as a short-term experience of estrangement from oneself, which can lead to feelings of detachment and disconnection from oneself when facing threat. It constitutes a temporary 'exit option' when faced with threat. Transient depersonalisation is different from denial because it does involve some acknowledgement of a threatening reality. However, the temporary engagement from oneself enables the individual to view the threat as also *separate* and *estranged* from the self. The strategy can temporarily shield the individual from the immediate effects of identity threat because the threatening stimulus is simply not viewed as being relevant to the self. For example, a MSM who engages in chemsex for the first time may experience feelings of shame after the initial experience, which could be attributed to his belief that this behaviour is stigmatised and problematic. Incidentally, such beliefs may be reinforced by others in one's social context who may also regard chemsex in similar terms. Given the potential difficulties of assimilating and accommodating this new behaviour in identity and the possible challenges that it can cause to the principles of self-esteem, continuity, self-efficacy and so on, the individual may initially experience transient depersonalisation and treat the experience as if it were related to somebody else. The individual will recollect the experience but view it as irrelevant to the self, due to his transient estrangement from it. It appears that transient depersonalisation is not within the individual's control – it occurs spontaneously in response to a threatening reality and functions in order to protect him from this reality. Due to its non-volitional nature, transient depersonalisation tends only to offer temporary respite from threat and is, thus, unlikely to be productive and effective in the long term.

Real and unreal selves

We tend to view our identity (or self-conception) as stable and enduring over time. This is essential to our sense of continuity. The self-conception tends to be construed in positive terms, which is important for our self-esteem. Yet, we also acknowledge that some self-images can be transient or 'not really me'. These self-images may refer to periods in our lives when we have thought or acted in particular ways. More specifically, those self-images that are perceived to be inconsistent with the current or desired self-conception may be dismissed as inauthentic, that is, 'not really me'. This enables the individual to differentiate between 'real' and 'unreal' selves. For instance, in the early stages of a romantic relationship, a MSM may decide to reveal to his partner information about his sexual history, which may include stigmatised behaviours, such as casual sex with multiple partners, sex work, or engagement in chemsex. However, aspects of his sexual past may subsequently be 'weaponised' by his partner and used against him in arguments. It is easy to see how this could disrupt one's sense of continuity and self-esteem, especially if the behaviours are stigmatised. Stigma itself can arise when one moves from a social context in which these behaviours were acceptable (e.g. being single) into to a new context in which they are now deemed to be unacceptable (e.g. being in a relationship). One possible method of coping with the consequential stigma and identity threat may be to differentiate between one's real and unreal selves, that is, to construe one's former behaviour as inauthentic to one's *real self*. The individual may attribute the stigmatised behaviours to the constraints of the social context, arguing that he had no choice, and consequently assert that they bear no correspondence to his real self. This can enable him to cordon off undesirable, threatening information about the self from his self-conception and, thus, minimise threats to identity. The effectiveness of this strategy is limited primarily because the individual cannot repeatedly attribute various self-images to an unreal self, as this may undermine feelings of authenticity and even lead to a fragmented sense of identity in which the real and unreal selves can no longer be easily distinguished.

Re-construal and re-attribution

The threatened individual may attempt to re-construe the threatening situation or its implications in order to reduce threat. This may involve re-defining the characteristics of the threatening position occupied by the individual. For instance, the MSM who is diagnosed with HIV may ignore the potential social and psychological implications of his diagnosis, such as the possibility that he might face stigma and rejection from potential sexual partners. He might reduce the experience of living with HIV to the necessity of taking a daily pill. This amounts to re-construing the nature of the position occupied, which shields identity from threat. It obviates the need to think about the more challenging aspects of living with HIV, which could plausibly abrogate continuity, self-efficacy and so on. On the other hand, it has been observed that some individuals may re-construe the meanings of their HIV infection and re-construe it in relatively positive terms. For example, some MSM who are diagnosed with HIV refer to maladaptive and sometimes self-destructive behaviours in which they engaged prior to their diagnosis, such as alcohol and substance misuse, sexual risk-taking, etc. Some may in fact re-construe their HIV diagnosis as a 'wake-up call', which compelled them to introduce positive change in their lives and, in some cases, to engage in HIV activism. In short, they may re-construe their HIV diagnosis as a catalyst for positive change in their lives, thereby reducing the power of HIV to threaten identity. It is no longer appended the negative valence that originally allowed it to threaten identity and takes on a more positive role in identity.

Re-attribution may also occur. The individual diagnosed with HIV may pose the question: why me? It is habitual for individuals facing psychological adversity to think through the possible reasons for being in that situation. A common strategy for deflecting identity threat is to attribute the causes of one's predicament to external factors and to distance responsibility from the self. For instance, the MSM who expresses shame about the number of sexual partners he has had and the transience of his sexual relationships may attribute his sexual behaviour to 'gay culture', rather than view this as a decision that he himself has made. This serves to protect identity from threat because the main cause of the behaviour is externalised and distanced from the self.

Compartmentalisation

This strategy entails the assimilation of threatening elements to identity without their accommodation. The individual accepts a particular trait or characteristic about himself but it is cordoned off from the rest of identity, which enables him to ignore its broader implications for other aspects of identity. In other words, he essentially compartmentalises a threatening element of identity by constructing walls around it and reducing its ability to 'contaminate' other elements of identity. For instance, the MSM who is newly diagnosed with HIV may accept this new information about himself and assimilate it to his identity but, given its threatening nature, he may isolate it within identity, thereby preventing it from affecting other identity aspects, such as his sexual behaviour. Although he is aware of his HIV status and thinks about it in some contexts, such as when he takes his medication or attends appointments with his HIV consultant, he may not think about it in others. For instance, he may continue to engage in condomless sex with partners because he fails to see the relevance of his HIV status for his sexual behaviour. He may smoke and engage in other risky health behaviours that are especially unadvisable for HIV patients. His compartmentalised HIV status is simply not viewed as being relevant to other identity elements – in this case, his identity as a sexual being or as a smoker. This strategy minimises the risk of threats to continuity that might usually arise as a result of needing to give up smoking or to self-esteem due to the possible rejection one may face from a sexual partner. The strategy has also been observed in research into MSM of religious faith, many of whom report avoiding thoughts about their sexuality when in religious settings and vice versa (Jaspal and Cinnirella 2010). This obviates the need to consider the coherence of these identity elements.

Salience of principles

Most threats to identity occur because a given situation or event abrogates one or two of the identity principles. The salience of principles strategy refers to the individual's ability to attenuate the importance of the threatened identity principles and instead to focus on other principles. For instance, breaking up with a long-term partner could severely compromise the individual's sense of continuity because he has become so accustomed to life with his partner and the break-up of course exposes him to change. The individual may move out of his shared accommodation with his former partner, miss spending time with him, and find it difficult to change his daily routine which consisted of joint activities. However, provided that the break-up does not challenge other principles of identity, it is quite possible for the individual to focus his attention on self-esteem, self-efficacy and distinctiveness. He may in fact begin to consider the potential benefits of the break-up for their self-esteem, perhaps because he no longer faces stigma or denigration from his partner, or for his self-efficacy if he feels more independent and empowered following his departure from the relationship. Salience of principles can be considered an acceptance strategy because the individual accepts the source of the threat but attempts to focus on other possible aspects of his situation. This strategy is in fact very common. Many changes do inevitably challenge the continuity principle of identity, given that they represent a rupture in the links between past, present and future, but these changes may be tolerated because of the potential benefits for other principles of identity. Given that individuals probably prioritise some identity principles over others due to their personality traits, in some cases it may be very difficult to attenuate the importance of, say, distinctiveness if this has always been important to the individual. A potential shortcoming of the salience of principles strategy is that some situations present 'hyper-threats' to identity in that they simultaneously abrogate all of the principles of identity. For many people newly diagnosed with HIV, their diagnosis does appear to constitute such a 'hyper-threat' – as it simultaneously threatens self-esteem, self-efficacy, continuity, distinctiveness and coherence – which can make the salience of principles strategy impossible. The individual essentially has nowhere to turn and must resort to other coping strategies.

Anticipatory restructuring

The individual may be aware of the social psychological demands associated with his threatening position some time before the threat actually materialises. It is possible that the individual who decides to have an HIV test knows that he will test positive, or that one suspects that one's romantic partner will eventually leave. Both of these scenarios can be construed as threats to self-esteem and continuity. In anticipation of the threats to identity, the individual may focus his attention on accommodating the threatening element in identity in the most effective way possible before the event has occurred. For instance, a gay man who has accepted and assimilated his sexual orientation to his identity may begin to re-think his friendship circles and to attenuate the importance of friendship with those individuals unlikely to accept his sexuality and to accentuate the importance of friendship with those more likely to accept it. Similarly, he may anticipate threats to, or even the loss of, other identity elements, such as his involvement in religious community, and thus attenuate the significance of this identity element prior to the event. He may begin to think about possible reactions from other people and rehearse explanations, which he may offer to people who learn that he is gay. Furthermore, practices and identity elements that were hitherto intended to deflect his sexual orientation may slowly be abandoned in order for him to prepare himself and others for his coming out. All of these practices reflect the re-structuring of identity *in anticipation of* the threatening event so that the impact for identity is minimised. The individual accepts that the event will pose a threat to identity but chooses to take pre-emptive action against the threat. It is important to note that, despite pre-emptive action against the threat, the individual may be unable to completely eradicate the threat to identity as there will be some aspects that are simply not foreseen or that cannot be alleviated. The accommodation component of the assimilation-accommodation process and the evaluation process can greatly facilitate this coping strategy.

Interpersonal strategies

Interpersonal strategies for coping with threats to identity focus on changing the nature or dynamics of relationships with others. The aim is always to minimise the potential for identity threat that can arise from the nature of one's relationships with other people by disclosing or concealing, in one way or another, the threatening stimulus. Interpersonal strategies can sometimes be deployed alongside other intrapsychic strategies in order to optimise the coping response. However, these strategies all have limited effectiveness.

Isolation

The threatened individual may attempt to shield identity from threat by avoiding contact with other people. In the case of threatened self-esteem, it is easy to see how isolation can minimise the risk of social stigma undermining a person's self-esteem. After all, if the individual isolates himself, he is not exposed to stigmatising, hostile or aggressive feedback from others. The isolation strategy goes hand in hand with deflection strategies operating at the intrapsychic level, such as denial or re-construal, since the lack of social contact reduces the chance that others can challenge the revised 'reality' that the individual constructs in attempting to cope with threat. In previous research, it has been observed that MSM newly diagnosed with HIV may initially isolate themselves from other people due to the feelings of shame and stigma that they anticipate (Jaspal and Williamson 2017). They may erroneously suspect that other people know their HIV status or fear exposure to stigmatising remarks about HIV, which could potentially threaten self-esteem and continuity. Isolation is generally a maladaptive coping strategy because it deprives the individual of social support, which conversely is associated with successful coping. Much research demonstrates significant benefits of social support for coping with psychological adversity – social support is, for instance, negatively correlated with depressive symptoms (Miller, Wakefield and Sani 2017).

It must also be acknowledged that in deriving social support by disclosing intimate and potentially stigmatising aspects of the self, such as one's HIV status, one does run the risk of stigma, pity, hostility and even aggression – the very reactions that often propel the individual towards isolation in the first place. The isolationist is unlikely to join an HIV support group or to seek counselling following his diagnosis, which can deprive him of the social and psychological resources necessary for combating psychological stress associated with HIV. His decision to isolate himself may be the result of problematic previous experiences of disclosure. For instance, HIV-positive MSM who face stigma and rejection following disclosure of their HIV status may come to believe that these are inevitable responses, which can lead to complete disengagement from other people. Indeed, research has shown that those individuals who received negative and stigmatising responses from others experienced poorer psychological outcomes (Dowshen, Binns and Garofalo 2009). It is easy to see how such responses could deprive the individual of faith in others and, thus, lead him to favour isolation as a coping strategy. However, isolationists do not always engage in all-out isolation – they may be selective about the groups from which they isolate themselves. Some MSM diagnosed with HIV report threats to self-esteem due to the stigma and rejection that they encounter from HIV-negative men – particularly from potential sexual partners. This can lead some individuals to discard the possibility of a serodiscordant relationship and to isolate themselves from HIV-negative people, viewing them as a threatening, hostile outgroup. This can in turn give rise to new social groups (HIV-positive versus HIV-negative) and intergroup tensions.

Negativism

Negativism entails direct confrontation with the source of the threat to identity by refusing to accept perceived requirements or pressures from other people. In short, it entails saying 'no' to other people, and refusing to accept stigma and the threats that might normally be generated by it. For instance, a gay negativist who overhears a homophobic remark would not just ignore it but directly confront the perpetrator, challenging the validity of the remark. Often, a stigmatising remark that goes unchallenged can continue to threaten an individual's identity while this event remains salient within the individual's consciousness. The individual may continue to experience obstructions to self-esteem, continuity and so on. However, the act of negativism can serve to protect those principles of identity particularly if one believes that one has been successful in counteracting the source of the threat. In so doing, the individual convinces himself that the remark (reflecting, in this context, the societal pressure to be heterosexual) lacks validity and it therefore loses its power to threaten identity.

The strategy can be effective but there are of course circumstances under which the strategy itself can compromise identity processes. For instance, Muslim MSM who overtly challenge homophobia that they encounter from fellow members of their ethno-religious group may risk their own membership in that group, which can deprive them of an important source of belonging. Loss of a valued group membership can also result in abrogation of the continuity principle of identity. It is also easy to see how the strategy of negativism could induce hypersensitivity among those individuals who become accustomed to facing and challenging stigma from others. Misattribution and even paranoia may dominate the individual's thinking and their behaviour with other people. Genuine ignorance or innocent remarks from others could invite unwarranted hostility from the individual who utilises negativism, which in turn could undermine the quality of relationships with others.

Passing

A possible protective response to occupancy of a threatening social position is simply for the individual to exit it. Some group memberships, such as social class, can be easily relinquished, while others can be more difficult or even impossible to exit. Passing refers to the process of concealing one's group origins and feigning membership in a group of which one is not really a member. One enters a new group or interpersonal network on false pretences so that others do not gain awareness of one's group origins. For instance, many MSM do initially assimilate and accommodate their sexual orientation in identity but may recognise that, if disclosed to others, this identity element could expose them to stigma and derision. This could potentially lead to threats to self-esteem, continuity and self-efficacy. They may therefore conceal their sexual orientation from others and feign heterosexuality in order to protect themselves from threats to the aforementioned principles.

The interpersonal strategy of passing can complement deflection strategies operating at the intrapsychic level, such as denial. Indeed, the denialist whose 'false world' is validated by others can continue to deny his threatening reality. However, it is equally possible that the individual does not in any way deny his sexual orientation at an individual level, but rather that he simply wishes to conceal it from others in order to avoid threats to self-esteem via stigmatisation. In attempting to pass himself off convincingly as heterosexual, the individual may adopt other traits and characteristics that reinforce his membership in the group that he has entered on false pretences. An unfortunate example of this is the way in which some gay adolescents who have not disclosed their sexual orientation may themselves deride and denigrate other gay people, sometimes perpetrating acts of bullying, aggression or violence against them, in a cynical attempt to protect themselves from being exposed as gay.

It is easy to see how the passing strategy, which is intended to protect identity from threat, can reinforce feelings of internalised homophobia and the negative emotions that often accompany this state. This can be attributed to the self-withdrawal from possible social networks that could provide exposure to positive social representations. Another example of passing is the way in which some individuals living with HIV may, on the one hand, accept their positive serostatus but, on the other hand, decide never to reveal this information to others due to fear of stigma and rejection. In attempting to protect self-esteem, the individual may pass himself off as HIV-negative and avoid all discussions concerning HIV – with friends, family and sexual partners. Passing is sometimes accompanied by a degree of 'hypersensitivity' as the individual may fear being 'outed' as a member of the stigmatised group or interpersonal network and, thus, go to great lengths to protect their feigned membership of the new group. An individual living with HIV might not insist on condom use with a 'serosorting' sexual partner who assumes that he is HIV-negative, as he might fear that insistence on condom use could lead to suspicions about his own HIV status.

Compliance

The interpersonal strategy of compliance entails adherence to the behavioural and social norms and prescriptions associated with the threatened position. In stark contrast to negativism, compliance reflects the individual's acceptance and, thus, enactment of what is expected of him. This strategy can of course have a number of drawbacks, some of which are discussed below, but a potential benefit is that it may gain one social approval due to conformity to stereotypes and non-disruption of social hierarchies. In reflecting on periods of their lives, some MSM report engaging in particular behaviours (e.g. casual sex with multiple partners, frequenting gay sex venues and chemsex) because they believed that this is what it meant to be gay. The meanings attached to being gay will depend on dominant social representations. MSM may report complying with prevalent norms on the gay scene, which can in turn have problematic outcomes for self-identity, wellbeing and sexual health. Some of the activities perceived to be normative on the gay scene can lead to exposure to HIV, which itself can be a catalyst for poor psychosocial outcomes. In such situations, MSM may derive social approval from other gay men, which can enhance feelings of belonging. Compliance with social and behavioural norms can sometimes alleviate the feelings of loneliness and social disconnectedness reported by some MSM. However, possible downsides include the fact that some individuals begin to experience a schism in their sense of identity, particularly if they do not perceive the social and behavioural norms, with which they are compliant, as being consistent with their individual beliefs and values. In attempting to cope with threats to some principles of identity, such as belonging and self-esteem, the individual could inadvertently introduce a new threat to coherence by deploying the compliance strategy. Furthermore, while the individual may gain some acceptance and approval from others, compliance with norms associated with their gay identity could potentially lead to alienation from other valued social contexts. Some gay men describe their growing distance from heterosexual friends and family members as a result of coming out, which can sometimes be attributed to restrictive self-immersion in social and behavioural norms associated with their sexual identity.

Self-disclosure

Self-disclosure to a trusted significant other can constitute a fruitful and productive strategy for coping with threat. The threatened individual and his trusted significant other may exchange confidences about their problems, which can provide the individual with the opportunity to obtain positive feedback about himself, to validate aspects of his identity, and to make sense of the source of the threat. This is central to acceptance and self-acceptance, which were described in relation to psychotherapeutic approaches in Chapter 3. Sharing one's predicament with a trusted other can also reduce fear, anxieties and uncertainties about the future, all of which are associated with threat. Accordingly, it is possible that positive feedback and the sense-making that results from self-disclosure can banish the original threat to identity. For instance, most gay adolescent boys come out to their mothers in the first instance, and the nature of the mother's response to their coming out often determines their willingness to disclose their sexual identity to others, as well as their psychological wellbeing in the long-term. Coming out tends to be construed as a significant step in one's identity development and the initial responses to this are equally as significant in determining the future.

It is generally important that self-disclosure be reciprocal in that there should be an *exchange* of sensitive and intimate information. The threatened individual may feel uncomfortable disclosing such information without reciprocation from his interlocutor. The exchange of information can cement the relationship, build trust and maintain a balance of power between the two individuals. There are of course potential drawbacks to the self-disclosure strategy. Self-disclosure can result in further stigma if one's interlocutor (unexpectedly) provides negative or stigmatising feedback or even in emotional exploitation if one's confidence is breached. It is easy to see how such negative responses to self-disclosure could further imperil identity and lead to further stress, shame and anxiety about one's predicament. The individual may begin to regard self-disclosure and social support (see below) as counterproductive or dangerous, and instead revert to maladaptive strategies, such as isolation.

Intergroup strategies

Some threats emanate from particular individual traits and characteristics, others are the result of membership in a stigmatised social group. In attempting to cope with threats to identity, some people turn to social groups in order to seek social support or attempt to revise group dynamics. Intergroup coping strategies are generally more effective than those operating at the intrapsychic and interpersonal levels, because they seek to change the social conditions and indeed the social representations that are often conducive to threats.

Multiple group memberships

A key observation of IPT is that identity is composed of multiple elements of which many are indeed group memberships. Ahmed, whose case was described in Chapter 1, may simultaneously identify as gay, a former university student, of British nationality, of South Asian ethnicity, of Muslim faith, and so on. When the individual faces threats to identity associated with one group membership, other group memberships can, either singularly or collectively, assuage the threat to identity. The strategy of multiple group memberships can be deployed in a number of ways. For instance, discrimination against a MSM on the basis of his stigmatised sexual identity may be moderated by his other more socially valued group memberships, such as his status as a university student. The individual may accentuate this element of his identity in order to avoid stigmatisation due to his homosexuality, thereby minimising the threat to self-esteem. This essentially entails shifting the focus from the socially stigmatised to the socially valued.

Additionally, individuals who experience threats to identity due to a minority group membership may emphasise a group membership that is shared with others in their group context. A shared, superordinate identity can encompass other group memberships and thus supersede them. The HIV-positive MSM may be marginalised by other MSM due to his positive serostatus but he may emphasise his sexual identity in order to derive a sense of belonging. In short, people who might usually perceive themselves to be different can come to view themselves as members of a larger, more inclusive group.

An additional sub-strategy is that of strategically revising the salience of group memberships in accordance with social context. It is possible to temporarily 'switch off' a group membership and to activate another. This is not the same as departing the group but rather it refers to the temporary attenuation of the group membership so that identity can remain intact. In research into identity conflict among British Muslim MSM (e.g. Jaspal and Cinnirella 2010), it has been found that in attempting to reduce threats to continuity and self-esteem some individuals may accentuate their British identity and attenuate their Muslim identity when thinking about their homosexuality. They remain both British and Muslim, but the shift in focus enables them to eschew negative social representations of homosexuality and to access more positive social representations of their sexual orientation.

Group support

One of the most effective coping strategies is that of seeking group support. Confronted with a threat to identity, the individual may seek others who share his predicament and create a new group network based around it. Being a MSM, living with HIV, and suffering from depression can all constitute potentially threatening identity elements. Some individuals may be motivated to join or create group networks on the basis of one or more of these shared elements. As indicated above, isolation is seldom an effective strategy for coping with threat. Group support acts as a buffer against isolation because it provides a safe and inclusive context for deriving acceptance and inclusion but also information and consciousness about the nature of the threat. Often, the threatened individual, and particularly the isolationist who is threatened, comes to believe that the threat is insurmountable and that they are alone in experiencing it. However, by engaging with other people who share his grievance, the individual is able to understand more extensively the nature of the threat and its likely implications. Many people diagnosed with HIV initially know little about the condition and may believe that it is invariably life-limiting. Social support can provide exposure to accurate information about HIV and assuage the mortality concerns held by some individuals.

Furthermore, in externalising the thoughts and feelings, which often accompany the threat, in a supportive and inclusive environment, the threatened individual is able to relate them to the experiences of other people, which can perform a normalising function. In short, these thoughts and feelings may no longer seem idiosyncratic or strange but rather habitual aspects of living with a particular condition. It is noteworthy that social stigma is a common antecedent to threatened self-esteem, which can lead to reluctance to discuss the stigmatised issue. Yet, self-disclosure and the sharing of experience lie at the heart of the group support strategy. People feel empowered to share their experiences, and derive satisfaction from the knowledge that others are willing to follow suit. Self-disclosure can provide cathartic relief to the silence that often envelops the threatened individual's identity, while also providing greater group cohesion.

The group – originally intended as a social and informational network focusing on a specific issue – can evolve into an important and meaningful group membership for the threatened individual deprived of interpersonal contact. Through the new group, the threatened individual may be able to access a stock of alternative, more empowering social representations of the source of their threat. Exposure to such social representations can constitute an important step in the process of surmounting a threat to identity. For instance, an HIV diagnosis may initially be construed as a catastrophic life event, and it can therefore undermine the individual's sense of continuity. Yet, the group support strategy can provide alternative ways of thinking about one's HIV diagnosis – possibly as a catalyst for positive change in one's life or as a reason for helping other people facing a similar situation, thereby providing a new sense of purpose. The new group – formed in response to identity threat – itself acquires the characteristics of any other social group and will present its members with norms, social representations and pressures for conformity. These group mechanisms can be greatly empowering for the threatened individual.

Group action

In response to threatened identity, the individual may engage in group action to minimise or remove the threat. While the group support strategy is inward-looking in that its principal objective is to change perceptions among threatened individuals, the group action strategy is outward-looking and aims to change social representations that can in turn threaten identity among group members. The strategy is predicated on the ability of threatened individuals to seek others who share a common grievance so that they can form either a pressure group or a social movement. The group action strategy aims to change the social conditions that lead to identity threat. This can be achieved in at least three ways.

First, the group may attempt to bring about a change in the value attributed to the characteristics that are associated with its members. The change will focus on promoting a more positive image of the group, which can reduce social stigma and, thus, safeguard self-esteem among group members. For instance, in the era of HIV/AIDS, unprotected anal sex among MSM has acquired considerable social stigma, due to the widespread social representation that, due to the high prevalence of HIV among MSM, they should always use condoms to avoid infection. Some MSM living with HIV have mobilised as a group to de-stigmatise condomless sex in some contexts and to argue that it is unfair to deride MSM for engaging in this behaviour. The aim is to challenge the negative valence appended to MSM who engage in condomless sex.

Second, the group may try to amend the characteristics associated with the group and to add new, alternative characteristics to the group's image. It is possible that a particular characteristic of the group acquires social stigma and, thus, the power to threaten self-esteem. Moreover, if group members do not regard the characteristic as a legitimate aspect of the group's image, focus on that characteristic could plausibly undermine the continuity principle of identity. For instance, MSM living with HIV may form a pressure group that attempts to replace negative social representations of people living with HIV with more positive representations – perhaps by challenging the stigmatising stereotypes that HIV-positive people are 'promiscuous' or that they are 'unclean'. Indeed, HIV charities and pressure groups have launched successful social media campaigns for challenging such stereotypes. The aim of such campaigns is to raise public awareness and understanding of HIV, which in turn should reduce social stigma, creating better psychosocial conditions for people living with HIV.

Third, it is easy to see how negativism, which functions at the interpersonal level, could be more successful if deployed at the level of the group. A group of individuals who collectively reject societal prescriptions and norms that threaten their identities can effectively create a new social and ideological context for their members. Moreover, they have the potential to mount a successful campaign for challenging social representations that threaten identity. A very clear example of this is Gay Pride, particularly when it takes place in contexts where homosexuality remains stigmatised. Gay Pride is a public celebration of LGBT identities and a demonstration to society that LGBT people too have the right to take pride in their sexual identities. This may be regarded as a collective attempt to counteract social stigma and the public silencing of LGBT identities.

Overview

Social representations influence how we understand and think about the world. They are context-dependent and are subject to change. Social representations play a significant role in determining how events, experiences and other stimuli impact our sense of identity.

For instance, if prevalent social representations of homosexuality in a given context are fundamentally negative, MSM in that context may be at risk of internalised homophobia and of developing a problematic relationship with their sexual identity. As demonstrated in this chapter, this can result in identity threat, thereby challenging psychological wellbeing.

IPT is proposed as a means of understanding the construction and protection of identity among MSM. The theory specifies two universal processes and several motivational principles, which can be affected by events, experiences and other stimuli encountered during the life course. The threatened individual is said to cope in a variety of possible ways. These coping strategies vary in their degree of effectiveness and, despite their short-term convenience, some are actually maladaptive. Perhaps the greatest strength in IPT lies in its ability to explain the link between social representation (the ideas that circulate in society), identity and behaviour. Thus, it is a multi-level model that can enable practitioners to understand the inter-relations between self-identity, wellbeing and sexual health, which is the principal objective of this volume.

As outlined in Chapters 1 and 2 of this volume, MSM may engage in maladaptive behaviours that increase their risk of poor wellbeing and sexual health outcomes. The challenge for the practitioner is to limit the risk of engaging in these behaviours, which of course requires an initial understanding of their antecedents and predictors. IPT proposes a series of principles that can enable the practitioner to understand what may be threatening for identity among MSM and how individuals are likely to behave in particular circumstances. It is argued that MSM facing adversity should be empowered and encouraged to adopt more effective strategies, such as anticipatory restructuring, self-disclosure and social support. In Part 3 of this volume, various case studies relating to sexual health, self-identity and wellbeing are described, and the therapeutic frameworks and behaviour change models from Chapter 3 are invoked in order to propose possible interventions. Crucially, it is demonstrated that tenets of both social representations theory and IPT can enhance these frameworks and models and, thus, optimise practice with MSM.

Part III

PRACTICE

Chapter 5

Promoting Psychological Wellbeing among MSM

The focus of this chapter is on the promotion of psychological wellbeing among MSM. In this chapter, two case studies are presented. The first outlines possible self-identity issues that can arise among BPM MSM as they attempt to reconcile the distinct tenets, norms and values associated with their religious and sexual identities. The second case study focuses on the psychosocial challenges associated with an HIV diagnosis among MSM, particularly in view of the social stigma that surrounds both HIV and homosexuality, the feelings of shame and self-stigma that can accompany this, and possible difficulties in developing and maintaining social relationships in the aftermath of an HIV diagnosis. In both case studies, some illustrative quotes from qualitative interview research into the experiences of BPM gay men and MSM living with HIV, respectively, are presented. Illustrative quotes from the interview studies highlight some of the psychosocial issues which may be presented by MSM in clinical settings. Accordingly, the final section of this chapter outlines potential approaches to psychological support for promoting wellbeing among MSM. Recommendations are made for enhancing psychological support with insights from IPT.

Self-identity conflicts in British Pakistani Muslim MSM

Over the last decade, there has been increased empirical focus on the lives, experiences and identities of BME MSM (Jaspal 2017a; Jaspal and Cinnirella 2010; Yip and Khalid 2010). Some of this work has focused on MSM of religious faith as it is recognised that sexual minority and faith identities may be viewed as being in conflict. More specifically, homosexuality may be perceived to be at odds with the dominant tenets, norms and values associated with one's religious identity, and some MSM of religious faith may feel that their sexual identities, feelings and behaviours make them less 'authentic' religious group members. This can present a series of psychological challenges for the individual, such as a sense of identity conflict, shame, guilt and other negative emotional experiences. As a case study, the identities and experiences of BPM MSM are presented to exemplify identity threat and the negative affective states associated with it.

On the whole, scholars are in agreement that mainstream Islam is opposed to any theological accommodation of homosexuality. Islamic scholars tend to invoke the Story of Lut in Islamic Holy Scripture (the Koran), which recounts the destruction of the Tribe of Lut due to their engagement in homosexual acts, as 'evidence' for Allah's condemnation of homosexuality. They also point to the verbal teachings attributed to the Prophet Mohammed (the Ahadith), which also appear to condemn homosexuality. There are some Muslim groups that have attempted to promote a 'reverse discourse' concerning the Islamic position on homosexuality, arguing that there is scope for the accommodation and acceptance of homosexuality within Islam. In his scholarly writings, Kugle (2010) has argued that the dominant interpretation of the Story of Lut may be erroneous and that the destruction of the Tribe of Lut can be attributed to the tribe's infidelity and inhospitality, rather than to their homosexuality *per se*. Although there are some support groups for LGBT Muslims, the reverse discourse promoted by Kugle and others has not gained widespread acceptance in the Islamic theological community and, in many cases, has faced opposition from mainstream Islamic groups.

In the remainder of this section, illustrative quotes from interview studies of identity among BPM MSM (e.g. Jaspal 2015; Jaspal and Cinnirella 2010, 2012, 2014) are presented in order to highlight some of the potential self-identity conflicts that can arise. Thematic analysis (Braun and Clarke 2006) was used to analyse the interview data. The following themes summarise the results of the analysis: (1) religious representations of homosexuality, (2) psychological threats, (3) threats to social relationships, and (4) managing group memberships.

Religious representations of homosexuality

Theological, legal and social condemnation of homosexuality in Muslim communities serves to create social representations that homosexuality is immoral, sinful and dangerous to society. Many Muslim MSM themselves are embedded within homonegative social representations and are compelled to construct their identities against this backdrop. This can result in threats to identity, negative emotional experiences and poor psychological wellbeing. In an interview study of British Muslim gay men, one participant illustrated this:

> In the mosque we're told that Shaitan [Satan] tries to tempt Muslims because he is evil and he makes us do evil things. I know that doing gay things is evil but I hope I'll change my ways and take the right path soon... It's all about temptation, really. Life is a big test.
>
> (Aziz)

This extract suggests that, while homosexuality has increasingly gained social acceptance in the UK, it remains highly stigmatised in Muslim societies. Some British Muslim MSM reportedly feel that they are viewed by other Muslims as being 'too British' (that is, as having assimilated the norms and values of British society) due to their sexual identity. This can make some individuals feel like less 'authentic' Muslims, potentially problematising their religious identity. On the other hand, British national identity can sometimes act as a buffer against threat. For instance, some individuals may reject the perceived 'Islamic stance' on their sexual identity and, conversely, embrace the 'British stance', which is perceived as more readily accommodating sexual diversity. Indeed, as one participant said:

> They're [Muslims] on another planet. We don't do this violent nonsense. We've moved on since the sixth century and we don't stone gay people any more. In this country we've all got our rights.
>
> (Kasim)

On the whole, BPM MSM face psychological challenges in managing their sexual, religious and ethnic identities, which in turn can problematise the construction of a psychologically satisfying sexual identity. They may perceive the norms, values and representations associated with their religious and sexual identities, respectively, as being incompatible. This can lead to a decreased sense of psychological coherence. More specifically, they may feel that, because their sexual identity is at odds with what God intended and with what their religion teaches, they are either not 'proper' Muslims or are engaged in sinful behaviour that will lead to divine retribution. This is reflected in the account of a British Muslim MSM who reflected on his experience of going to a gay nightclub in London:

> Well I sat down [in the gay nightclub] and I kept thinking the roof was going to fall in any minute and that we'd all die there and then… I knew it was a bad place with bad stuff going on around me. I hated that night.
>
> (Aziz)

Individuals may feel that two identities, which are socially represented as being 'inter-connected' (because Islam appears to have a stance on homosexuality), are fundamentally incompatible. Like Aziz, some believe that this incompatibility is insurmountable and that homosexuality could invite negative consequences.

Psychological threats

It is easy to see how negative perceptions of homosexuality can challenge self-esteem. Many feel unable to derive a positive self-conception on the basis of their sexual identity, because they are exposed to homonegative representations associated with a group membership that they value, namely their religion. Group memberships that matter to an individual will have clout in shaping their personal beliefs and representations – people use their group memberships, and particularly valued group memberships, as sources of knowledge about the world. Consequently, it comes as no surprise that Muslim MSM may exhibit signs of internalised homophobia:

> *Interviewer:* And how does [the idea that homosexuality is wrong] make you feel?
>
> *Rasool:* Bad. [Being gay is] wrong and I'm doing wrong. I need to be a better Muslim.
>
> *Interviewer:* And what does it mean to be a better Muslim?
>
> *Rasool:* Well not gay for starters.

There is evidence that some Muslim MSM experience guilt, shame and self-hatred, potentially leading to mental distress and suicidal ideation. They may reach the conclusion that their sexual identity is wrong and that it must and, with God's help, *will* change. However, as individuals begin to realise that it is impossible to change one's sexual orientation, they may experience feelings of helplessness, hopelessness and anxiety. The negative affective states of shame and guilt are also observable in their accounts.

We know from decades of empirical research that sexual minority youth can experience challenges in developing a sexual identity due to the initial confusion that arises upon recognition of difference from the dominant heterosexual majority (e.g. Cass 1979; Corrigan and Matthews 2009). Change is inherent to the developmental journey. A number of coming out models have been proposed, which highlight the changes in self-definition that arise amid social developmental processes and more general social change. Research with Muslim MSM clearly demonstrates the potential threats of coming out to the continuity principle of identity, especially if the act of coming out entails negative changes to one's life, such as stigma or rejection from others (Jaspal and Siraj 2011):

> It was a big shock afterwards, the change from being not totally gay to being gay because I'd like acted on it, it was stressing me out.
>
> (Faisal)

> I knew I couldn't get married but I didn't want to disappoint my family because it like meant a lot to them, you know. Nothing made sense about where to turn.
>
> (Iqbal)

Muslim MSM tend to be socialised in a theological, social and familial environment that appends hegemony to heterosexuality and, in many cases, to arranged (heterosexual) marriage. They themselves may aspire to fulfil this religious and cultural expectation of an arranged heterosexual marriage due to religious/cultural pressures (Jaspal 2014a). This can create a rupture between past, present and future, as individuals fail to construct a coherent temporal narrative. They may feel unable to get married and, thus, see no acceptable future for themselves as sexual minorities. As highlighted in Iqbal's account, this can pose difficulties for the continuity principle of identity.

Threats to social relationships

In addition to the social challenges that are experienced as threatening at a psychological level, Muslim MSM may face social challenges in that they may question their position within relevant social groups and categories and fail to derive feelings of acceptance and inclusion from significant others. This can threaten the belonging principle of identity. Family identity is central to many Muslims, who generally adhere to a collectivist cultural orientation and patriarchal hierarchy. Family and cultural honour are key for many Muslims, and premarital chastity and an arranged (heterosexual) marriage are widely perceived as central to maintaining honour. Muslim MSM often feel compelled to behave and to construct their identities in ways that enhance family honour. Typically, many conceal their sexual identities from their families, which can lead to a decreased sense of identity authenticity:

> I'll never tell my parents because it would kill them. They wouldn't be able to cope with it, you know. Yeah, I'm keeping them out of this but it's like living a lie really. That's not the real me.
>
> (Ali)

Interpersonal difficulties can arise when parents obliviously encourage their children to get married. Muslim MSM have reported problems in interpersonal relations with parents and other family members, as they feel unable to disclose their sexual identities, on the one hand, and are unwilling to enter into an arranged heterosexual marriage, on the other (Jaspal 2014a). Moreover, some may decide to come out to family members, which can result in ostracisation, disownment and even psychological/physical abuse.

Given the perception of incompatibility between Islam and homosexuality among many sexual minority Muslims and the theologically-based homonegativity that many are exposed to, they may themselves begin to question the *authenticity* of their religious identity. This may lead them to seek strategies for affirming their Muslim identity, often at the expense of their de-valued sexual identity, which, for many Muslim MSM, is an identity that they wish to reliniquish. There is some evidence of a 'hyper-affiliation' to the religious group, as a means of compensating for any potential doubts surrounding their identity authenticity (Jaspal and Cinnirella 2014). Some have reported using Ramadan (a Muslim festival of fasting) as a symbolic opportunity for asserting their piety and for dispelling accusations of inauthenticity, while others may espouse what they regard as prototypically 'Muslim attitudes' concerning society, such as homonegativity. These attempts to 'prove' one's Muslim identity can result in psychological distress, especially as individuals may perceive this to undermine their feelings of authenticity. They may also be fearful of being 'outed' as gay, despite their attempts to conceal it.

Managing group memberships

The late British social psychologist Henri Tajfel, who developed social identity theory, described the exit option, that is, the individual's self-removal from a threatening social group (Tajfel 1981). The process of self-removal from a group may not be so simple, given that for many Muslims their faith constitutes a meaning system and an overarching 'superordinate' identity that is entwined with other identity elements, such as the family. Departure from a valued social group potentially requires modification of the structure of identity, such as loss of other identity elements. Some Muslim MSM have, however, reported distancing themselves from their religious/ethnic ingroups in order to align themselves with sexual ingroup members, that is, other (largely non-Muslim) MSM. Interview data indicate that Muslim MSM may feel otherised and discriminated against on the (predominantly White) gay scene, due to Islamophobia and racism, in general:

> They have all these stereotypes about Asians, like 'Oh, you're a Muslim so you must be all messed up', like 'You are never gonna tell your parents that you're gay'... I hate all these damn baseless assumptions.
>
> (Mohammed)

Racism is said to occur not only on the gay scene but also in online settings, such as on geospatial gay social networking applications, where messages like 'no Asians' are often interpreted as rejection. In short, Muslim MSM may feel rejected and excluded from the sexual ingroup, which can challenge their sense of *belonging* and lead to feelings to isolation.

Social support is known to buffer threats to identity and wellbeing, but Muslim MSM may feel that they simply have no access to social support — from neither their families nor sexual ingroup — which can aggravate their threatening position. This has been highlighted in Jaspal's (2015) research into how Muslim MSM cope with relationship dissolution:

> When [my former partner] left me I was totally alone and nobody knew. I couldn't talk to anyone. I never felt so alone in my life. I still haven't got over it.
>
> (Faisal)

Due to the general lack of social support, individuals may deploy deflection strategies, such as denial and depersonalisation, in order to cope with threat and further minimise contact with others (from whom they anticipate little or no support). This may be conducive to further isolation and stress, which can undermine psychological wellbeing.

Decreased wellbeing among MSM newly-diagnosed with HIV

As indicated in Chapter 2 of this volume, although HIV is now considered a manageable chronic condition, the social, psychological and indeed physical aspects of living with HIV continue to be challenging for most patients (Arseniou, Arvaniti and Samakouri 2014). In 2015 15 HIV-positive MSM aged between 18 and 36 were recruited in the English Midlands and in London for a qualitative interview study concerning the experience of an HIV diagnosis and the implications for identity processes. The data, which were analysed using qualitative thematic analysis, are categorised into the following themes: (1) HIV stigma, (2), HIV and mental health issues, (3) deriving a positive self-conception, and (4) positive coping with HIV-related stressors.

HIV stigma

Given the stigma appended to HIV, even in groups in which prevalence is relatively high, such as among MSM, individuals who test positive may choose not to disclose their HIV status to others. They may fear stigma, judgement and rejection. This may in turn impede access to social support groups and contexts, which can enhance identity among those diagnosed with HIV. It is easy to see how psychological health may be adversely affected following diagnosis, given that individuals may experience fear and uncertainty in relation to their physical health:

> When they told me, I just thought 'that's it, I'm going to die' and yes at the moment I'm fine but I could get ill. The meds could just stop working.
>
> (Tom)

Individuals may themselves associate HIV with poor physical health and mortality, and worry about the possible impact of ART on their physical health. Moreover, HIV infection may render salient one's mortality at a psychological level, as some patients fear that their infection will decrease their life expectancy.

Social representations play an important role in shaping psychological and physical health outcomes among HIV-positive individuals. They can give rise to distinct 'cultures' of HIV, which in turn shape the social and psychological experience of HIV diagnosis. For instance, widespread access to high-quality HIV care in the UK may create a culture in which patients who test positive can experience more favourable outcomes for their sense of self-efficacy:

> Diagnosis was a nightmare but the doctors are amazing. My consultant is really good and so you know I feel like this isn't the end of the world because I've got the help and I'll get through this. I can do this.
>
> (Mike)

Indeed, the self-efficacy principle has been associated with engagement with HIV care as patients come to feel empowered vis-à-vis their chronic condition (Chen *et al.* 2013). Conversely, patients who perceive barriers to accessing HIV care, for instance, because they express trepidation about engaging with health services, would not experience high levels of self-efficacy in relation to their HIV infection. Moreover, in many major cities with large populations of MSM, there is a sense of community among HIV-positive MSM which can create opportunities for those living with HIV (Courtenay-Quirk *et al.* 2006).

The sense of social support and empowerment may facilitate access to services, leading to better health outcomes.

HIV diagnosis, in particular, can be a challenging psychological event, which merits close empirical attention (Flowers, Davis, Larkin, Church and Marriott 2011). It requires the assimilation and accommodation of a stigmatised identity element. One must absorb in identity new information about oneself, that is, one's new HIV status. The assimilation of this novel information may lead some MSM to feel ashamed of their sexual identity, leading to avoidance of sexual relations (Bernier *et al.* 2016):

> Sex has been difficult for me. There's always that fear that you might like give it to someone or they might freak out…sometimes I feel a bit ashamed of my past and it makes me, you know.
>
> (James)

One's diagnosis may be construed as reflecting a flaw in one's identity which can induce feelings of guilt, shame and self-deprecation (Bennett *et al.* 2016). It has been found that HIV diagnosis can pose threats to the individual's self-esteem given the social stigma that is appended to HIV and, particularly, in view of its association with stigmatised sexual behaviours. More generally, there is evidence that HIV diagnosis can affect several aspects of the patient's identity, such as their sexual identity (Bourne *et al.* 2012), family identity (Sachperoglou and Bor 2001), and occupational identity (Hunt *et al.* 2003).

Partly in view of the associated social stigma, HIV diagnosis and the experience of living with HIV can give rise to post-traumatic stress disorder. In a systematic review of HIV infection associated with post-traumatic stress disorder and post-traumatic growth (Sherr *et al.* 2011b), it was found that there was a 5 per cent to 74 per cent prevalence of the disorder in HIV patients compared to 7 per cent to 10 percent in the general population. There was also evidence of a link between HIV-related trauma and post-traumatic stress disorder. This can have considerable implications for health behaviours, such as decreased adherence to ART and general difficulties in engaging with HIV care (LeGrand *et al.* 2015). Furthermore, initiation of ART, which must be continued for the rest of the individual's life, might plausibly represent a threat to continuity, as it can serve as a daily reminder of one's infection:

> It's been hard starting on medication because I haven't completely got my head around being positive and each time I take [the medication] I spend some time thinking about my life and everything. Bad things.
>
> (Mike)

HIV and mental health issues

In a recent article by Sherr *et al.* (2011a), it was argued that depression is an important correlate of HIV. Poor self-esteem associated with HIV stigma can escalate into depression. It was observed that pre-existing depression can put an individual at risk of HIV infection, that the experience of HIV-related illness can cause depression, and that some HIV medications can exacerbate or precipitate mood disturbance. This suggests that depression is a key psychopathology that needs to be addressed in interventions designed to improve health outcomes among people living with HIV (Jaspal and Dhairyawan 2018). Indeed, as suggested by Arseniou *et al.* (2014), treatment of HIV-related depression can improve the individual's quality of life, which in turn can lead to better disease prognosis. Chronic threats to identity that remain unresolved can lead to psychopathological states, such as depression and depersonalisation. Two young MSM living with HIV described this in their accounts:

> It just reached a point where I was thinking 'I just want this all to end'. I was really depressed for months about it.
>
> (Will)

> I wasn't myself for ages and like I didn't feel myself... When [the health advisor] was telling me, I couldn't feel my legs and it was like they were talking about someone else, not me.
>
> (James)

An HIV diagnosis can have a profound impact on affect. Carrico and Moskowitz (2014) indicate that positive affect of individuals living with HIV was positively associated with entry into HIV care three months after diagnosis and with adherence to ART over the 18-month follow-up period. The social stigma that links HIV diagnosis to promiscuity and immorality can threaten self-esteem in the newly diagnosed individual, leading to feelings of self-disgust, guilt and shame (Lee, Kochman and Sikkema 2002). Threats to self-esteem, and the negative affective experiences associated with them, may serve as a barrier to entry into HIV care, thereby undermining physical health outcomes. Indeed, as Castrighini *et al.* (2010) have argued, low self-esteem can reduce the level of confidence required to seek HIV care. More generally, self-esteem has been described as a primary motivational principle for help-seeking (Wakimoto 2008), which is echoed in the following account:

> I actually started caring about getting on meds and looking after myself when I started caring about myself. When you find out you're positive, you go through a weird thing about like hating yourself for what you did and I knew like I made mistakes and I was beating myself up over it all.
>
> (Sanj)

As reported by Flowers *et al.* (2011) and the aforementioned studies of HIV and mental health, the psychosocial impact of HIV diagnosis can be considerable. While policy efforts mainly focus on HIV prevention, it is important to consider the psychosocial burden of HIV diagnosis among those already living with the condition. In their early research into the link between sense-making vis-à-vis HIV diagnosis and physical health, Segerstrom *et al.* (1996) argued that attributions involving negative beliefs of the self, the future and perceived control over HIV risk events (e.g. a condomless sexual encounter) were associated with a decline in CD4 cell count. This early study provides some evidence that construal of one's diagnosis and HIV status, such as the identity attributions that individuals may make in the process of making sense of their diagnosis, can affect physical health outcomes. With the demonstrated impact of psychological construal for HIV disease progression (i.e. CD4 decline), acknowledgement of the role of identity processes is key.

Deriving a positive self-conception

The attributions that individuals make are drawn at least in part from dominant social representations, that is, social images and ideas about HIV that circulate in society. The long-standing social stigma appended to HIV is a key area of enquiry in social sciences studies of HIV. The stigmatisation of those infected can plausibly affect not only their self-identity but also their interpersonal relationships. This is exemplified by Toppenberg *et al.*'s (2015) experimental study which revealed that patients with HIV (and specifically MSM with HIV) were more marginalised than patients with cancer or patients with a broken leg, suggesting that HIV, in particular, is a chronic condition that can invite negative responses from others due to the associated stigma and negative stereotypes.

HIV stigma can lead to rejection of seropositive MSM with implications for their health outcomes. Cole *et al.* (1997) demonstrated that accelerated HIV disease progression was detected among rejection-sensitive individuals in the US who did not conceal their sexual identity. The rejection-sensitive personality trait predisposes the individual to identity threat when he is rejected. This research suggests that the physical health of seropositive MSM can deteriorate when an important social identity (in this case, being MSM) is stigmatised. It is easy to see why some MSM living with HIV anticipate stigma and rejection from others:

> For me the hardest thing has been the stigma because it's so hard when someone tells you to your face 'no' and you know it's because you're positive. Like you're damaged goods in a way.
>
> (Peter)

The negative correlation between the experience of social stigma and self-esteem is well documented, particularly when there is no cohesive group membership to buffer the negative effects of stigma (Crocker and Major 1989). For instance, it has been observed that Greek MSM living with HIV may experience difficulties in disclosing their HIV status to significant others, such as family members, which can deprive them of social support (Sachperoglou and Bor 2001), while Londoners diagnosed with HIV appear to be more likely to disclose their status to significant others (Petrak *et al.* 2001). Research conducted by Cole *et al.* (1997) suggests that social support and social acceptance may help decelerate HIV disease progression, and that identity is a key variable in physical health outcomes (see also Segerstrom *et al.* 1996). Some MSM appear to cope better with experiences of rejection on the basis of their HIV status if they have access to social support:

> Yeah, [rejection] hurts but at the end of the day it's something we all go through as positive people and we get it. We talk about it.
>
> (Sean)

Positive coping with HIV-related stressors

Aspects and constructs related to identity (such as self-esteem) play a key role in how individuals respond to a positive diagnosis. According to Nicholson and Long (1990), HIV-positive MSM in Canada react either proactively or avoidantly when confronted with a positive diagnosis. In explaining their findings, the authors argued that increased homophobia and decreased self-esteem predicted engagement in avoidant behaviours while less homophobia and greater self-esteem could induce a proactive coping style. This study identifies self-esteem, which may be challenged by the experience of homophobia (Zervoulis, Lyons and Dinos 2015), as a key predictor of coping style. Individuals appear to cope with HIV-related stressors when they have higher levels of self-esteem and self-efficacy:

> When I was diagnosed I felt like my life was a mess but when I got it back on track it almost sort of got me thinking that you only live once, make the most of it.
>
> (Andrew)

> HIV shouldn't define me. I am the same guy I was when I was negative so I don't let it define me even though it's with me and always with me.
>
> (Peter)

As suggested by these extracts, there are positive approaches to coping with HIV. Post-traumatic growth is one example. Milam (2006) investigated the relationship between post-traumatic growth and HIV disease progression. He found that there was a positive association between growth and CD4 count which was moderated by level of optimism (low vs high). The study reported a negative correlation between growth and viral load among individuals who reported low levels of pessimism. Hence, culture and personality traits (both aspects of identity) can have a significant impact on physical health outcomes among patients. Results from a study of stress and ART adherence and viral load conducted by Weaver *et al.* (2005) suggested that negative mood and lower social support among patients are closely related to poorer ART adherence and hence higher viral load. Moreover, a range of contextual factors such as time since diagnosis and initiation of ART can determine the effectiveness of coping (Moskowitz *et al.* 2009).

In a systematic review of interventions for anxiety for people with HIV (Clucas *et al.* 2011), it was found that psychological interventions were more effective than pharmacological ones, further demonstrating the need for social psychological investigations of HIV diagnosis and for a shift from solely biomedical approaches to HIV treatment. Given that interventions can be effective in reducing risk behaviour and in improving health outcomes among patients (Sikkema *et al.* 2011) it seems reasonable to explore aspects of identity and coping and to develop interventions on the basis of these data.

The implications for practitioners

The two case studies presented in this chapter focus on distinct areas of psychological distress: the first case study outlines the challenges to self-identity that can arise from perceived incompatibility in being MSM and of religious faith (see Case 2 in Chapter 1) and the second case study describes the threats to wellbeing that can emanate from an HIV diagnosis (see Case 3 in Chapter 1). Yet, both case studies point to the relevance of psychosocial factors, such as self-construal, attributions, self-esteem, interpersonal relations and social stigma, in predicting psychological health. Furthermore, these psychosocial concerns are linked to behavioural outcomes, such as disclosure of one's identity to others, patterns of social interaction, adherence to ART and so on.

Drawing upon IPT, this chapter offers a particular focus on the identity principles that may be affected by the events and experiences described in each case study, as well as the coping strategies that may be deployed in response to ensuing threats. The case studies converge in demonstrating the importance of attempting to understand how social, cultural and economic factors relate to the experience of being gay and of religious faith, on the one hand, and that of being diagnosed with HIV, on the other. Such an understanding can enable practitioners to develop therapeutic, and indeed behavioural, interventions for enhancing psychological wellbeing in MSM from diverse backgrounds. Therapeutic and behavioural interventions may also lead to better physical health outcomes given the established link between psychological and physical health (Fish *et al.* 2016).

The evidence and the empirical data presented in this chapter indicates that both intrapsychic factors and interpersonal relationships determine how individuals respond to the interface of sexual and religious identities and an HIV diagnosis, respectively. Practitioners may draw upon psychodynamic principles, such as those associated with relational psychoanalysis, in their therapeutic engagement with MSM facing these issues. In the remainder of this chapter, recommendations for optimising therapeutic practice are presented.

In identifying the patient's relational configurations with others, the practitioner must understand and acknowledge the psychological functions that are likely to be performed by these configurations. In other words, why does the individual develop particular relational configurations and what psychological benefits do they appear to have? On a basic level, IPT might suggest that the relational configuration provides a sense of *continuity* because it facilitates a psychological connection between one's past, present and future patterns of interpersonal relations. One remains consistent and uses past relational experiences to inform relationship formation in the present and future. This is an important motivation to maintain a particular configuration, despite its potential social and psychological shortcomings. Furthermore, the relational configuration is likely to enhance feelings of *self-efficacy* because it empowers the individual to navigate through new relationships, to reduce uncertainty associated with the future and, crucially, to predict outcomes associated with new relationships. For instance, if a British Muslim MSM has developed a relational configuration based around secrecy and concealment that characterised his relationship with his parents, he may derive feelings of competence and control (that is, self-efficacy) from applying this configuration to men whom he meets in later life.

Similarly, an individual living with HIV who has developed a relational configuration that is emotionally avoidant due to previous experiences of HIV stigma may nonetheless derive feelings of control and competence in relation to future interpersonal encounters. This way of thinking allows the individual to feel 'safe' and confident about the outcomes of his subsequent relationships just as his tendency to be secretive and to conceal intimate information from his significant others provides feelings of safety and confidence. Furthermore, previous relationships may have been detrimental to the individual's self-esteem and, thus, the relational configuration developed may aim to protect him from subsequent threats to *self-esteem*. It is easy to see how an avoidant relational configuration can shield the individual from potential stigma and rejection associated with one's identity incompatibility or HIV status.

The practitioner may work with the patient to develop a more productive and psychologically beneficial relational configuration, which enables him to form personally meaningful relationships with others. It has been recommended that therapists working with gay men assess the quality of their patients' friendships with other gay men and that they collaboratively carve out pathways for developing mutually satisfying, high-quality friendships with sexual ingroup members (Kocet 2014). Gay friendships can provide the individual with access to more positive social representations of their sexual identity, facilitate the coming out process, and enhance psychological wellbeing on the basis of this shared identity. In the case of MSM living with HIV, this strategy could be extrapolated to friendship formation and maintenance with other HIV-positive MSM. The aim is to create a supportive 'space' with other individuals who share a given identity element. However, it is important that the new relational configuration is sufficiently protective of the identity principles that seem to be most susceptible to threat in the individual or population of interest.

Research into British Muslim MSM suggests that self-esteem, continuity and psychological coherence seem to be especially vulnerable to threat, while self-esteem, self-efficacy and continuity appear to be most susceptible to threat among MSM living with HIV. On the one hand, the new relational configuration should be designed in ways that actively enhance these vulnerable identity principles. More specifically, it should provide exposure to social representations of homosexuality or HIV that are conducive to increased self-esteem. Meaningful relationships with other ingroup members could also provide insight into narratives of coming out or self-disclosure that enhance continuity, which may replace individuals' construal of their own narrative as discontinuous and disjointed. Moreover, these relationships may enable individuals to explore ways of establishing connections between potentially conflicting identity elements, thereby enhancing psychological coherence.

It would be necessary to avoid developing a new relational configuration that potentially continues to expose the individual to threats to psychological coherence, for instance, by uncritically submitting to orthodox views concerning the relationship between Islam and homosexuality. Similarly, a new configuration that potentially undermines continuity would need to be avoided. For example, a new relational configuration could result in the breakdown of valued relationships, such as with one's parents, family members and members of one's cultural and religious ingroups. On the one hand, an element of distance from these individuals and groups may be deemed necessary in order to reduce exposure to stigmatising social representations but, on the other hand, this could lead to feelings of loss and undesired change. Thus, the new relational configuration would need to safeguard existing valued relationships, as well as to facilitate the formation of new ones. For MSM living with HIV in particular, novel relationships should enable individuals to build feelings of self-efficacy in relation to their infection so that they are better positioned to cope with the potential stressors associated with it. This may increase feelings of hope and resilience in the face of HIV diagnosis. Similarly, while it is important to encourage and to facilitate a relational configuration that is conducive to contact with others living with HIV, it must not induce isolation from, or feelings of hostility towards, people who are HIV-negative, as this can undermine the quality of interpersonal relations and access to a wide range of social networks.

The new relational configuration must be conducive to effective strategies for coping with threats to identity associated with occupancy of a stigmatised position. As highlighted above and in Cases 2 and 3 presented in Chapter 1, British Muslim MSM and MSM living with HIV may have experienced judgement and stigma on the basis of their identities, leading to decreased willingness to disclose this and other intimate self-relevant information to others. It is easy to see why some may develop a relational configuration that fosters avoidant behaviours and that encourages isolation. This may also enable the individual to deny their homosexuality or their HIV-positive status, as these are psychologically distressing. Moreover, they may seek to isolate themselves from other people who are stigmatising towards them. This can cut off potential sources of social support, which, in both cases, would be beneficial for enhancing wellbeing.

A relational configuration that provides social support is key. Social support enables the individual to self-disclose, to revise the meanings that he appends to potentially stigmatised identity elements (e.g. being gay or HIV-positive) and to derive a positive self-conception despite the presence of these stigmatised identity elements. Patients ought to develop relationships that enable them to assimilate and accommodate in identity their homosexuality or HIV status. A relational configuration that allows the threatened individual to derive social support is important, not only because this is an especially effective coping strategy, but also because social support can develop into social action. As outlined in Chapter 4, the social action strategy aims to improve the social conditions surrounding the potentially threatening stimulus. For instance, Muslim MSM who engage in social support groups may collectively seek to campaign in order to challenge homonegativity within religious settings, while MSM living with HIV may lobby to promote HIV education in order to challenge the stigma surrounding their condition. While social support benefits the threatened individual, social action can lead to benefits for the wider community within which the threatened individual is embedded.

As demonstrated above, there are clearly negative social representations of homosexuality and HIV, respectively, which can make it difficult for individuals to derive a positive self-conception. The new relational configuration must facilitate exposure to positive and empowering social representations. However, there may be aspects of one's experience that do lead to identity threat and that simply cannot be evaded. The strategy of anticipatory restructuring is important and effective. The patient should be in a position to anticipate the potential threats that can arise and to make changes to identity in order to decrease the magnitude of these threats when they do occur. Contact with others in a similar situation may enable individuals to anticipate future threats.

Care should be taken when developing a relational configuration that could lead to the patient's departure from social groups and contexts that are stigmatising. These social groups and contexts may nonetheless be important for other elements of identity and departure from them could compromise the patient's sense of continuity. Identifying ways of challenging stigmatising representations may constitute a more viable strategy, rather than total departure from these social groups and contexts. In short, the 'exit option' is not always possible even though it may appear a desirable means of enhancing the patient's wellbeing. Furthermore, the new relational configuration must promote a sense of authenticity in that individuals should be encouraged to avoid the passing strategy. For instance, some Muslim MSM may feign heterosexuality and some individuals living with HIV may present themselves as HIV-negative, as a means of avoiding the associated stigma. Isolation, avoidance and passing may initially protect the individual from threat but they are not considered to be productive strategies in the long-term.

Overview

In this chapter, two examples of decreased wellbeing among MSM were presented. The qualitative data provided outline the nature of the threats that can accompany potentially conflicting identities and diagnosis with a stigmatised health condition. Multiple principles of identity appear to be susceptible to threat. It is proposed that in these particular cases, principles of relational psychoanalysis could be useful for managing psychological distress and improving wellbeing in MSM facing adversity. The notion of the relational configuration is useful, particularly because the primary source of threats described in the two case studies above appear to be social in nature. The most significant source of threat is social stigma – manifested in terms of homonegativity and HIV prejudice. On the basis of the discussion in this chapter, the following recommendations are offered to practitioners:

- It is important to acknowledge that the patient's existing relational configuration will be designed to serve identity processes – most notably, continuity, self-efficacy and self-esteem. Thus, change may be resisted and successful change may induce residual threats to identity.

- The practitioner should endeavour to assist the patient in developing a relational configuration that facilitates exposure to positive social representations of identity elements that are stigmatised (e.g. one's sexual identity, one's HIV status). A successful type of relationship may be friendship with others who share one of these identity elements with the patient.

- It is advantageous to facilitate self-disclosure and the derivation of social support. This is especially important in the case of identity elements that are stigmatised and, thus, concealed by the patient. Self-disclosure can decrease internalised stigma and promote feelings of authenticity, which are essential for a positive self-identity.

- It must be acknowledged that some social group memberships and social relationships will be important for identity processes in spite of their role in stigmatising identity elements that are important to the individual. This can make it difficult for the patient to exit these groups.

It is suggested that, regardless of the focus of one's practice (e.g. medicine, health advice, counselling, psychotherapy), practitioners should attempt to work with MSM to develop more fruitful, productive and meaningful social and interpersonal relationships that can provide exposure to positive social representations and to social support. It is important that practitioners are cognisant of the possible ways in which identity could be compromised among MSM with decreased wellbeing and the possible strategies for coping – both negative and positive – that may be deployed in response. As demonstrated earlier in this volume, the use of effective coping strategies may be conducive to improved and sustained wellbeing, on the one hand, and to better behavioural and health outcomes, on the other. This could in turn lead to less engagement in sexual risk-taking behaviours and improved engagement in healthcare. Consequently, awareness and acknowledgement of self-identity issues are certainly an important component of the practitioner's remit, regardless of their specialty.

Chapter 6

Developing Effective Sexual Health Interventions for MSM

Sexual health interventions generally attempt to address the factors that can lead to poor sexual health outcomes. Some of the risk factors among MSM were discussed in Chapter 2. There is a recognised need to develop effective sexual health interventions that can reduce the incidence of HIV and other STIs in MSM, a population at risk of poor sexual health outcomes. Accordingly, in this chapter, two case studies are presented. The first focuses on an intervention to enhance sexual health outcomes among MSM in sex-on-premises venues given that this constitutes a physical space within which risky sexual behaviour may occur. The second case study examines a multi-dimensional intervention for improving sexual health outcomes among BME MSM who, as highlighted in Chapters 1 and 2, are at particularly high risk of HIV and other STIs. Both interventions are described and data from the evaluation projects that accompanied them are presented. The evaluation data elucidate the effectiveness of the interventions and the areas in which improvement may be required. The principal purpose of presenting these evaluation data is to highlight major observations concerning sexual health knowledge and behaviour in these contexts so that evidence-based recommendations can be made for future interventions informed by social psychological theory. In the third and final section of this chapter, insights from social psychology (focusing on IPT and models of behaviour change) are provided to facilitate the development of more effective sexual health interventions for MSM.

Enhancing sexual health in gay saunas

Sex-on-premises venues (e.g. saunas, bathhouses and sex clubs) are businesses which provide a physical space in which MSM can meet and engage in sexual behaviour (Binson, Blea, Gotten, Kant and Woods 2005). They are therefore a key context in which sexual health promotion and HIV prevention efforts need to be targeted. Despite the controversial nature of sex-on-premises venues, research conducted globally has shown that they are ideal locations for on-site sexual health interventions for MSM, and especially for those at elevated risk of HIV and other STIs but who may otherwise be difficult to reach (Debattista 2015; Genoway, Caine, Singh and Estefan 2016; Pollack, Woods, Blair and Binson 2014). Some MSM who use gay saunas are not openly gay and do not frequent LGBT community settings and, thus, they may not access sexual health promotion and HIV prevention messages in the same way that MSM who do frequent LGBT community settings do. In recent years, there has been an increase of on-site HIV testing in the US where approximately 75 per cent of the saunas provide this kind of service (Pollack *et al.* 2014). The fact that HIV testing programmes reach high-risk MSM by providing a safe and anonymous environment is greatly advantageous for prevention efforts.

The importance of a safe space for HIV testing has also been echoed in research conducted in the UK. Buckley *et al.* (2010) argue that HIV testing interventions provided in sex-on-premises venues can be highly efficacious since they facilitate increased opportunities for reaching individuals who do not otherwise test in traditional settings, such as in GUM clinics. Indeed, it has been found that MSM may avoid testing for HIV in GUM clinics due to fear of stigma, both from the public and from healthcare professionals (Jaspal 2017c). Conversely, on-site testing and sexual health awareness services are located in what is perceived to be a safe and supportive environment, catering for the specific needs of MSM (Debattista 2015). On-site screening services and outreach opportunities are often provided in collaboration with the managerial teams of saunas. These partnerships between sauna owners, voluntary agents, and statutory public health departments are essential for the maintenance of HIV prevention intervention strategies, which can reach high-risk MSM (Huebner *et al.* 2012).

Although there have been promising results from small scale studies in the UK context vis-à-vis HIV prevention interventions (Buckley *et al.* 2010), there is a need for further research and additional innovative approaches in taking this work forward. Consequently, a sexual health charity based in in the English Midlands developed and delivered the Sauna Online Assessment Project (SOAP), which was funded by the Public Health England 2015/2016 HIV Innovation Fund (see below). The project was targeted in the city of Leicester due partly to epidemiological data presented in Public Health England HIV surveillance reports (Public Health England 2017a), which report a rise in HIV incidence among MSM in the Midlands and in East England. It was reported that in these regions there was a higher increase in HIV exposure through sex between men (7.3 per cent increase in 2015 compared to 2014) than HIV exposure through heterosexual contact (4.82 per cent increase in 2015 compared to 2014). Although HIV prevalence in Leicester can be considered low compared to other areas in England (see Chapter 2), it has the highest prevalence of all local authorities in the East Midlands: approximately four out of every 1000 residents aged 15 to 59 are living with HIV.

The SOAP project – a sexual health intervention

The SOAP project set out to deliver a certification scheme to recognise sexual health promotion efforts in three gay saunas in Leicester. Its principal objectives were to set up an online assessment tool for assigning to gay saunas an excellence certification for performance in relation sexual health promotion and HIV prevention; to design an excellence certification to reflect the sauna's level of engagement with sexual health issues; and to promote greater collaboration between gay saunas and local sexual health agencies in promoting good sexual health outcomes and HIV prevention among sauna users. The three saunas were evaluated by the sexual health charity and given a certification based on their performance vis-à-vis sexual health promotion/HIV prevention. The certification levels consisted of gold (the highest), silver (medium) and bronze (the lowest). The principal aim of the intervention was to ascertain the effect of a particular certification on the sexual health knowledge and behaviours of sauna attendees. Some of these data are presented in this section.

Sauna A is the largest and the newest of the three saunas. It is comprised of two clearly distinguished levels. The ground level is the social space which includes the bar and the lounge area, the changing rooms, the sauna and stream room, and the bathtub. There is a strict policy of no sexual activity in this part of the sauna. The upper-level consists of private cabins, a sling room and a movie-projecting room (pornographic material). This area is used for sexual activity. The sauna collaborates with local sexual health charities (for outreach work), and the NHS (to provide sexual health screening and basic sexual health counselling). The NHS clinic and its staff are present twice a week. In general, the daily number of visitors ranges from 13 to 110. Sauna A was given gold certification.

Sauna B is the smallest of the three saunas. It also consists of two levels. The upper level is comprised of a small lounge area, the changing rooms, the dry and wet saunas, the private cabins and rooms for sexual activity (e.g. projector room, sling room, etc.). The lower level caters for the needs of individuals interested in fetishistic activities. The specific sauna caters for MSM and heterosexual men and women. Furthermore, it is used by transgender individuals and by cross-dressers. Therefore, its user base is remarkably diverse. The sauna collaborates with the NHS by providing spaces for sexual health screening, twice a week. In general, five to 25 people visit the sauna daily. Sauna B was given lower silver certification.

Sauna C is comprised of one level and a basement sling and gloryhole room. MSM constitute the majority of visitors to this sauna. In general, five to 30 people visit the sauna daily. Sauna C was given upper silver certification.

The evaluation project

The evaluation project set out to ascertain the effect of a particular sauna certification on sexual health knowledge and behaviours among sauna users. The project consisted of a mixed methods approach, drawing upon both quantitative and qualitative research methods from social psychology research. Semi-structured individual interviews were used to generate qualitative data from 20 sauna users involved in the SOAP project. The aim was to obtain in-depth insights into sexual behaviours, sexual health knowledge and the overall sexual health 'culture' in each of the three saunas. A quantitative survey was administered to 45 sauna users, tapping into demographic issues, perceived access to condoms, sexual health literature and HIV testing in the sauna, perceived risk of HIV infection, HIV knowledge, and actual sexual behaviour in the sauna.

In the remainder of this section, key findings from the evaluation project are presented. The objective is to present some of the evaluation data in order to illustrate the potential challenges and opportunities associated with the design and implementation of an effective sexual health intervention for MSM in gay saunas. The data are drawn upon to sketch out what an effective intervention might look like. The findings are divided into sub-sections that focus on particular areas, such as sexual health knowledge and awareness, interactions with others, and sexual behaviour.

HIV status

- At Sauna C, 66.7 per cent believed themselves to be HIV-negative and 33.3 per cent were unaware of their HIV status.
- At Sauna B, 71 per cent believed themselves to be HIV-negative and 28.6 per cent were unaware of their HIV status.
- At Sauna A, 90 per cent believed themselves to be HIV-negative and 10 per cent were unaware of their status.

This suggested that attendees at Sauna A were more likely to be aware of their HIV status than attendees at other saunas, due partly to the encouragement of HIV testing and the dissemination of HIV-related information in this setting.

Knowledge of Post-Exposure Prophylaxis (PEP)

- At Sauna C, 47.1 per cent of participants had heard of PEP and 52.9 per cent had not.
- At Sauna B, 57.1 per cent had heard of PEP and 42.9 per cent had not.
- At Sauna A, 81.8 per cent had heard of PEP and 18.2 per cent had not.

These data suggest that Sauna A attendees were more likely to have heard of PEP, an important emergency HIV prevention method, than attendees at the other saunas.

Knowledge of PrEP

- At Sauna C, 45.5 per cent was aware of PrEP and 54.5 per cent unaware.
- At Sauna B, 35.7 per cent had heard of PrEP and 64.3 per cent had not.
- At Sauna A, 58.8 per cent had heard of PrEP and 41.2 per cent had not heard of it.

These data suggest that Sauna A attendees were more likely to have heard of PrEP, an important HIV prevention method, than attendees at other saunas.

HIV testing

- At Sauna C 23.5 per cent had never tested for HIV and 29.4 per cent reported testing every few years.
- At Sauna B, 42.9 per cent tested for HIV every six months and 28.6 per cent had never tested for HIV.
- At Sauna A, 45.5 per cent get tested every three months and 27.3 per cent get tested every few years.

These data suggest that Sauna A attendees were more likely to get tested for HIV every three months and less likely to get tested every few years than attendees at other saunas.

Hepatitis B vaccination

- At Sauna C, 44.4 per cent had received the hepatitis B vaccine and 50 per cent had not.
- At Sauna B, 50 per cent had received the hepatitis B vaccine and 50 per cent had not.
- At Sauna A, 63.6 per cent had received the hepatitis B vaccine and 36.4 per cent had not.

These data suggest that Sauna A attendees are more likely to have had the hepatitis B vaccine than attendees at the other saunas.

Perceived personal benefits of PrEP

There were significant differences between the perceived personal benefits of PrEP among attendees at the three saunas. Sauna A attendees were more likely to perceive PrEP as personally beneficial than Sauna B and C attendees. Previous research (Jaspal and Daramilas 2016) suggests that MSM may not view PrEP as personally beneficial given low risk appraisal (see also Chapter 7). Thus, Sauna A attendees may have exposure to more affirmative images of PrEP.

Perceived easiness of negotiating condom use in the sauna

There were significant differences between the perceived easiness of negotiating condom use with sexual partners at the three saunas. Sauna B attendees found it easier to negotiate condom use than Sauna A and C attendees. This was an unexpected finding given that in the silver certified sauna condom negotiation appears to be easier than in a gold certified sauna.

Sexual risk-taking behaviours

In general, levels of sexual risk-taking behaviours were low among attendees at all three saunas. However, there was a marginally significant difference in the frequency of oral sex without a condom. Attendees at Sauna B more frequently performed oral sex without a condom than Sauna A and C attendees. Thus, sexual risk-taking (measured on one dimension) was lower at the gold certified sauna.

Perceived risk of HIV infection

There was a marginally significant difference between perceived risk of HIV infection among attendees at the three saunas. Sauna A attendees saw themselves as being at higher risk than Sauna B and C attendees. It has been observed that perceived HIV risk may be inaccurately low among some MSM, despite high objective risk (Jaspal et al. 2016). Sauna A attendees may have internalised more accurate information regarding HIV, leading to more realistic and accurate HIV risk appraisals.

Saunas as spaces of social interaction

The saunas were seen not only as spaces of sexual engagement and interaction with like-minded individuals but also as spaces of social interaction, and as a context which facilitates freedom of sexual expression, 'a secluded space' without stigma *(P3, Sauna B)*. Furthermore, some sauna users were eager to socialise both with other users and with the management team. Management teams appeared to support this (e.g. Sauna A had plans for further expanding, and separating, the lounge/bar area from the rest of the sauna, for this purpose). This need of social connectedness (even in the form of a casual chat) was expressed particularly by older sauna users but not exclusively so. For example, a younger participant claimed that he used the sauna precisely for this social purpose *(P8, Sauna A)*.

Saunas as spaces of safe sexual interaction

The saunas were also construed as spaces for safe sexual interaction with a specific etiquette which is directly and indirectly 'learned' and followed by most sauna users who engage in any form of sexual contact. They considered the management team an asset in maintaining this safe space which allowed for sexual and social interactions. The concept of safe sexual connectedness has an added value, in view of the complex ways in which sauna users self-identify in terms of their sexual orientation and in view of the desire for discretion among many sauna users. Sauna B users self-identified mostly as MSM or in ways other than 'gay' (e.g. bi-curious, straight interested in t-girls, etc.). Several users were heterosexually married, and their spouses were reportedly unaware of their visits to the sauna.

Sexual behaviour

Participants engaged in a variety of sexual practices in the saunas. Participants reported engaging in, or observing, anal sex, oral sex, masturbation, threesomes, group sex, voyeurism and exhibitionism. Interestingly, a high number of the participants tended not to engage in anal sex themselves and those who did engage in anal sex generally reported condom use or other methods of HIV prevention (e.g. PrEP, *P14, Sauna A*). Only one participant reported condom use during oral sex (*P10, Sauna B*). None reported engaging in drug use on the sauna premises, and only one person reported observing drug use once (*P6, Sauna A but not in Sauna A*). It is noteworthy that, although most participants reported safer sex, some reported observing other people engaging in unsafe sex:

> 'I've seen it. One, two youngsters. I've seen one young bloke going from one to another, two, three blokes.'
>
> (P10, Sauna B)

Perceived access to condoms and lubricant

The majority of participants in all three saunas agreed that condoms and lubricant were easily accessible throughout all the premises. More specifically, in Sauna A and C there were condoms and lubricant in strategically located spots within the spaces where sexual activity took place. In Sauna B, every patient received condoms and lubricant with their towel in the changing areas, before entering the sauna.

Interaction with staff

In terms of interactions with the management team, most participants expressed their belief that all staff members were helpful, personable and sociable. Some participants contrasted this with other saunas in larger cities (e.g. Birmingham, London, etc.) where the setting could reportedly be more 'clinical' (*P1, Sauna C*) and the management team more 'disconnected'. This point should be considered in the context of saunas as sites for social interaction, as outlined above. Moreover, sauna users were generally pleased with the knowledge and support obtained in the saunas in relation to sexual health. Many found that the mere presence of the NHS sexual health clinical staff led them to think more about sexual health issues.

Effectiveness of the sexual health intervention

This evaluation of the SOAP certification scheme demonstrated moderate effectiveness in regards to sexual health promotion and HIV prevention. It is possible that the project could have achieved greater effectiveness if aspects of social psychological theory were incorporated in its design and implementation. However, the data do shed light on the ways in which MSM construe and utilise gay saunas; they are not just spaces for sexual contact but also for social interactions. Moreover, this section highlights some of the potential challenges that must be acknowledged and overcome in order to increase the effectiveness of such a sexual health intervention. For instance, MSM who use particular saunas appear to have different levels of knowledge and awareness of sexual health issues and manifest distinct patterns of HIV testing. Furthermore, there are observable differences in perceived HIV risk and in perceived suitability of PrEP, which can in turn affect uptake of HIV testing and PrEP, respectively. More generally, the data emphasise the importance of considering gay saunas as a viable context for promoting sexual health and for preventing HIV infection. In the third section of this chapter, some of these challenges are revisited and recommendations are offered regarding the optimisation of sexual health interventions.

Enhancing sexual health outcomes among BME MSM

As indicated in Chapter 2, MSM are disproportionately affected by HIV, whose incidence is increasing in those of BME background: 14.6 per cent of the total number of MSM diagnosed with HIV in 2014 (6,654 of 45,679) are BME (Public Health England 2015b). There has been a more than 82 per cent increase in new HIV diagnoses among MSM categorised as Other or of Mixed Heritage (242 to 442). The number of HIV-positive BME MSM seen for HIV care has increased greatly in recent years. Among Black-Caribbean men there has been a more than 100 per cent increase (408 in 2005 to 837 in 2014) and among Black African men there has been a 126 per cent increase (267 to 605).

Although there is growing incidence of HIV among BME MSM, there is still relatively scarce understanding of the specific risk factors associated with this population. In a survey study conducted at a London sexual health clinic (Soni et al. 2008), it was found that BME MSM were more likely to report condomless anal intercourse with casual partners in the preceding three months than White British respondents, demonstrating the high risk of HIV infection in this group. A meta-analysis of studies of BME MSM from Canada, the UK and the USA revealed that BME MSM engaged in fewer sexual risk behaviours and reported fewer instances of unprotected anal sex, fewer male sexual partners and more condom use during anal sex than other MSM (Millett *et al.* 2012). Regardless of their greater likelihood of adopting safer sex behaviours, Black MSM were three times more likely to test HIV-positive and six times more likely to have undiagnosed HIV than MSM of other ethnicities (Millet *et al.* 2012). These findings demonstrate significant sexual health inequalities between BME MSM and White MSM. Moreover, the meta-analysis revealed numerous differences in HIV risk between MSM in the UK and the USA. BME MSM are more likely than White MSM to test HIV-positive or to ever have had a STI. BME men in the UK were more likely to have a history of substance misuse. Black MSM in the UK were more likely to have been tested for HIV, but less likely to have heard of PEP or PrEP than White MSM. Black MSM living with HIV were less likely to have access to ART than White MSM.

The small number of studies of South Asian MSM in the UK generally suggest a low HIV prevalence in this population, although there is emerging evidence of high-risk behaviours in this group (Griffiths 2015). For instance, in survey research, it has been argued that South Asian MSM are less likely to report sexual activity with a known HIV-positive partner (Hickson *et al.* 2004). This may actually be construed as a risky sexual behaviour given that individuals may be engaging in 'sero-guessing', that is, they may erroneously guess the HIV status of their sexual partner. In a survey of BME MSM (Jaspal *et al.* 2016), it was found that South Asian MSM were more likely to seek sex in gay saunas and on gay geospatial social networking applications than Black MSM. There has also been some work on South Asian MSM's engagement with GUM clinics. Survey research conducted at GUM clinics suggests that South Asians may be more reluctant than other ethnic groups to seek care in this setting due to cultural stigma (Dhar *et al.* 2010). Similarly, a national survey of MSM living in Britain found that South Asians were more likely to express anxiety in relation to attendance at a sexual health clinic due to the possibility that others in their community might find out that they have sex with men (McKeown *et al.* 2012). Although the prevalence of diagnosed HIV remains low among South Asians in the UK, a year on year increase in HIV incidence has been observed in this group (Desai *et al.* 2015). In short, existing research in this area demonstrates the importance of developing effective sexual health interventions for

BME MSM to reduce the incidence of HIV and other STIs in this population.

The BME MSM Project – a sexual health intervention

As a key national public health agency, Public Health England is committed to promoting and protecting public health and to addressing health inequalities in society. In 2014, Public Health England launched the BME MSM project, in order to pilot models of direct behaviour change interventions for BME MSM aimed at reducing sexual health risk behaviour and building resilience. The interventions set out to promote positive changes on the following dimensions: sexual identity, sexual risk behaviour, mental health, wellbeing, smoking status, alcohol use, recreational drug use, employment, social isolation, and use of public services. As indicated in Chapter 2, many of these factors are known to impinge on sexual health outcomes in MSM. Although the project included a series of behavioural interventions led by various community organisations in London, this section focuses only on one of the interventions – the 'Selfie' intervention for BME MSM, which was led by a sexual health charity in London.

The Selfie intervention aims to inform and empower BME MSM in relation to their sexual health and decision-making, and to facilitate a positive sexual identity in this population. An overall aim of the programme is to enhance the social and psychological wellbeing of participants and to decrease engagement in sexual risk behaviours, thereby reducing the incidence of HIV and other STIs in BME MSM. The following Selfie groups were evaluated as part of the current project: (1) a group for Spanish-speaking MSM (mainly from Latin America), (2) a group for Portuguese-speaking MSM (mainly from Brazil), (3) a group for Black and mixed heritage MSM, and (4) a group for South Asian MSM. The Spanish- and Portuguese-speaking groups consisted of separate sessions for HIV-negative and HIV-positive MSM. The Black/mixed heritage and South Asian groups consisted of sessions for HIV-negative MSM only. The programmes included seven sessions over a period of seven weeks. The following areas were covered to varying degrees in all of the sessions: (1) sexual health, (2) addictive behaviours, (3) identity, (4) self-esteem and wellbeing,

(5) leadership and self-development, (6) relationships and intimacy, (7) religion, (8) anger management, and (9) nutrition. Each workshop was facilitated by a staff member at the charity (e.g. the psychosexual therapist, the group coordinator) or an external volunteer (e.g. an HIV doctor, a nutritionist).

The evaluation project

The evaluation project set out to ascertain the effect of the sexual health behaviour change interventions on the following indicators and risk factors: sexual identity, sexual risk behaviour, mental health, wellbeing, smoking status, alcohol use, recreational drug use, employment, social isolation and use of public services.

A quantitative survey, which tapped into aspects of identity, perceived stigma, social inclusion, quality of life and wellbeing, was administered to participants once before the intervention began and then once again after the intervention had concluded. For the quantitative component, a total of 33 BME MSM completed pre-intervention and post-intervention questionnaires. Four defined themselves as African, three as Caribbean, one as Indian, six as Pakistani, fifteen as Latino/Hispanic, one as mixed White/Black heritage, and two as 'Other'. Seventeen individuals were HIV-negative, twelve were HIV-positive, and four were unaware of their HIV status. Responses on each of the aforementioned scales were compared using the t-test statistical technique.

In addition, one focus group was conducted for each intervention group to examine qualitatively the perceived impact of the intervention. The focus group interview schedule tapped into participants' perceptions of the aforementioned foci of the interventions. For the qualitative component, there was a focus group for each of the Selfie programmes. Five men participated in the HIV-positive NAZ Latina group, ten in the HIV-negative NAZ Latina group, six in the HIV-positive NAZ Vidas group, four in the HIV-negative NAZ men group, and six in the HIV-negative NAZ Asia group.

In this section of the chapter, key quantitative and qualitative findings from the evaluation project are presented. The findings are divided into sub-sections that focus on particular areas, namely reductions in sexual health risk factors, the communication of sexual

Reductions in sexual health risk factors

In view of the similar content across all of the Selfie programmes, the quantitative data were not split by ethnic group but rather analysed as a single cohort. A comparison of the pre-intervention and post-intervention data from the 33 men using the t-test statistical technique exhibited statistically significant improvements on measures of attitudes towards condom use, sexual risk-taking, attitudes towards alcohol, sense of continuity, perceived access to public services, and participation in chemsex. In general, there were no significant changes in reported or intended sexual behaviours.

Invaluable source of sexual health information

Participants reported perceiving greater access to important sexual health information to which they would not ordinarily have access. Participants across all of the cohorts hoped to modify their sexual risk-taking behaviours in view of the information they obtained regarding the prevalence and transmission of STIs among MSM. The Portuguese-speaking cohort in particular derived information about the potential risks of using recreational drugs in sexualised settings, which was useful particularly for HIV-positive MSM concerned about the risks surrounding interactions between ART and recreational drugs. All of the Portuguese- and Spanish-speaking cohorts greatly benefitted from the delivery of this important information in their own language, given that many reported difficulties in communicating in English and expressed anxiety about having to discuss their sexual health with monolingual English-speaking healthcare professionals (see also Jaspal 2017c).

Re-thinking the value appended to sexual identity

Most respondents described the challenges of identifying and coming out as gay in their communities, which in some cases led to internalised homophobia, but reported that the Selfie sessions had enabled them to re-evaluate their sexual identities in more positive and accepting ways.

The sessions had reportedly exposed them to more positive social representations of their sexual identities, which enabled them to view it in a more affirmative manner. This led the Black and Latin American participants, in particular, to seek closer ties with other MSM in their respective ethnic communities, which provided a sense of social identity. Participants overwhelmingly identified an improvement in their sense of self-esteem on the basis of their sexual identity since beginning the programme.

Coping with depression

Most participants described past and ongoing experiences of anxiety and depression, which they attributed to homonegativity and/or their HIV diagnosis. However, participation in the Selfie programme provided the social and psychological 'resources' for beginning to cope with depression (primarily through the derivation of social support). Experiences of homophobia had led some individuals to feel marginalised but the Selfie groups provided a supportive network which reportedly decreased feelings of anxiety and depression. HIV-positive respondents in particular expressed their pleasure at their ability to attend sessions tailored to those living with HIV, in which they felt more comfortable disclosing mental health issues they had experienced, such as depression. A key aspect of the Selfie programmes is the encouragement of sexual health leadership roles among participants so that they can further promote sexual health in their respective communities. The qualitative data suggested that this scheme provided some individuals with increased self-efficacy and, thus, a further boost to their wellbeing.

Effectiveness of the sexual health intervention

The Selfie programme provided a space that was construed by participants as being socially and psychologically 'safe'. In view of reported experiences of homophobia and racism, this safe space was key for promoting wellbeing and for encouraging thinking and discussion in the important area of sexual health. Moreover, it was clear that many of the participants had had little exposure to positive social representations concerning sexual identity and to important sexual health information prior to their engagement with the intervention.

The affirmative social representations of sexual identity and sexual health information were communicated in highly effective ways in participants' own languages (e.g. Spanish, Portuguese, Urdu), which had a discernibly positive impact on them. Overall, the data suggest significant improvements particularly in the domain of psychological wellbeing with some evidence of improvement on attitudes towards health behaviours.

The implications for practitioners

As outlined in Chapter 3, the theory of planned behaviour could provide a robust theoretical underpinning to interventions for enhancing sexual health outcomes among MSM in gay saunas and for BME MSM, respectively. The key is to promote the adoption of safer sexual behaviours among MSM, that is, consistent condom use, reduced number of sexual partners, awareness and uptake (if necessary) of biomedical prevention approaches such as PEP and PrEP, and regular HIV testing (see Case 1 in Chapter 1). The data presented in the two case studies suggest that the impact of the interventions for self-identity and wellbeing was more significant than their impact for actual sexual behaviour among participants. Thus, one should consider how behavioural interventions could be improved through the incorporation of tenets from social psychology.

First, it is important to understand the individual's attitudes towards particular behaviours and, more specifically, to ascertain whether the behaviour and its consequences are evaluated positively or negatively. Behavioural interventions seek primarily to change risky behaviours but, in order to do so, it is vital to attempt to change attitudes towards those behaviours and the behaviours that the intervention attempts to promote. The processes of anchoring and objectification are central to the formation of social representations. As outlined in the second case study, the communication of social representations that are intelligible and that make sense to members of a given community are more likely to be adopted and internalised by them. Information should be linguistically and culturally appropriate. BME MSM, the target population of the second intervention presented in this chapter, may have distinct ethnic, cultural and linguistic requirements from the general population. However, there is a more general need to incorporate identity factors (relevant to the target population) in the design of behavioural interventions. The social representations to be disseminated must relate to existing representations held by individuals in the specific population so that they can be more readily assimilated and accommodated.

The intervention should seek to challenge positive social representations of undesirable behaviours and to introduce more positive representations of those that the intervention seeks to promote. For instance, as highlighted in Chapter 2, chemsex may be regarded in positive terms due to one's ability to engage in sex with multiple partners without inhibition, which can be a sexually exciting experience for some individuals. However, many participants simultaneously recognise the disadvantages of chemsex, which can cause disruption in their lives. Through the promotion of conversational exchange and in-depth critical thinking, the intervention could seek to draw out some of the disadvantages of chemsex. The potential psychosocial benefits of chemsex, such as non-disclosure of HIV status, and avoidance of HIV stigma in these contexts, can sometimes override the disadvantages of the practice.

Conversely, it would be advantageous to explore alternative behaviours that could replace one's engagement in chemsex and to focus on the potential advantages and benefits of adopting such alternative behaviours. The role of social representations is once again key, since through discussions it is possible to gain exposure to, and to promote, a more positive social representation of the new behaviour. Chemsex is but one example. HIV testing is another behaviour that needs to be encouraged in order to improve HIV disease prognosis in patients and to reduce onward HIV transmission. A behavioural intervention to increase HIV testing among MSM might aim to improve attitudes towards testing primarily by normalising the practice so that it is no longer associated with those 'at high risk' or those who engage in particular sexual behaviours that may be stigmatised. This would likely improve attitudes towards HIV testing among individuals who may feel uneasy about seeking, and/or disclosing their uptake of, HIV testing (Jaspal 2017c).

Second, it is necessary to explore the subjective norms surrounding the behaviour, which entails researching the individual's belief about what significant others will think about the behaviour. In the case study on enhancing sexual health outcomes among BME MSM, the strategy of dividing BME individuals into distinct intervention groups by ethnic group and HIV status was described. This can have both advantages and disadvantages. On the one hand, individuals may come to regard their specific group (e.g. HIV-positive South Asian MSM) as their principal source of subjective norms. They may feel comfortable disclosing their experiences and debating social representations with fellow ingroup members. Indeed, the most effective strategy for coping with the high levels of anxiety and depression observable in BME MSM, due to homonegativity and other social stressors, is self-disclosure and social support, which may be easier to derive from ingroup members. On the other hand, individuals may feel overly immersed in their specific ingroup and become less able to derive social support from outgroup members, that is, others who do not share their ethnicity or HIV status. Moreover, they may continue to perceive negative subjective norms from outside their specific group. Individuals may thus face continued exposure to negative social representations when they do come into contact with outgroup members.

In the case study on enhancing sexual health outcomes in gay saunas, it appeared that the saunas had distinct 'cultures' that might in turn result in particular patterns of HIV testing and distinct levels of knowledge around HIV status, PrEP and PEP. Furthermore, in some gay communities, practices such as non-monogamy and chemsex have become normalised over time, which can lead to stigma around what may sometimes be construed as 'heteronormative' practices such as monogamy or marriage. This can make it difficult for individuals to adopt behaviours that they perceive to be stigmatised in the groups and communities in which they are embedded. This can potentially be remedied in at least two ways.

On the one hand, a large-scale intervention might attempt to produce a shift in social representations within the entire group or community. For instance, the practitioner might seek to encourage and promote positive social representations of PrEP and to dispel stigmatising social representations of PrEP which currently impede uptake of this biomedical prevention method. While it is recognised that it can be difficult to challenge long-standing social representations and to introduce new representations at a community level, this is an effective long-term strategy for encouraging a subjective norm that is conducive to effective behaviour change.

On the other hand, the intervention could encourage the individual to broaden his social networks to increase exposure to positive social representations of a given behaviour. For instance, MSM who could benefit from PrEP could be encouraged to associate with current PrEP users which would allow exposure to distinct social representations of the prevention tool. In other words, the significant others change so that one is exposed to more positive social representations of the desirable behaviour. However, it must be acknowledged that the new social representations that the intervention seeks to promote may prove to be inconsistent or incompatible with existing representations held by the individual or even with other identity elements. This could potentially challenge the psychological coherence principle of identity.

Third, the practitioner must ascertain the individual's level of perceived behavioural control, that is, the individual's belief regarding their ability to perform the behaviour. Any sexual health behaviour, such as condom use, HIV testing or PrEP use, may be construed by the individual as difficult or obstructive. For instance, some men prefer not to use condoms due to erectile dysfunction, the cause of which is often psychological in that the individual *believes* that he will not be able to get and maintain an erection. HIV testing may be associated with the fear of testing positive or of being seen in the clinic by somebody one knows, which can lead individuals to disengage. The very prospect of taking daily PrEP may appear to be too difficult due to concerns around one's ability to adhere to the medication (see Chapter 7). It is essential that behavioural interventions attempt to bolster self-efficacy in the individuals targeted. Participants must come to believe that they *can* adopt the new behaviour – be it consistent condom use, HIV testing or PrEP adherence.

As discussed above, social representations play an important role in the development of self-efficacy in relation to a given behaviour. For instance, when PrEP is anchored to first generation ART, it may plausibly be perceived as toxic and difficult to adhere to. The intervention should therefore acknowledge existing social representations held by the individual and seek to challenge them in order to build feelings of control and competence. This process may involve exposure to more favourable social representations through discussion with individuals who currently engage in the desired behaviour. For instance, during HIV Testing Week, a principal objective of HIV testing campaigns is to dispel the social representation that HIV testing is difficult, time-consuming and painful – often by depicting an actual HIV test with a celebrity who later attests to the ease with which he or she was tested.

In addition to self-efficacy, other motivational principles are important to consider in the behavioural intervention. Awareness of risk does not have an automatic effect on behaviour in that individuals may continue to engage in risk behaviours despite their awareness and understanding of the risks involved. It is likely that behaviours and practices that satisfy identity processes will be enacted and maintained in spite of risk (see Chapter 4). For instance, MSM who engage in chemsex are generally aware of the (sexual) health risks associated with this practice but they may continue to engage in it because it enhances self-esteem. As outlined in Chapter 2, benefits for self-esteem may be derived from the fact that individuals feel more desirable and that they do not face HIV stigma in chemsex settings. Similarly, individuals may continue to engage in condomless sex with their partner(s) because continued engagement in this practice enhances their sense of continuity. Condom use would conversely constitute a lifestyle change, and perhaps an undesirable one, thereby challenging continuity. It can plausibly be argued that when a (risk) behaviour is central to identity it will be maintained. Thus, the intervention must acknowledge the identity functions performed by any given behaviour, as well as the potential impacts that the new behaviour (e.g. sober sex, condom use) might have for identity in members of the target population. This requires in-depth cultural understanding of the population. Moreover, greater understanding of the identity functions performed by relevant behaviours would allow the practitioner to develop ways of limiting the negative effects of behaviour change for identity processes. This would increase the likelihood of *sustained* behaviour change.

As outlined in IPT, identity is also contingent on the physical spaces within which individuals are embedded. The data presented in the first case study, in particular, demonstrate the importance of acknowledging the physical spaces and structures of the settings within which HIV prevention efforts are to be targeted. The physical layout of the gay sauna must be factored into the design of the intervention. How is the physical space organised and how does this in turn shape the nature of interaction between individuals within that space? The data demonstrate that, contrary to expectations, the gay sauna may also be utilised as a space for social interaction rather than solely sexual behaviour. This provides an opportunity for disseminating and indeed debating particular social representations of sex and sexual health in this context. Thus, prior to designing an intervention, the practitioner must acquire an in-depth understanding of the nature of the physical spaces and the meanings appended to them by users themselves.

The practitioner must consider attitudes, the subjective norms, and perceived behavioural control, as they collectively contribute to the formation of a *behavioural intention*, which in turn constitutes a key predictor of whether or not the desired behaviour is adopted. If even one of the three factors (e.g. the subjective norm concerning the new behaviour) is weak, then the overall behavioural intention will decrease. Perceived behavioural control is likely to be an especially important factor given that the individual must believe that behaviour change is actually possible. This amounts to self-efficacy concerns. However, as indicated above, other motivational principles of identity must be factored in.

Overview

In this chapter, two interventions for enhancing sexual health outcomes among MSM and the data from the studies to evaluate their effectiveness are presented. These data are utilised to highlight the potential achievements and shortcomings of these interventions and to sketch out possible pathways for developing more effective interventions for sexual health, self-identity and wellbeing among MSM. The most effective behavioural interventions are those that are informed by robust social psychological theory. Drawing upon insights from the theory of planned behaviour and IPT, the following recommendations can be offered:

- Existing social representations held by participants in the intervention must be acknowledged, as must the general 'cultures' in which participants are embedded. These will inform awareness and understanding of the new social representations that are introduced as a result of the intervention.

- The intervention should provide exposure to social representations that are likely to lead to the desired behaviour change.

These representations will be disseminated and internalised through the medium of discussion and debate.

- The social representations that are introduced, disseminated and encouraged in the intervention must be linguistically and culturally appropriate for the target population, as they are unlikely to be accepted and internalised if individuals cannot identify with them.

- The potential significance of existing behaviours and the potential impact of new behaviours for identity processes should be considered. Behaviour change should be presented in a non-threatening manner and strategies should be in place for minimising threats arising from behaviour change.

- It is especially important to empower participants in the intervention to build self-efficacy in relation to behaviour change so that they feel sufficiently competent to make the desired changes to their behaviour.

The overall aim of the intervention is to facilitate the assimilation and accommodation of sexual health behaviours in identity without causing excessive disruption to the identity structure. IPT outlines the various principles of identity that are susceptible to threat. Crucially, behaviour change that is minimally threatening is likely to be adopted and sustained. Effective strategies must be in place for coping with potential threats that arise. These factors must be acknowledged and incorporated in behaviour change interventions in order to improve effectiveness.

Chapter 7

Integrating Tenets of Identity Theory into HIV Medicine

The aim of this chapter is to outline how tenets of IPT can enhance the practice of HIV medicine. In this chapter, two case studies are presented. The first outlines the potential challenges associated with the roll-out of PrEP for preventing HIV infection among MSM at high risk. In addition to the challenges associated with obtaining PrEP in the UK, there are psychosocial barriers to accessing PrEP, some of which are discussed in this chapter. The second case study focuses on the psychosocial difficulties associated with adherence to ART in MSM living with HIV. Despite the physical benefits of ART, both for individual and public health, many patients experience psychosocial challenges which can inhibit uptake of and adherence to ART. These barriers may be grounded in fear, misinformation and stigma. In both case studies, data from qualitative interview research into social representations of PrEP and ART among HIV-negative and HIV-positive MSM, respectively, are presented. The aim is to provide illustrative quotes from affected individuals in order to highlight some of the psychosocial issues which may be encountered by HIV healthcare providers in clinical settings. Accordingly, the final section of this chapter outlines potential ways in which tenets of IPT can be acknowledged and incorporated into clinical practice in order for the practitioner to facilitate better outcomes in patients. Recommendations are made for enhancing HIV clinical practice through the use of identity theory.

The challenges of rolling-out PrEP

The psychosocial challenges of rolling-out PrEP among MSM are multifarious. In 2015, 11 HIV-negative MSM aged between 18 and

48 were recruited in the English Midlands and in West London for a qualitative interview study of social representations of PrEP (Jaspal and Daramilas 2016). The data, which were analysed using qualitative thematic analysis, suggest that the (1) uncertainty and fear associated with HIV and PrEP, (2) challenges in managing relationships with others, and (3) stigma and categorisation in relation to HIV and PrEP collectively, constitute key barriers.

Uncertainty and fear

There is an established empirical link between uncertainty and fear (Grupe and Nitschke 2013). A large body of research indicates that uncertainty surrounding future health outcomes can fuel fear around medication. The two constructs are considered in tandem because interview data regarding MSM's social representations of PrEP suggest that uncertainty about the effectiveness of PrEP can generate fear of HIV infection despite adherence to the preventative drug. Despite evidence from clinical trials that PrEP is highly effective in preventing HIV infection (see Chapter 2), HIV-negative MSM may still manifest uncertainty and fear about its effectiveness. Individuals have described their anxiety after sexual encounters even when they have used condoms, highlighting the general fear of HIV infection among MSM (Prestage *et al.* 2012), and contrasted them with the prospect of using PrEP (an *invisible* prevention method). Accordingly, MSM may anticipate greater anxiety about HIV infection after sex (with PrEP):

> Well, they say it's effective but it isn't exactly a vaccine is it? Scientists can make mistakes too… With a condom you put it on and that's it. You know what the score is.
>
> (Joel)

> I don't trust the scientists. One minute it's OK to just take it and then the next 'oh sorry, we misjudged that'… It's like when they didn't get the whole blood transfusions issue and loads of people wound up getting infected.
>
> (Keiron)

As a relatively novel prevention tool, PrEP may be perceived by some as an uncertain method of protecting oneself against HIV. This is in contrast to previous research that has found that PrEP can reduce fear of HIV (Koester *et al.* 2014). Interestingly, there is sometimes a clear orientation towards a one-shot HIV vaccine as the desired HIV prophylaxis. Indeed, in an analysis of the press coverage of PrEP (Jaspal and Nerlich 2017), it has been found that some journalists in favour of the prophylactic tool anchor it to vaccination and, in some cases, construct it as surpassing a vaccine in terms of its benefits. Despite this misleading press tendency, there is evidence that some MSM reject this notion but, due to the cultural desirability of a vaccine, also appear to reject the effectiveness of PrEP. Fear and uncertainty vis-à-vis PrEP may additionally stem from general mistrust of scientists and public health experts who 'can make mistakes too'. Keiron described his fear that PrEP may fail by anchoring scientists' knowledge on PrEP to their lack of knowledge concerning the contamination of blood products which led to HIV infections among recipients. This early error in the HIV/AIDS crisis may resurface in people's minds and fuel scepticism towards PrEP.

Much trepidation in relation to PrEP stems from uncertainty and, thus, fear surrounding its potential (long-term) side effects (Grant *et al.* 2014). Some MSM may anchor PrEP to earlier generations of ART which did cause side effects:

> It freaks me out, taking those pills and you don't know the effects they will have... You know, people on medication wasting away. I do look after myself and my body and skin. All of that matters to me.
>
> (Ian)

> You know, you hear the stories about, you know, being forced to pump drugs into your body and people dying from it. What's the need to pump drugs in your body unnecessarily?
>
> (Andy)

Some individuals may focus on the potential physical side effects of using, as prophylaxis, drugs currently used to treat HIV infection. Ian believed that PrEP might cause undesirable physical changes, thereby undermining his efforts to 'look after myself and my body and skin'. Upon close scrutiny, it is clear that he anchors PrEP to first-generation ART which could cause lipodystrophy and other physical changes. In short, MSM may fear that they will become identifiable as PrEP users, due to the physical changes that they believe to be associated with its use. This anchoring process is observable in MSM's reflections on PrEP. Indeed, Andy associates it with 'people dying from' the use of azidothymidine (AZT) in the early stages of ART development.

In addition to the tendency to anchor PrEP to first-generation ART, there may be more general negative perceptions of PrEP. The objectification of taking PrEP as 'being forced to pump drugs into your body' constructs a decreased sense of agency and self-efficacy in relation to sexual health. This metaphorical theme is in stark contrast to the perception among some users of PrEP that it conversely does provide greater choice and agency in protecting their sexual health (Grant and Koester 2016). Although MSM may acknowledge their own inconsistent use of condoms, as a concept condoms tend to be evaluated by some as a more logical approach to HIV prevention than a biomedical approach involving 'drugs'.

The impact of PrEP on one's own sexual behaviour constitutes an additional source of uncertainty for some individuals, who believe that they might find it more difficult to use condoms consistently:

> In a way it sounds good I agree because I do sort of have [condom] slip ups quite a bit, like I have had unprotected sex a few times… But I think maybe it's something to like improve on and with PrEP I reckon I'd stop altogether and that does worry me.
>
> (Kyle)

Kyle refers to condomless sexual encounters as 'slip ups' as he acknowledges the associated risks. Use of this term also suggests that condomless encounters are undesirable and that he wishes to change this risky behaviour. This may be attributed to the social stigma appended to condomless sex in the MSM community (Shernoff 2006), which is also sometimes reproduced by medical professionals (Grant and Koester 2016). Upon reflection, Kyle fears that PrEP might accentuate his existing habit of not using condoms in casual sexual encounters, because it would provide protection against the STI he feared most, namely HIV. In short, Kyle expresses uncertainty about his future sexual behaviour which increases his fear of possible HIV infection. Like Kyle, many MSM quite honestly acknowledge the 'competition' between PrEP and condoms and do not seriously believe that they would use condoms consistently while taking PrEP (Brooks *et al.* 2012). This is in contrast to the recommendation made by both the Food and Drug Administration in the US and the research team leading the PROUD Study in the UK that condoms be used alongside PrEP (see Chapter 2).

Managing relationships with others

There may be concern among MSM about the impact that PrEP use could have on their personal relationships. There appears to be widespread awareness of the social stigma surrounding PrEP, embodied by references to the 'Truvada Whore' in the US context (Spieldenner 2016). Individuals' awareness of this stigma may inform their own evaluation of PrEP:

> There is a bit of shame, you know, when you don't use condoms and like what you supposed to do? Tell a guy 'oh, we don't need to worry about using condoms because I'm taking a tablet that lets me fuck raw?' It is a bit slutty-sounding.
>
> (Ian)

> I often wonder how people would judge me for taking PrEP. In my culture (South Asian) let's say we have a conservative culture... My parents don't even know I'm gay.
>
> (Raj)

Like Ian and Raj, MSM may feel uneasy about the potential social consequences of disclosing PrEP use to others. This could be attributed to the coercive social norm of using condoms in this community and the consequential social stigma appended to non-use of condoms among MSM. While non-use of condoms may be socially represented as irresponsible and reckless, condomless sex is nevertheless practised though not discussed openly (Shernoff 2006). There may be a pervasive perception among MSM that PrEP and condoms are mutually exclusive and would therefore not be used in conjunction. There is an element of stigma appended to non-use of condoms as some may feel that this would portray them as 'slutty' and 'irresponsible'. There is, thus, a discernible sense of shame surrounding PrEP use in lieu of condoms (McDavitt and Mutchler 2014).

Similarly, Raj fears judgement from others, although his account exhibits an additional layer of complexity. While many MSM consider

PrEP through the lens of their sexual identity, which is generally recognised as placing them at increased risk of HIV exposure, some may also consider PrEP from the perspective of other identities, such as their ethno-cultural group membership. Raj describes his ethno-cultural ingroup as 'conservative' which has discouraged him from disclosing his sexual identity to his parents and other ingroup members. Raj's socialisation in his ethno-cultural group appears to have led to increased shame surrounding aspects of his sexual identity, including how to safeguard his sexual health as a MSM. Consequently, he worries about the added stigma that he might face as a PrEP user, and he anticipates difficulties in concealing his PrEP use from family members.

There are also positive observations about PrEP among HIV-negative MSM:

> PrEP seems to give you a lot of choice though, I've got to say… I mean that sometimes you can't really have that conversation about what you want to do and don't want, like in a condom kind of sense, but with PrEP you'd take it in the morning right? That's good.
>
> (Andy)

MSM may find it difficult to discuss HIV and to negotiate condom use particularly before or during a sexual encounter (Shernoff 2006). Andy, who previously used the metaphor of 'pumping drugs into your body' in his reflections on PrEP, does acknowledge the self-efficacy that PrEP might provide in relation to sexual health. He feels that this would enable individuals to take control of their sexual health without external pressures from others. Some HIV-negative MSM may acknowledge that PrEP is safer than relying on one's sexual partner to report their HIV status accurately, but may simultaneously manifest decreased willingness to use it themselves. This could be attributed to the social stigma surrounding it.

Stigma and categorisation

Many MSM are acutely aware of the social stigma surrounding PrEP due to its anchoring to condomless sex and sexual risk-taking, which leads some to distance themselves from it:

> [PrEP] wouldn't benefit me. I don't take many risks, not much more than most guys on the scene. I suppose it's for someone high-risk.
>
> (Alan)

> Jack: I'm not like taking that many risks really so I've never thought this is for me.
>
> Interviewer: What do you see as a risk?
>
> Jack: Someone who is out at chemsex parties every weekend.

MSM may accept the social representation that PrEP is intended for individuals at high risk of HIV while also acknowledging the social stigma surrounding the category 'high-risk'. Accordingly, HIV-negative individuals may seek to disassociate themselves from this category in their reflections on PrEP. Alan resists the category 'high-risk' by attenuating the magnitude of the sexual risks that he takes. Social psychologists discuss the strategy of 'downward comparison', which refers to the process of comparing oneself to others on dimensions that will lead to a more favourable self-evaluation and, thus, to enhanced self-esteem (Wills 1981). Alan engages in a form of downward comparison with 'most guys on the [gay] scene' in order to present his own risk-taking as relatively trivial in contrast to others' risk-taking. Furthermore, Jack anchors the high-risk category to participation in chemsex which itself carries the double stigma of casual sex with multiple partners and drug use (Bourne *et al.* 2014). He is able to avoid self-positioning in this stigmatised category by constructing participation in chemsex as a central criterion for PrEP use. Although Jack does not engage in chemsex, he does report condomless sexual encounters with multiple casual partners, which in fact highlights his risk of HIV exposure. In resisting the stigmatised category 'high risk', Alan and others hastily conclude that PrEP would not be of benefit to them. Furthermore, PrEP is anchored to sexual promiscuity, which further accentuates its stigma:

> I read an article that said 'Truvada Whore'... It must be because this pill lets you have sex without condoms with loads of guys. I don't really want to be that guy, to be fair.
>
> (Ian)

Ian invokes the category 'Truvada Whore' (an objectification of PrEP users) in order to illustrate the stigma of PrEP. It is perceived as facilitating condomless sex with multiple partners. The desire to resist the stigmatised category of 'Truvada Whore' may lead some MSM to reject the prospect of PrEP, despite its potential benefits for HIV prevention efforts.

Non-adherence to ART among MSM living with HIV

As indicated in Chapter 2, linkage into HIV care is associated with better disease prognosis as disease progression can be monitored and patients can be given the opportunity to initiate ART as part of their care. Moreover, as the objective of ART is to reduce the patient's viral load to 'undetectable' levels, the risk of onward HIV transmission is greatly reduced. It is important to promote patient retention in care and adherence to ART. However, numerous studies have found that HIV patients can experience difficulties in continuing to engage in care and in adhering to their medication (de Bruin *et al.* 2010; Cambiano *et al.* 2010; Gross *et al.* 2006). In a meta-analysis of 569 studies, it was found that patients with a variety of illnesses manifested a non-adherence rate of approximately 25 per cent (DiMatteo 2004). We might expect this to be more acute for HIV patients in view of the side effects associated with some drug regimens and the mental health issues that frequently accompany HIV infection (Jaspal and Dhairyawan 2018).

In 2014, 15 HIV-positive MSM aged between 18 and 35 were recruited in five cities in the UK for a qualitative interview study of their experiences of living with HIV, including their relationship with ART. In the remainder of this section, data from that study are presented in order to elucidate the potential barriers to ART adherence. The data, which were analysed using qualitative thematic analysis, describe participants' (1) challenges in managing change, (2) engagement in maladaptive behaviours, (3) mental health issues, and (4) social stigma and social support.

Challenges in managing change

Sustaining satisfactory levels of ART adherence in HIV patients can be a challenge for healthcare professionals. The initial task is to understand the potential antecedents to non-adherence. According to the existing body of research in this area, there are multifarious reasons underpinning non-adherence to ART among HIV patients (Gifford *et al.* 2000). ART initiation represents a major lifestyle change for patients who are required to take daily medication for an indefinite period of time. Some individuals may have a multi-pill ART regimen, which can make adherence especially difficult:

> Before I was just taking the one pill but then the clinic asked me if I'd change to three a day because of, you know, cost-cutting. I said yes but since then I've missed the odd dose now and then but before it was just popping a pill a day.
>
> (Mark)

While some patients may seamlessly transition from a single- to a multi-pill regimen without adverse outcomes for adherence, others clearly find this transition more difficult and struggle to maintain optimal adherence. Given the risk of virological failure and of onward HIV transmission, the risk of non-adherence must be considered carefully before any changes to the drug regimen are implemented. On a related note, some patients simply forget to take their medication due, for instance, to other lifestyle-related issues, such as work responsibilities:

> I don't like taking my meds to work but if I'm on the morning night shift I have to do that and it's got to be constantly on my mind but sometimes you know I forget and then at work I'm like 'oh shit'.
>
> (Jason)

There is also some evidence that both actual and perceived side effects of ART can impede satisfactory adherence. As highlighted in Case 3 in Chapter 1, Juan had a negative experience when he initiated ART in his country of origin, which in turn led him to interrupt but also to avoid re-engaging with HIV care and re-initiating ART. The fear of negative side effects after an initial poor experience can hinder re-engagement:

> A week after starting on my meds I had diarrhoea non-stop and life was hell so I just thought to myself that it isn't worth it. That isn't life, is it?
>
> (Peter)

> There's a lot of different kind of info. You read the warning stuff and it makes it sound like the side effects of the drugs will kill you so there's that to worry about too.
>
> (Kyle)

As indicated in these extracts, patients may manifest concerns about side effects which can inhibit optimal drug adherence. There is evidence that concerns about body image can play an important role in considerations about side effects. Although uncommon with newer anti-HIV agents, ART can sometimes cause lipodystrophy and lipoatrophy in patients, which in turn can induce body change distress in affected patients (Martinez *et al.* 2005; Peterson, Martins and Cofrancesco 2008). Moreover, some patients may not have an adequate level of knowledge concerning HIV and the necessity of adhering to ART, namely that non-adherence can result in virological failure and drug resistance. Lack of clarity regarding the necessity of ART and concerns about a variety of side effects can interfere with adherence (Nieuwkerk 2008). Social representations of HIV and ART are key factors in adherence. For instance, there is evidence of a negative correlation between belief in conspiracy beliefs concerning HIV and ART and non-adherence (Bogart *et al.* 2010). Some individuals may hold the belief that pharmaceutical companies exploit people living with HIV in order to improve drug sales, which can sometimes decrease patient trust in both ART and care providers:

> The doctor I was with was insisting on Eviplera and I told him that my friend had side effects with that one but it's like he wanted me to take that and it makes you think like if there's some agreement they sell a set number of drugs or whatever.
>
> (Kyle)

Engagement in maladaptive behaviours

In this volume, several potential risk factors for poor ART adherence have been noted, including childhood sexual abuse, experiences of prejudice and chemsex. It is worth homing in on some known correlates of decreased adherence. There is a high prevalence of substance and alcohol misuse in MSM, which is more acute in those living with HIV (e.g. Dirks *et al.* 2012). This may constitute a form of escapism for some patients who may self-medicate against depression and other mental health issues (Jaspal *et al.* 2018). Substance and alcohol misuse are also associated with poor adherence to ART (Azar *et al.* 2010), which could be attributed to decreased cognitive abilities when in a state of intoxication:

> When you're using chems, it's like another world, you know. I know my meds are important but it's not number one in your head when you're high.
>
> (Peter)

Furthermore, some research suggests that HIV patients who are non-adherent to ART are more likely to engage in sexual risk-taking behaviours, which can lead to poor sexual health outcomes, such as hepatitis C co-infection, and to onward HIV transmission (Remien *et al.* 2007). It is important to explore the factors that have led to non-adherence to ART in the first place. In some cases, this can be attributed to decreased self-esteem, which is generally associated with decreased self-care, such as non-adherence to ART and inconsistent condom use. Moreover, as reported by some MSM living with HIV, low self-esteem due to HIV stigma and rejection from (potential) sexual partners may lead to situations of vulnerability in which the patient avoids HIV status disclosure and engages in sexual risk behaviours (in order to conceal successfully their HIV status):

> There's times when I don't bother using a condom even though you know there's a risk there because I can't be arsed with the aggro of telling them and then the whole debate about how I got it or even them legging it when the secret's out.
>
> (James)

Sexual risk may be augmented through engagement in sex with multiple partners. As discussed in Chapter 2, sexual compulsivity is related to poor wellbeing and sexual health outcomes. In a study of ART adherence, it was found that HIV patients with high levels of sexual compulsivity were more likely to manifest poor ART adherence (Halkitis *et al.* 2014).

Mental health issues

There appears to be a high prevalence of mental health disorders in HIV patients (Vranceanu *et al.* 2008). High levels of psychiatric disorders in HIV patients can complicate engagement with and retention in HIV care and, by extension, uptake of and adherence to ART. Decreased quality of life, depressive symptoms and higher levels of HIV stigma are significant risk factors for non-adherence (Protopopescu *et al.* 2009). Depression is one of the most common comorbidities of HIV infection (Jaspal and Dhairyawan 2018). It is associated with decreased energy, inconsistent memory and pessimism, all of which can plausibly impact on one's ability to adhere to ART. This is clearly observable in interview data from MSM living with HIV and depression:

> For at least a year after my diagnosis I was a bit like a living zombie because I didn't see the point in anything. I hated myself. Getting out of bed was hard enough and then the whole meds thing was a massive burden on me, mentally speaking. I just didn't want to know.
>
> (Rick)

It has been found that post-traumatic stress disorder and depression predict lower adherence to ART and that depression, in particular, is associated with poorer CD4 count and a detectable viral load (Boarts *et al.* 2006). Negative affect is associated with decreased self-efficacy to engage in care and to adherence to ART. High levels of anxiety have been observed in MSM living with HIV, which can constitute a cognitive barrier to adherence (Orlando *et al.* 2002). The high prevalence of anxiety can be attributed to fears of decreased life expectancy, health problems associated with HIV infection and ART use, negative expectations about the consequences of HIV status disclosure, and HIV stigma. In particular, a lack of accurate information about ART and its potential long-term effects appear to be related to high levels of anxiety, which in turn can adversely impact adherence.

Patients who construe their medication as beneficial for their health and wellbeing develop a more positive relationship with it:

> It's since I got involved [in an HIV charity] I'm seeing this from a different angle now. The meds are what keep me healthy and we're lucky to like have them because 20 years ago this would be a death sentence.
>
> (Jamie)

Anxious symptoms can adversely affect self-care behaviours, including engagement with HIV care and ART adherence. These symptoms can be manifested in terms of excessive worrying, preoccupation and the inability to perform everyday tasks. As indicated in earlier chapters of this volume, social stigma is a significant contributor to poor mental health outcomes among MSM living with HIV.

Social stigma and social support

The social stigma that is appended to HIV can greatly interfere with ART adherence. One of the insidious consequences of HIV stigma is indeed the negative health outcomes among HIV patients themselves. HIV stigma affects willingness to disclose one's positive serostatus to others as one may experience fear and anxiety about how others will react to this information. Previous experiences of rejection from sexual partners, for instance, may lead individuals to be fearful of HIV status disclosure:

> It is a horrible feeling. I remember one guy I hooked up with. Completely my type. I was at his place and told him 'I'm positive' and he actually moved back, like sat back in his seat, like to get away from me and he said he can't do it with me and I remember walking out of his place and crying because it was devastating... Since that day I hesitate about HIV topics of discussion.
>
> (Chris)

It is noteworthy that ART may need to be consumed at inopportune times or places, which can increase the fear of involuntary disclosure of one's HIV status. For some individuals, it may be preferable to miss doses of ART in order to avoid damaging important social relationships (Ware, Wyatt and Tugenberg 2007). This can be dilemmatic for the patient who may ultimately decide that the risk of involuntary disclosure is excessively high and that the preferable solution is not to adhere to one's medication (Wolf et al. 2005):

> [My family and I] spent the weekend at the beach and we all slept in one room, all of my cousins, and I knew I had to take my pills out my bag and then go into the bathroom to take them and they're just nosy. I just didn't want to risk doing that and then them like quizzing me on what it is.
>
> (Adrian)

Non-adherence to ART is likely to be prevalent among those patients who are particularly concerned about, and sensitive to, HIV stigma. However, this will vary as some individuals are less exposed to HIV stigma than others and have greater social and psychological resources for buffering the negative psychosocial effects of stigma. One such resource is social support, which is a known predictor of increased retention in HIV care and adherence to ART (Catz et al. 2000; DiIorio et al. 2009). There is considerable support for the hypothesis that social support decreases negative affect, thereby enhancing self-efficacy to adhere to ART (Simoni, Frick and Huang 2006). Positive interpersonal relationships appear to enhance engagement with care and indeed adherence to ART. This can be manifested in terms of being reminded to take one's medication or feeling the need to engage in self-care behaviours due to the presence of significant others in one's life:

> The thing for me was actually my boyfriend at the time. He got me on medication and then supported me through it and told me it's time to take it. Just basically giving me the support I needed.
>
> (Jamie)

> Well, [my partner] is a reason to be happy, yeah? And to go on and just get on with it.
>
> (Max)

Social support, especially in the form of close interpersonal relationships, can be beneficial for deriving a positive identity and, crucially, for optimising ART adherence. Yet, it is easy to see how social stigma can impede social support. Individuals living with HIV may avoid disclosing their serostatus to others for fear of social stigma, as outlined above, thereby limiting their ability to derive social support.

The implications for practitioners

The two case studies focus on the potential obstacles to promoting PrEP use among MSM at risk of HIV and on the possible barriers to adherence to ART among MSM living with HIV (see Cases 1 and 3, respectively, in Chapter 1). PrEP is an effective HIV prevention tool, and ART is highly beneficial for both individual and public health as it improves disease prognosis and prevents onward HIV transmission. As exemplified by the research presented in this chapter, clinical practitioners may face overlapping challenges in dealing with both cases. More specifically, the research points to the potential ways in which identity concerns may affect PrEP uptake and ART adherence in HIV-negative and HIV-positive patients, respectively. The desire to maintain a sense of self-esteem, self-efficacy and continuity in the face of social stigma seems especially important. In the remainder of this chapter, identity concerns and possible coping strategies in patients are discussed.

PrEP may induce feelings of uncertainty and fear among patients, largely due to the concerns around its effectiveness, mistrust of science and medicine, and potential side effects. Similarly, unfavourable previous experiences of ART and negative social representations of ART that have developed over time can produce similar concerns in HIV patients. It is also noteworthy that ART initiation – a life-long commitment – can represent a significant change to one's lifestyle, especially in the case of a multi-pill regimen. Side effects may also be challenging, and the (sometimes unfounded) *fear* of potential side effects may be especially distressing at a psychological level. These issues may collectively compromise the individual's sense of continuity, since PrEP or ART and the factors perceived to be associated with either medication can disrupt the psychological thread between past, present and future. In other words, PrEP and ART can represent for the individual undesirable change and an uncertain future. As indicated in the second case study presented in Chapter 5, HIV diagnosis itself can be severely threatening for continuity and, thus, daily medication to control one's infection can constitute a reminder of this threat. This is a matter of perspective since some patients, conversely, come to view their medication as a means of regaining a sense of control over their health and lives.

MSM at risk of HIV may be reluctant to initiate PrEP due to the perceived repercussions for valued social relationships, as they may anticipate stigma and social judgement from sexual partners and/or family members. This can be attributed *inter alia* to awareness of negative social representations of non-use of condoms, to homophobia and indeed to HIV stigma. Indeed, some people worry that others may confuse PrEP with ART and, thus, think they are living with HIV. HIV-positive MSM too may worry about the effect of taking daily ART for valued social relationships, especially as many are uneasy about disclosing their positive serostatus to friends, family and, in some cases, to sexual partners. In order to avoid involuntary disclosure of their HIV status, individuals may resort to poor adherence to ART. The disruption or rupture of valued social relationships can curtail continuity given the introduction of undesirable change in one's life, that is, the loss of significant others in one's life. Moreover, it can severely compromise the individual's sense of self-esteem, since we derive our sense of self-worth at least in part from what significant others think about us.

One of the most significant barriers to both PrEP uptake and ART adherence is social stigma and indeed this underpins many of the barriers outlined above. In spite of their actual risk of HIV, some individuals may resist the category 'high risk' and, thus, perceive PrEP as unsuitable. Indeed, 'high risk' may be interpreted in terms of specific (stigmatised) activities, such as chemsex, sex with multiple partners and extreme sexual practices. It is easy to see how the stigmatised category of 'high risk', which may be associated with immorality, recklessness and stupidity in the minds of some individuals, might threaten identity processes. The need to think of oneself as 'high risk' constitutes undesirable change and can, thus, challenge one's sense of continuity. Given the associated stigma, self-perception in this way is unlikely to enhance self-esteem. It may also be incompatible with other elements of identity, potentially jeopardising psychological coherence. Given the multiple threats associated with the category 'high risk', the patient may simply reject it from identity and refuse to assimilate and accommodate it. More generally, social stigma and indeed other psychosocial factors outlined earlier in this volume, can contribute to poor mental health among patients, such as depression, anxiety and difficulties in adjusting to HIV-positive status. Indeed, there is a high prevalence of poor wellbeing and risk behaviours, which can inhibit medication uptake and adherence. Conversely, one of the most significant correlates of PrEP uptake and ART adherence is social support.

Principles from social cognitive theory may be especially useful for practitioners working with patients for whom either PrEP or ART would be beneficial. As indicated in this chapter, negative expectations regarding the outcomes of either PrEP or ART constitute a significant barrier to uptake and adherence. These expectations will stem from the social representations held by the individual, which will be influenced both by those representations that are prevalent in his context and, if applicable, by personal experience. Juan's case in Chapter 1 demonstrates the effect of a negative past experience of HIV care on his social representation of ART. As demonstrated in Chapter 4, identity constitutes an important source of social representations in that some social group memberships may provide the individual with exposure to taken-for-granted, uncritically accepted ideas and images regarding PrEP or ART. Some social representations, such as the representation that ART invariably causes lipodystrophy, may be out-dated or erroneous, and should be challenged. It is acknowledged that it can sometimes be difficult to challenge some representations, given their association with valued group memberships. This highlights the importance of approaching this task with sensitivity and understanding. The patient should be exposed to alternative social representations of medication, which can provide more accurate and realistic expectations of the outcomes of uptake and adherence.

Patients may append negative meanings to PrEP or ART as a result of stigmatising social representations surrounding them. Some HIV-negative MSM may, for instance, construe PrEP primarily as facilitating promiscuity or as a 'party drug' (Jaspal and Nerlich 2017), while some HIV-positive MSM may regard ART as a daily reminder of their infection, which, as highlighted earlier in this volume, may constitute a traumatic life event. Practitioners should work with their patients so that they can come to append alternative, more favourable meanings to PrEP or ART. If PrEP is regarded principally as an additional layer of protection against HIV and ART as an effective means of controlling one's HIV infection, the patient is more likely to evaluate the medication favourably, to regard it as enhancing self-efficacy (due to the increased control it affords the individual over their health) and, crucially, to assimilate and accommodate it in identity. It is important to remember that, if medication is understood in a way that threatens identity, it will likely be resisted and the barriers outlined in this chapter will remain. Conversely, understanding it in more favourable terms (for self-esteem, self-efficacy and so on) is likely to lead to uptake and maintenance. In short, the potential *benefits*, rather than disadvantages, for identity should be explored.

Social cognitive theory points to self-efficacy as an important motivational principle in the adoption of new behaviours, such as PrEP uptake and ART adherence. As highlighted above, more positive meanings appended to medication can enhance self-efficacy. However, patients must feel that they are actually capable of performing this new behaviour. Fear of negative side effects, as a result of feedback from others or of negative previous experiences, can decrease feelings of self-efficacy. Indeed, Juan's case, described in Chapter 1, highlighted this very issue. The patient should be informed about the risk of (transient) side effects but also reassured that any potential side effects will be taken seriously and dealt with by practitioners.

It would be beneficial to provide the patient with opportunities to discuss their medication with other patients willing to disclose their experiences of ART. The provision of first-hand accounts regarding one's treatment experience could be reassuring for new patients, thereby bolstering their own beliefs regarding their ability to adhere to their medication. This could be facilitated by the availability of social and peer support networks for new patients. Furthermore, the practitioner may explore with the patient possible solutions to other perceived barriers that may limit their self-efficacy, such as managing medication around one's work schedule or other lifestyle factors. It is possible that the patient engages in other practices (e.g. recreational drug use, chemsex, sex work), which could potentially interfere with medication adherence, but which are nonetheless valued and significant elements of identity. Some patients may derive self-esteem and self-efficacy from their engagement in chemsex and may therefore be reluctant to relinquish this behaviour. It is important that the practitioner acknowledge the psychosocial importance appended to these other practices and that they work with the patient to formulate a viable plan of action, so that self-efficacy in relation to their medication is not curtailed as a result of these other practices.

IPT identifies several other motivational principles of identity that should be acknowledged in the promotion of behaviour change. As indicated in this chapter, the principles of continuity, self-esteem and coherence are especially vulnerable to threat as HIV-negative and HIV-positive patients contemplate the uptake of PrEP and ART, respectively. In particular, the patient may construe the uptake of medication as disrupting the psychological thread between past, present and future and, thus, may require assistance in assimilating and accommodating what may constitute a significant change to their lifestyle. Providing the patient with the opportunity to think and talk about the future could be beneficial for continuity, as it may enable him to work through potential inconsistencies, and to develop 'connections', between present and future, potentially bolstering continuity. On a related note, coherence may be curtailed by the perception that medication is inconsistent with other elements of one's identity. Developing connections and consistency between the actual elements of identity, such as being a MSM *and* taking PrEP, could enhance coherence. As indicated above, novel, more positive meanings appended to PrEP and ART may enable the patient to develop greater feelings of self-esteem in relation to the medication. The practitioner should seek to challenge meanings appended to medication which might put the patient at risk of decreased self-esteem and, thus, inhibit their access to it.

Social cognitive theory emphasises the importance of environmental factors in the promotion of behaviour change. It is hypothesised that feedback from significant others, social norms and social representations will collectively shape individual behaviour. On the one hand, these factors contribute to the individual's expectations regarding the outcomes of a given behaviour and, on the other hand, they inform the individual's evaluation of the behaviour. In thinking about environmental factors in the context of behaviour change in HIV medicine, it is important to acknowledge the reality that patients sometimes perceive a power differential and/or status differential between themselves and clinical practitioners. They may regard their practitioner as lacking understanding of their predicament and, in some cases, as lacking empathy (Daramilas and Jaspal 2017). In short, some patients may wonder how their practitioner could possibly understand what it is like to live with HIV or to be at risk of HIV and, thus, append little credibility to their advice. This can constitute a challenge as credibility is central to the successful dissemination of social representations. Put simply, a credible individual is more likely to be able to influence patients. In some cases, it may be necessary for the practitioner to accept that they will be less successful in disseminating a given social representation than people with whom the patient more closely identifies. Thus, in addition to disseminating accurate and favourable social representations of PrEP and ART for patients who may benefit from them, the practitioner should facilitate the patient's involvement in supportive social groups and networks that can provide exposure to feedback, norms and social representations that are conducive to medication uptake and adherence.

In other words, peer support is crucial. More specifically, this may involve enabling patients who are eligible for PrEP to liaise with other PrEP users to discuss with them their experiences of using this prevention drug. It is important that eligible patients are able to align themselves with, and to seek information from, other users of PrEP and to identify in their communities role models who can shape their thinking around the medication. This may dispel some of the myths and erroneous social representations clearly held by some individuals at risk of HIV who reject the suitability of PrEP. As demonstrated in this chapter, some HIV-negative MSM erroneously attenuate their risk of HIV because they associate the condition exclusively with specific behaviours and practices (e.g. chemsex, sex with multiple partners) in which they personally may not engage. Thus, it could be beneficial to be peer mentored by others with whom patients themselves identify, that is, with people who share their HIV status and with whom they share other identity elements. It is encouraging to observe that the emergence of social support movements around PrEP, which can provide patients with access to positive social representations of this biomedical prevention tool. There are a growing number of awareness-raising events and paraphernalia concerning PrEP that provide accurate information and access to positive social representations about it.

HIV patients benefit greatly from peer support with ART. Contact with other patients who have initiated ART can promote the development of more accurate and favourable social representations about it. Individuals are able to gain first-hand exposure to narratives of viral suppression, undetectability (that is, having an undetectable viral load), and treatment success, while also gaining realistic knowledge concerning the potential challenges faced by peers in initiating and adhering to ART. This can bolster self-efficacy, as well as other principles of identity, in relation to ART adherence, empowering them to take greater control of their health. This may also dispel erroneous social representations regarding ART and replace them with more empowering representations of patients doing well on treatment and living healthy and fulfilling lives while being HIV-positive.

It is important to encourage patients to derive social support from relevant social groups in order for them to access life-saving medication. Self-association with particular social groups is likely to encourage the adoption of more positive social representations. Yet, the practitioner must be aware of the social representations held by the patient. These social representations will in turn inform their awareness and understanding of PrEP or ART, as well as their behaviour in relation to it. The practitioner must be mindful of the vast array of coping strategies that may be deployed by the patient in response to potential threats associated with PrEP or ART.

Denial of one's risk (e.g. of HIV infection, of becoming ill without ART) is a common impulsive response to this threatening information. Patients may compartmentalise their risk behaviours from 'who they really are', thereby decreasing the likelihood of productive action to mitigate the risk. Practitioners must facilitate acknowledgement and awareness of risk and work with patients to decrease their engagement in maladaptive deflection strategies. Patients should be encouraged to engage in anticipatory restructuring (see Chapter 4) so that they can begin to plan and re-structure their identities as PrEP or ART users. It is not an exaggeration to state that the sexual health and wellbeing of MSM depend on their ability to select fruitful and effective coping strategies in response to threat. The practitioner can play a central role in facilitating this.

Overview

In this chapter, there is a focus on the potential barriers to PrEP and ART among HIV-negative and HIV-positive patients, respectively. Drawing upon principles from social cognitive theory and IPT, various suggestions for enhancing clinical practice for patients who may benefit from PrEP or ART are provided. Specific recommendations can be summarised as follows:

- Practitioners should explore ways of incorporating medication into the patient's existing lifestyle with minimal disadvantages for continuity.
- It is advisable to work with patients to facilitate HIV status disclosure and medication use to significant others. This promotes feelings of authenticity and is likely to be associated with the assimilation and accommodation of the medication in identity.
- It is necessary to avoid categorising the patient in ways that may be experienced as threatening for identity. The category 'high risk' is one that appears to be associated with threats to self-esteem and that may be resisted by the patient. Language that is more neutral and less threatening is likely to be more effective.
- It is recommended that the practitioner acknowledge the patient's existing social representations of HIV, PrEP and ART, as they will shape their understanding of new information that is provided and will have an impact for their response and behaviour.
- Practitioners should promote exposure to positive and empowering social representations by informing the patient and by facilitating engagement with social and peer support networks.

Social and peer support is especially important. Social cognitive theory hypothesises that one will observe and repeat the behaviours observed in significant others, that is, in individuals with whom one identifies and who are fellow members of groups that one values. This is referred to as 'modelling' behaviours. Practitioners should enable both HIV-negative and HIV-positive patients to access social support group networks for PrEP and ART, respectively, so that they can potentially acquire behaviours that are more conducive to better health outcomes. While this chapter outlines a series of potential barriers to uptake and adherence, it is clear that peer support will harness both the personal and environmental factors that are likely to promote uptake and adherence to PrEP or ART.

Part IV

CONCLUSION

Chapter 8

Integrating Theory into Practice

The focus of this chapter is on the integration of theoretical tenets from social psychology in practice with MSM. First, the challenging questions concerning the inter-relations between self-identity, wellbeing and sexual health, which are evoked in the cases and cases studies outlined in this volume, and the potential pathways for addressing them are discussed. Second, an integrative framework for understanding self-identity, wellbeing and sexual health is presented and its relevance for practitioners working with MSM is highlighted. Third, a series of overarching recommendations for integrating theory in practice are outlined.

The challenging questions

In this volume, a multitude of social stressors potentially faced by MSM have been outlined and discussed, as well as the possible effects of these stressors for identity processes. The epidemiological and social psychological data presented in this volume demonstrate the insidious consequences of these social stressors for self-identity, wellbeing and sexual health. In Chapter 1, three distinct cases of MSM facing identity threat and an increased risk of poor sexual health outcomes were presented. The distinct cases collectively exemplify the tripartite relationship between self-identity, wellbeing and sexual health. The common thread in all three cases was that MSM face a series of social stressors in their lives, which can lead them to experience a fragile sense of identity and to engage in behaviours which, in one way or another, aim to protect their sense of identity. Some of these behaviours are adaptive while others are maladaptive, but they all aim to provide some protection from threat. The cases gave rise to a series of challenging questions, namely:

- How can HIV risk and HIV prevention methods be effectively communicated to MSM at risk of poor wellbeing or sexual health so that sustained behaviour change can be produced?
- Why do particular 'identity configurations' (e.g. being MSM and of religious faith) cause some MSM significant distress while others experience no distress at all?
- Why might some life events, apparently unrelated to sexuality, increase engagement in sexual risk behaviours?
- How can MSM be supported to disengage from behaviours that put them at increased risk of decreased wellbeing or poor sexual health outcomes?
- Why might behaviours which, to practitioners, may seem obvious ways of improving wellbeing and sexual health not readily be adopted by MSM?

These questions regularly arise in practice with MSM. The aim of this volume was to sketch out possible pathways for addressing these and indeed other challenging questions that emerge not only from the cases presented in Part 1 of this volume but also in Part 2 in which epidemiological data and the possible social stressors faced by MSM were presented, and in Part 3, in which data from empirical studies focusing on distinct aspects of MSM's lives were explored. It is argued that theoretical tools from social psychology can enable practitioners to respond to these questions and to attempt to overcome the barriers that they may create in practice. These tools were applied to the case studies in Part 3 of this volume.

Physicians, nurses, health advisors, psychologists and those involved in the design of public health interventions are just some of the practitioners who may encounter these issues in the course of their practice. While some practitioners may view these questions as relevant to their practice and actively seek to address them, others may regard them as falling outside of their remit and delegate the task of addressing them to colleagues working in 'relevant' specialties. A key conclusion of the discussion that unfolds in this volume is that these issues are pertinent to practice with MSM regardless of one's specialty.

In Chapter 3, a series of possible therapeutic frameworks and behaviour change models were presented. The therapeutic frameworks included psychodynamic approaches, the humanistic person-centred approach and cognitive-behavioural therapy, and the behaviour change models included social cognitive theory, theory of planned behaviour and transtheoretical stages of change model. Collectively, these frameworks and models provide the practitioner with robust hypotheses for beginning to address the aforementioned questions:

- MSM form 'relational configurations', that is, templates for forming relationships that are based on previous experiences and relationships.
- The perceived 'conditions of worth' imposed by significant others can impede self-actualisation among MSM and should therefore be challenged.
- Negative core beliefs – the product of earlier experiences and interactions with others – inform negative automatic thoughts, which can cause distress and undesirable patterns of actions. These too must be challenged.
- Self-efficacy is a key motivator of sustained behaviour change.
- The views, assumptions and expectations of others play a significant role in determining attitudes and behaviour among MSM.

Unsurprisingly therefore, it has been demonstrated in evaluation studies that therapeutic and public health interventions that draw upon empirically tested theories are more likely to be successful than those not underpinned by theories (Fish *et al.* 2016; Jaspal *et al.* 2016). The aim of this volume was not to provide an exhaustive list of frameworks and models, but rather to exemplify their application to the real-world problems evoked in the three cases and in the case studies presented in this volume. It is suggested that relevant tenets of these frameworks and models, or indeed others that may be applicable to a particular case, ought to be drawn upon in all forms of practice. They should inform, rather than necessarily drive, practice. It has also been shown how frameworks and models can be further enriched through the incorporation of theories of identity in order to promote a more nuanced and holistic understanding of self-identity, wellbeing and sexual health among MSM.

In order for practitioners to understand the antecedents to and consequences of poor wellbeing and sexual health outcomes in MSM, they must acknowledge the importance of identity processes in attitudes and behaviours. It is important to draw upon an integrative framework within which self-identity, wellbeing and sexual health can be collectively examined. IPT (described in Chapter 4) constitutes one such framework, which can be fruitfully incorporated in practice – both in therapeutic practice and in the design of public health interventions.

An integrative framework for self-identity, wellbeing and sexual health

The integrative framework for self-identity, wellbeing and sexual health draws upon social representations theory and IPT. It attempts to articulate the multiple 'levels' (intrapsychic, interpersonal and intergroup) at which MSM think and act in relation to their wellbeing and sexual health.

As demonstrated in Figure 5, the individual is confronted with a range of social representations, some of which will be stigmatising towards elements of identity, such as sexual orientation or HIV status. The individual is aware of these social representations even if he does not fully understand or accept them himself (see Breakwell 2001). For instance, it is possible to be aware of the social representation that homosexuality is a sin without necessarily understanding the theological aspects of this argument or the scripture upon which the argument is based. Social representations may become salient in particular temporal or social contexts. They can be rendered salient by other people or become salient because of the existence of social stressors. As highlighted in Chapter 2, social stressors can include homonegativity, childhood sexual abuse experiences, and so on. Specific life events, such as childhood sexual abuse, and negative psychological states and dispositions, such as internalised homophobia, may reinforce or render salient stigmatising social representations concerning one's sexual orientation. Conversely, negative social representations may accentuate the psychological salience of these negative past events and psychological states.

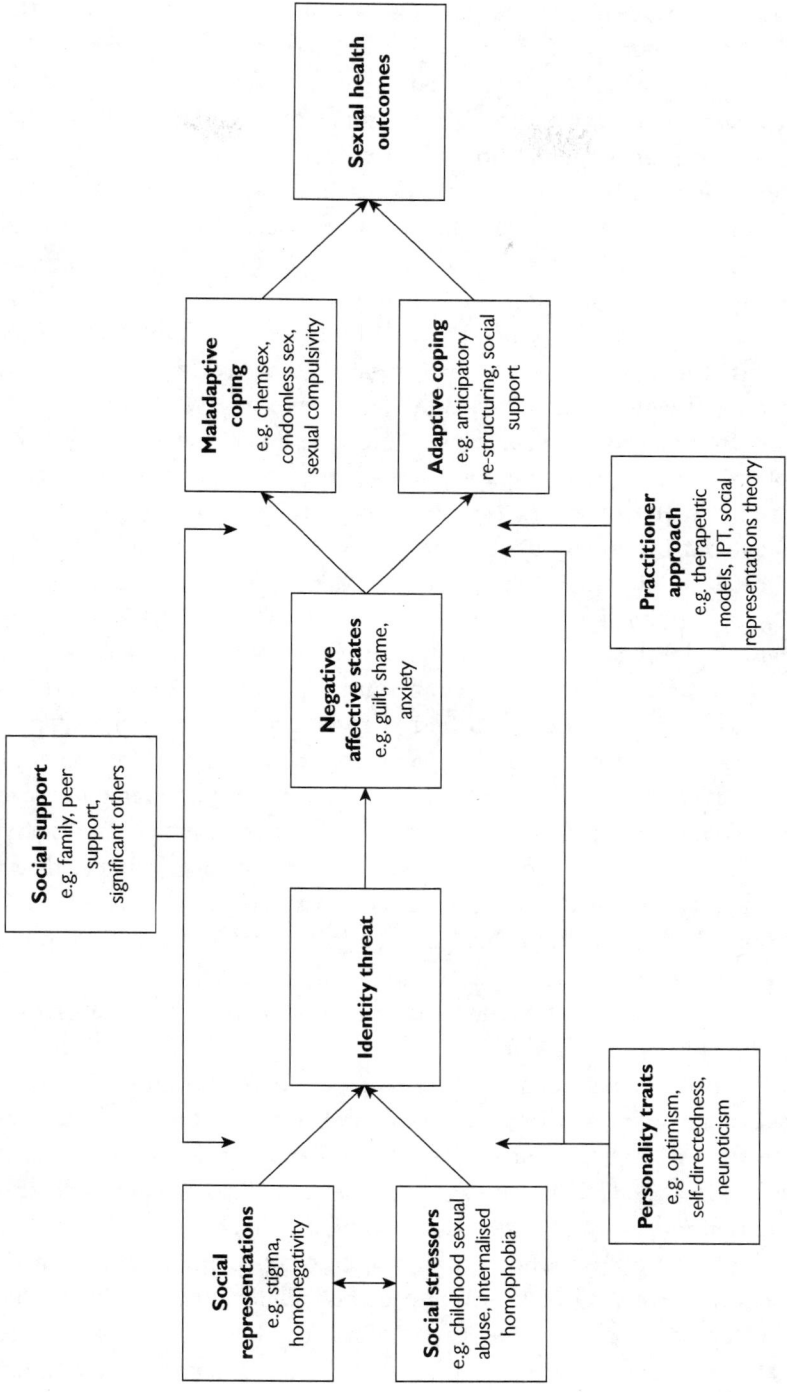

Figure 5: A framework for understanding self-identity, wellbeing and sexual health among MSM

Collectively, social representations and social stressors have the potential to curtail the identity principles of self-esteem, continuity, distinctiveness, self-efficacy, belonging and psychological coherence. However, what the practitioner may assume to be a threatening position, such as the experience of homonegativity or that of childhood sexual abuse, may not be subjectively experienced as such by the individual himself. Indeed, the relationship between social representations and social stressors is likely to be moderated by personality traits and social support mechanisms that the individual has in place. For instance, it is easy to see why a person with high levels of optimism might dismiss the significance of homonegativity expressed by others and therefore be minimally affected by it or, conversely, why an individual with high levels of neuroticism might respond negatively to any potential social representations or social stressor with the capacity to curtail identity processes. Moreover, as highlighted in Chapter 4, it is likely that the individual's value orientations (e.g. valuing tradition) might lead him to favour particular identity principles over others (e.g. continuity if one values tradition) (Bardi *et al.* 2014). The fact that a social representation or stressor challenges a principle that one does not hold in high priority may mean that the threat to identity is minimal or non-existent. Furthermore, the presence of social support mechanisms, such as family members, peer support, a romantic relationship or simply a strong social identity in whatever guise, can greatly mitigate the negative effects of social representations and social stressors for identity processes. Social support can eradicate the threat to identity before it even occurs. For instance, the MSM who has strong friendships with other gay men (see Kocet 2014) may respond with indifference to homonegativity – this is not allowed to threaten belonging because his friendships with other gay men already satisfy the belonging principle of identity.

Identity threat can be aversive for psychological wellbeing and acute forms of threat are associated with the onset of negative affective states. As demonstrated throughout this volume, MSM who face threats to identity may experience the negative affective experiences of guilt, shame, fear and anger (Jaspal 2012). Guilt refers to the sensation that one has done something wrong and that one is therefore deserving of some form of punishment. As a more 'social' emotion, this may be especially relevant to the principles of identity that focus on one's relationship with others, such as belonging.

An example of this is that Muslim MSM may feel guilty about their sexual orientation due to the perception that they are letting down their religious ingroup, their family and their relatives, thereby jeopardising their sense of acceptance and inclusion (i.e. belonging) in these networks. Shame relates principally to self-perception in that one comes to feel that one has fallen short in one's own eyes but also in the eyes of others. Accordingly, shame is likely to constitute an affective reaction to threats to self-focused identity principles, such as self-esteem and continuity. For instance, HIV stigma from others but also the internalised stigma that HIV patients often report may collectively undermine self-esteem and induce shame (Bennett et al. 2016). Anger may arise from curtailed self-efficacy in that the individual feels incompetent and perceives a loss of control. This has been observed in relation to low self-efficacy in relation to computer use (Wilfong 2006) but could potentially be relevant to other manifestations of self-efficacy. Guilt, shame and anger are of course not the only reactions to identity threat. The main point is that these negative affective experiences prompt the individual to make attempts to cope with identity threat, that is, to eradicate the threat or at least to minimise its negative social, psychological and emotional consequences. It is likely that identity threat that does not provoke negative affect will be benign and eventually wane without the need for the individual to deploy any reactive measures against it. In short, the role of emotion and affect is important in determining how individuals will respond to identity threat.

The threatened individual will deploy either adaptive or maladaptive strategies for coping. Some of these strategies have been described in Chapters 2 and 4 of this volume. Adaptive strategies to combat identity threat and associated negative affect include reconstrual and reattribution, such as rethinking the meaning of one's HIV infection, thereby replacing negative meanings with more positive ones; anticipatory restructuring, such as anticipating what a positive HIV test result might mean for one's life and identity and pre-emptively making changes to one's identity to accommodate this impending threat; self-disclosure, that is, disclosing to significant others social stressors, such as homonegativity; multiple group memberships, such as the act of emphasising one's British national identity and attenuating one's Muslim identity when thinking about what it means to be gay; and the derivation of group support in the face of adversity, such as engaging with an HIV support service following one's diagnosis. Conversely, some MSM engage in maladaptive coping strategies. These too function at the three levels of human interdependence: intrapsychic, interpersonal and intergroup. They include those strategies that seek to deflect the threat or its implications, such as denial of one's HIV status or transient depersonalisation in relation to one's drug use in sexualised settings; those that encourage avoidance of, and isolation from, other people, such as withdrawal from one's friendship circles and family networks in order to avoid involuntary disclosure of one's sexual orientation or HIV status, or the attempt to feign heterosexuality to conceal one's homosexuality; and behaviours that have clear pathways towards further psychological adversity and/or poor health outcomes, such as engagement in chemsex, condomless sex with partners of unknown HIV status, or engagement in sexually compulsive behaviours.

The evidence presented in this volume points to at least two factors that will determine whether an adaptive or a maladaptive coping strategy is selected by the MSM who faces identity threat and associated negative affect. First, it is important to acknowledge distinct personality types which will predispose MSM to favour particular coping strategies. For instance, the individual who values conservation (i.e. tradition and conformity) may be resistant to anticipatory restructuring because this strategy would require the anticipation and acceptance of change, thereby contradicting the individual's value priority. It might be expected that the MSM at risk of HIV who values conservation would resist the possibility that he might test positive for HIV and continue to expect a negative test result, despite his awareness of his high-risk behaviour. Given the non-availability of adaptive strategies of this kind, the threatened individual may be more inclined to engage in maladaptive strategies, such as denial of his reality, engagement in chemsex or in sexually compulsive behaviours, which may provide some cathartic relief of the symptoms of identity threat but which do not resolve the threat definitively. It is noteworthy that use of a maladaptive strategy may in turn give rise to additional secondary threats to identity. Conversely, the MSM whose personality profile is characterised by openness to change (i.e. self-directedness and stimulation) might be expected to be more creative in his attempt to cope with threat. He is more likely than the conservation-valuing MSM to seek novel perspectives on his predicament, to meet and liaise with others in a similar situation, and to embrace change in his life. It is easy to see why the adaptive strategies of anticipatory restructuring, reconstrual and reattribution, and group support would be more psychologically available to MSM who value openness to change.

The practitioner may legitimately wonder about the extent to which personality traits are mutable and about the extent to which patients with personality traits that predispose them to maladaptive coping strategies will actually be amenable to adaptive strategies. It has long been argued by personality psychologists that personality traits are stable, immutable and resistant to change (e.g. Tellegen 1988; West and Graziano 1989), which may plausibly lead some practitioners to believe that little can be done to promote a coping strategy that is inconsistent with the patient's particular personality profile. There is now a body of research that demonstrates that personality traits may be more amenable to change than previously thought. For instance, there is evidence that people's value orientations (a form of personality trait) can change, thereby impacting on attitudes and behaviours (Bardi 2009; Bardi and Goodwin 2011). Value change may constitute a component of future interventions for enhancing self-identity, wellbeing and sexual health among MSM. Furthermore, there is growing consensus among social psychologists that personality is not the sole determinant of attitudes and behaviour, which are likely to be the product of other psychosocial variables, including social representations, group memberships and socio-structural factors. The focus of this volume is of course on the role that practitioners can play in promoting positive psychosocial and health outcomes in MSM. Indeed, the role of the practitioner is a key moderator of the relationship between identity threat/negative affective states and coping strategy.

Recommendations for practitioners

In view of the important role of the practitioner in determining how patients will respond to identity threat and associated negative affect, it seems important to sketch out pathways for incorporating theory in practice with MSM. On the basis of the evidence presented in this volume, the following overarching recommendations can be offered to practitioners:

- Social representations surround us. They guide our ability to think and converse about a given topic and shape our attitudes and behaviours in relation to it. Practitioners should be mindful of relevant social representations (e.g. regarding sexual health, HIV) operating in the target population, and their ability to shape the patient's identity, wellbeing and sexual behaviour. They should use, disseminate and encourage social representations cautiously and acknowledge the potential impact of these representations.

- There is often a divergence between awareness of risk and engagement in risk behaviours due to various psychosocial factors, not least identity processes. Thus, while communication of risk is important, communication alone is often insufficient for promoting positive change. It is important to increase awareness of risk representations in patients but also their understanding and acceptance of these representations. Risk communication must be structured and presented in a way that draws upon the social representations (i.e. values, ideas and practices) of the target population so that they are intelligible to patients in that population. Moreover, they should not threaten identity as threatening social representations are unlikely to be accepted by the patient.

- It is essential to acknowledge the multiplicity of the patient's identity, which will consist of personality traits, group memberships, particular life events and so on. Identity is multifaceted and dynamic. On a related note, what may appear to be threatening for the identity of the patient may not actually be experienced as such. In short, the practitioner should seek to learn as much as possible about relevant aspects of the patient's identity and tailor their practice accordingly. Communication with the patient is key. The therapeutic frameworks discussed in this volume are designed to facilitate greater rapport and self-disclosure in consultations with patients.

- A common but ineffective strategy for responding to threatening information, such as an HIV diagnosis or awareness of one's sexual minority identity, is deflection (i.e. denial and rejection). The patient may seek to distance this threatening information from conscious awareness. Yet, all of the available evidence points to the benefits of self-acceptance, and assimilation and accommodation in identity. The practitioner should work with patients to facilitate self-acceptance, assimilation and accommodation so that information, initially deemed to be threatening, can become part of the patient's identity and become a source of positive action. An example of this is to accept one's positive HIV status and to begin to engage with care.

- In response to exposure to new knowledge, such as a positive HIV diagnosis, the individual will begin the process of evaluating this knowledge. This process will be undertaken against the backdrop of social representations operating in one's social context. Practitioners should work with patients to facilitate access to positive and empowering social representations of identity elements, such as their HIV status or sexual minority identity, in order to promote a more positive evaluation of these elements. Deflection is a common response to an identity element that is evaluated negatively. A more positively evaluated identity element is likely to lead to engagement, rather than disengagement and paralysis.

- The therapeutic frameworks described in this volume point to the centrality of self-efficacy in human functioning. IPT identifies several other motivational principles. The practitioner should acknowledge that identity processes are in fact guided by multiple, and sometimes competing, identity principles, such as self-esteem, continuity, belonging and so on. The relationships between the identity principles are complex; some are diametrically opposed, such as distinctiveness and belonging. Individuals attempt to acquire an 'optimal balance' between them. While some events, activities and behaviours may satisfy one principle, they can undermine the operation of another. Furthermore, in behaviour change interventions, the aim is usually to replace one behaviour with another. It is important to be mindful of the potential impact of behaviour change for identity processes, so that the change is sustained.

- It is crucial that the practitioner anticipate the various strategies that may be deployed by the patient in response to threat. The availability of coping strategies is determined by personality traits but also by social and cultural factors, such as the social context in which the patient is embedded. The practitioner should be aware of the risk that the patient may resort to particular maladaptive coping strategies, such as chemsex or condomless sex, and actively intervene to mitigate this risk. Interventions may include discussing these maladaptive coping strategies, exploring the possibility of using others, and referring the patient for additional social support. This naturally requires an understanding both of the patient's individual identity but also of broader social and cultural factors. Crucially, what may be considered an adaptive strategy in the grand scheme of things may actually be experienced by the patient as threatening. In such cases, harm reduction, rather than complete removal of the behaviour, may be preferable.

Concluding thoughts

Self-identity, wellbeing and sexual health are important, but challenging, areas of practice. In this volume, empirical evidence has been presented and discussed to demonstrate the inter-relations between these factors. The relationships between them are by no means unidirectional. A threatened identity due to stigma may induce engagement in behaviours that increase one's risk of poor sexual health, but it is equally possible that poor sexual health, and the associated stigma, will lead to identity threat and decreased wellbeing. This situation is further complicated by the multitude of social stressors, such as stigma and childhood adversity, that characterise the lives of many MSM. It is essential that practitioners acknowledge the inter-relations between these factors, that they understand the identities of patients and, crucially, that they anticipate possible coping responses in a given context. MSM are enveloped in a social and psychological world characterised by potential threats to identity. Coping effectively is key to wellbeing and sexual health. Practitioners in all specialties can help.

References

Ajzen I. (1985) 'From Intentions to Actions: A Theory of Planned Behavior.' In Beckmann, K.J. (ed.), *Action Control*. SSSP Springer Series in Social Psychology. Berlin: Springer.

Anderson, P.L. *et al.* (2012) 'Emtricitabine-tenofovir concentrations and pre-exposure prophylaxis efficacy in men who have sex with men.' *Science Translational Medicine, 4*, 151, 25.

Arreola, S.G., Neilands, T.B. and Diaz, R. (2009) 'Childhood sexual abuse and the sociocultural context of sexual risk among adult and Latino gay and bisexual men.' *American Journal of Public Health, 99,* S2, S432–438.

Arseniou, S., Arvaniti, A. and Samakouri, M. (2014) 'HIV infection and depression.' *Psychiatry and Clinical Neurosciences, 68,* 96–109.

Azar, M.M. *et al.* (2010) 'A systematic review of the impact of alcohol use disorders on HIV treatment outcomes, adherence to antiretroviral therapy and health care utilization.' *Drug and Alcohol Dependence, 112*, 3, 178–93.

Baeten, J.M. *et al.* (2010) 'Antiretroviral prophylaxis for HIV prevention in heterosexual men and women.' *The New England Journal of Medicine, 367*, 399–410.

Bager-Charleson, S. and van Rijn, B. (2013) *Understanding Assessment in Counselling and Psychotherapy*. Poole: Learning Matters.

Bancroft, J. *et al.* (2003) 'Sexual risk-taking in gay men: The relevance of sexual arousability, mood, and sensation seeking.' *Archives of Sexual Behavior, 32*, 555–572.

Bandura, A. (1986) *Social Foundations of Thought and Action: A Social Cognitive Theory*. Englewood Cliffs, NJ: Prentice-Hall.

Bardi, A. (2009) 'The structure of intraindividual value change.' *Journal of Personality and Social Psychology, 97*, 5, 913–29.

Bardi, A. and Goodwin, R. (2011) 'The dual route to value change: Individual processes and cultural moderators.' *Journal of Cross-Cultural Psychology, 42*, 2, 271–87.

Bardi, A. *et al.* (2014) 'Values and Identity Process Theory: Theoretical Integration and Empirical Interactions.' In Jaspal, R. and Breakwell, G. M. (eds) (2014) *Identity Process Theory: Identity, Social Action and Social Change*. Cambridge: Cambridge University Press.

Beck, A.T. (1976) *Cognitive Therapy and the Emotional Disorders*. New York: Meridian.

Bennett, D.S. *et al.* (2016) 'Shame among people living with HIV: A literature review.' *AIDS Care, 28*, 1, 87–91.

Bernier, A. *et al.* (2016) 'HIV seropositivity and sexuality: cessation of sexual relations among men and women living with HIV in five countries.' *AIDS Care, 28*, 1, 26–31.

Bérubé, A. (2003) 'The history of gay bathhouses.' *Journal of Homosexuality, 44*, 3–4, 33–53.

BHIVA (2012) *Standards of Care for People Living with HIV 2013.* London: Mediscript Limited.

Binson, D., Blea, L., Cotton, P., Kant, J. and Woods, W. (2005) 'Building an HIV/STI prevention program in a gay bathhouse: A case study.' *AIDS Education and Prevention,* 17, 4, 386–399.

Blackwell, C. and Birnholtz, J. (2015) 'Seeing and being seen: Co-situation and impression formation using Grindr, a location-aware gay dating app.' *New Media & Society,* 17, 7, 1117–36.

Blais, M., Gervais, J. and Hébert, M. (2014) 'Internalized homophobia as a partial mediator between homophobic bullying and self-esteem among youths of sexual minorities in Quebec (Canada).' *Ciência & Saúde Coletiva,* 19, 3, 727–735.

Boarts, J.M. *et al.* (2006) 'The differential impact of PTSD and depression on HIV disease markers and adherence to HAART in people living with HIV.' *AIDS and Behavior,* 10, 253–261.

Bogart, L.M. *et al.* (2010) 'Conspiracy beliefs about HIV are related to antiretroviral treatment nonadherence among African American men with HIV.' *Journal of Acquired Immune Deficiency Syndrome,* 53, 5, 648–55.

Boroughs, M.S. *et al.* (2015) 'Complexity of childhood sexual abuse: Predictors of current PTSD, mood disorders, substance use, and sexual risk behavior among adult men who have sex with men.' *Archives of Sexual Behavior,* 44, 7, 1891–1902.

Bourne, A. *et al.* (2012) 'Problems with sex among gay and bisexual men with diagnosed HIV in the United Kingdom.' *BMC Public Health,* 12, 916. DOI: 10.1186/1471-2458-12-916.

Bourne, A. *et al.* (2014) *The Chemsex Study: Drug Use in Sexual Settings among Gay & Bisexual Men in Lambeth, Southwark & Lewisham.* London: Sigma Research, London School of Hygiene & Tropical Medicine. Accessed 7 December 2016 at www.sigmaresearch.org.uk/chemsex

Braun, V. and Clark, V. (2006). 'Using thematic analysis in psychology.' *Qualitative Research in Psychology,* 3, 77–101.

Breakwell, G.M. (1983) 'Identities and conflicts.' In Breakwell, G.M. (ed.), *Threatened Identities.* Chichester: Wiley.

Breakwell, G.M. (1986) *Coping with Threatened Identities.* London: Methuen.

Breakwell, G.M. (1988) 'Strategies adopted when identity is threatened.' *Revue Internationale de Psychologie Sociale,* 1, 189–204.

Breakwell, G.M. (1992) 'Processes of self-evaluation: efficacy and estrangement.' In Breakwell, G.M. (ed), *Social Psychology of Identity and the Self Concept.* London: Academic Press/Surrey University Press.

Breakwell, G.M. (2001) 'Social representational constraints upon identity processes.' In Deaux, K. and Philogene, G. (eds), *Representations of the Social: Bridging Theoretical Traditions.* Oxford: Blackwell.

Breakwell, G.M. (2014) 'Identity process theory: Clarifications and elaborations.' In Jaspal, R. and Breakwell, G.M. (eds), *Identity Process Theory: Identity, Social Action and Social Change.* Cambridge: Cambridge University Press.

Breakwell, G.M. and Millward, L.J. (1997) 'Sexual self-concept and sexual risk-taking.' *Journal of Adolescence,* 20, 1, 29–41.

Brooks, R.A. *et al.* (2012) 'Sexual risk behaviors and acceptability of HIV pre-exposure prophylaxis among HIV-negative gay and bisexual men in serodiscordant relationships: A mixed methods study.' *AIDS Patient Care and STDs,* 26, 87–94.

Brown, A.E. et al. (2017) 'Fall in new HIV diagnoses among men who have sex with men (MSM) at selected London sexual health clinics since early 2015: Testing or treatment or pre-exposure prophylaxis (PrEP)?' *Euro Surveillance, 22* (25), 30553.

Brown, D.W. et al. (2009) 'Adverse childhood experiences and the risk of premature mortality.' *American Journal of Preventive Medicine, 37*, 389–396.

Buckley, E.J. et al. (2010) 'The effects of community-based sexual health testing and health promotion on gay men's sexual risk-taking behaviour.' *International Journal of Health Promotion and Education, 48*, 4, 123–128.

Cambiano, V. et al. (2010) 'Long-term trends in adherence to antiretroviral therapy from start of HAART.' *AIDS, 24*, 8, 1153–62.

Carlisle, N. and Rofes, E. (2007) 'School bullying: Do adult survivors perceive long-term effects?' *Traumatology, 13*, 16–26.

Carrico, A.W. and Moskowitz, J.T. (2014) 'Positive affect promotes engagement in care after HIV diagnosis.' *Health Psychology, 33*, 7, 686–689.

Cass, V. (1979) 'Homosexual identity formation: A theoretical model.' *Journal of Homosexuality, 4*, 3, 219–235.

Cassidy, J. and Shaver, P.R. (eds) (1999) *Handbook of Attachment: Theory, Research and Clinical Applications.* New York: The Guilford Press.

Castrighini, C. et al. (2010) 'Depression and self-esteem of patients positive for HIV/AIDS in an inland city of Brazil.' *Retrovirology, 7*, S1, 66.

Catz, S.L. et al. (2000) 'Patterns, correlates, and barriers to medication adherence among persons prescribed new treatments for HIV disease.' *Health Psychology, 19*, 2, 124–133.

Centers for Disease Control and Prevention (2016) *HIV Infection Risk, Prevention, and Testing Behaviors among Men Who Have Sex With Men—National HIV Behavioral Surveillance, 20 U.S. Cities, 2014.* HIV Surveillance Special Report 15. Accessed 22 June 2017 at www.cdc.gov/hiv/library/reports/surveillance/#panel2

Chaney, M.P. and Burns-Wortham, C.M. (2015) 'Examining coming out, loneliness, and self-esteem as predictors of sexual compulsivity in gay and bisexual men.' *Sexual Addiction & Compulsivity: The Journal of Treatment & Prevention, 22*, 1, 71–88.

Chen, W. et al. (2013) 'Engagement with health care providers affects self-efficacy, self-esteem, medication adherence and quality of life in people living with HIV.' *Journal of AIDS & Clinical Research, 4*, 11, 256.

Clark, A. (2012) 'Working with guilt and shame.' *Advances in Psychiatric Treatment, 18*, 137–143.

Cloete, A. et al. (2008) 'Stigma and discrimination experiences of HIV-positive men who have sex with men in Cape Town, South Africa.' *AIDS Care, 20*, 9, 1105–10.

Clucas, C. et al. (2011) 'A systematic review of interventions for anxiety in people with HIV.' *Psychology, Health & Medicine, 16*, 5, 528–547.

Cole, S.W., Kemeny, M.E. and Taylor, S.E. (1997) 'Social identity and physical health: Accelerated HIV progression in rejection-sensitive gay men.' *Journal of Personality and Social Psychology, 72*, 2, 320–335.

Coleman, E. et al. and Men's INTernet Sex (MINTS-II) Team (2010) 'Compulsive sexual behavior and risk for unsafe sex among internet using men who have sex with men.' *Archives of Sexual Behavior, 39*, 5, 1045–1053.

Corrigan, P. and Matthews, A. (2009) 'Stigma and disclosure: Implications for coming out of the closet.' *Journal of Mental Health, 12*, 3, 235–48.

Courtenay-Quirk, C., Wolitski, R.J., Parsons, J.T., Gomez, C.A., and Seropositive Urban Men's Study Team (2006) 'Is HIV/AIDS stigma dividing the gay community? Perceptions of HIV-positive men who have sex with men.' *AIDS Education and Prevention, 18*, 1, 56–67.

Crocker, J. and Major, B. (1989) 'Social stigma and self-esteem: The self-protective properties of stigma.' *Psychological Review, 96*, 608–630.

Crocker, J., Major, B. and Steele, C. (1998) 'Social stigma.' In Gilbert, D., Fiske, S.T. and Lindzey, G. (eds) *The Handbook of Social Psychology.* Boston, MA: McGraw-Hill.

Daramilas, C. and Jaspal, R. (2017) 'Measuring patient satisfaction: Insights from social psychology.' *Social Psychological Review, 19*, 1, 20–35.

de Bruin, M. *et al.* (2010) 'Electronic monitoring-based counseling to enhance adherence among HIV-infected patients: a randomized controlled trial.' *Health Psychology, 29*, 4, 421–8.

Debattista, J. (2015) 'Health promotion within a sex on premises venue: Notes from the field.' *International Journal of STD and AIDS, 26*, 14, 1017–21.

Desai, S. *et al.* (2015) 'An overview of the HIV epidemic among men who have sex with men in the United Kingdom, 1999–2013.' *Euro Surveillance, 20*, 14, pii=21086. Accessed 4 January 2018 at www.eurosurveillance.org/ViewArticle.aspx?ArticleId=21086

Dhar, J., Griffiths, C.A., Cassell, J.A., Sutcliffe, L., Brook, G.M. and Mercer, C.H. (2010) 'How and why do South Asians attend GUM clinics? Evidence from contrasting GUM clinics across England.' *Sexually Transmitted Infections, 86*, 5, 366–70.

DiIorio, C. *et al.* (2009) 'Adherence to antiretroviral medication regimens: A test of a psychosocial model.' *AIDS and Behavior, 13*, 1, 10–22.

DiMatteo, M.R. (2004) 'Variations in patients' adherence to medical recommendations: A quantitative review of 50 years of research.' *Medical Care, 42*, 3, 200–209.

Dirks, H. *et al.* (2012) 'Substance use and sexual risk behaviour among HIV-positive men who have sex with men in specialized out-patient clinics.' *HIV Medicine, 13*, 9, 533–540.

Dodge, R. *et al.* (2012) 'The challenge of defining wellbeing.' *Journal of Wellbeing, 2*, 3, 222–35.

Dolling, D.I. *et al.* on behalf of the PROUD Study Group (2016) 'An analysis of baseline data from the PROUD study: An open-label randomised trial of pre-exposure prophylaxis.' *Trials, 17*, 163.

Dorahy, M.J. and Clearwater, K. (2012) 'Shame and guilt in men exposed to childhood sexual abuse: a qualitative investigation.' *Journal of Child Sexual Abuse, 21*, 2, 155–75.

Dowshen, N., Binns, H.J. and Garofalo, R. (2009) 'Experiences of HIV-related stigma among young men who have sex with men.' *AIDS Patient Care and STDs, 23*, 5, 371–376.

Earnshaw, V.A. and Chaudoir, S.R. (2009) 'From conceptualizing to measuring HIV stigma: A review of HIV stigma mechanism measures.' *AIDS and Behavior, 13*, 1160–77.

Easton, S.D. (2012) 'The disclosure process for men with histories of sexual abuse.' *Clinical Social Work Journal, 12*, 1–12.

Easton, S.D., Saltzman, L.Y. and Willis, D.G. (2014) '"Would you tell under circumstances like that?" Barriers to disclosure of child sexual abuse for me.' *Psychology of Men & Masculinity, 15*, 4, 460–69.

Emlet, C.A. (2007) 'Experiences of stigma in older adults living with HIV/AIDS: A mixed-methods analysis.' *AIDS Patient Care and STDs, 21*, 10, 740–52.

Eysenck, H. (1960) *Behaviour Therapy and the Neuroses.* Oxford: Pergamon Press.

Fekete, E.M., Williams, S.L. and Skinta, M.D. (2017) 'Internalised HIV-stigma, loneliness, depressive symptoms and sleep quality in people living with HIV.' *Psychology & Health.* DOI: 10.1080/08870446.2017.1357816

Fish, J., Papaloukas, P., Jaspal, R. and Williamson, I. (2016) 'Equality in sexual health promotion: a systematic review of effective interventions for black and minority ethnic men who have sex with men.' *BMC Public Health, 16,* 810. DOI: 10.1186/s12889-016-3418-x

Flowers, P. et al. (2011). 'Understanding the impact of HIV diagnosis amongst gay men in Scotland: An interpretative phenomenological analysis.' *Psychology and Health, 26,* 10, 1378–1391.

Flowers, P. et al. (1997) 'Health and romance: Understanding unprotected sex in relationships between gay men.' *British Journal of Health Psychology, 2,* 1, 73–86.

Freud, S. (1949) *An Outline of Psychoanalysis.* New York: W.W. Norton & Co.

Friedman, M.S. et al. (2011) 'A meta-analysis of disparities in childhood sexual abuse, parental physical abuse, and peer victimization among sexual minority and sexual nonminority individuals.' *American Journal of Public Health, 101,* 1481–1494.

Frost, D.M. and Meyer, I.H. (2009) 'Internalized homophobia and relationship quality among lesbians, gay men, and bisexuals.' *Journal of Counseling Psychology, 56,* 1, 97–109.

Genoway, S., Caine, V., Singh, A.E. and Estefan, A. (2016) 'Point-of-care testing in bathhouses: A narrative inquiry into the experience of receiving a positive preliminary HIV test result.' *JANAC: Journal of the Association of Nurses in AIDS Care, 27,* 4, 430–443.

Gifford, A.L. et al. (2000) 'Predictors of self-reported adherence and plasma HIV concentrations in patients on multidrug antiretroviral regimens.' *Journal of Acquired Immune Deficiency Syndromes, 15,* 23, 386–395.

Gini, G. and Pozzoli, T. (2009) 'Association between bullying and psychosomatic problems: A meta-analysis.' *Pediatrics, 123,* 1059–1065.

Goedel, W.C. and Duncan, D.T. (2015). 'Geosocial-networking app usage patterns of gay, bisexual and other men who have sex with men: Survey among users of Grindr, a mobile dating app.' *JMIR Public Health and Surveillance, 1,* 1, e4.

Gold, S.D. et al. (2011) 'Childhood physical abuse, internalized homophobia, and experiential avoidance among lesbians and gay men.' *Psychological Trauma: Theory, Research, Practice, and Policy, 3,* 1, 50–60.

Grant, R.M. and Koester, K.A. (2016) 'What people want from sex and preexposure prophylaxis.' *Current Opinion in HIV and AIDS, 11,* 1, 3–9.

Grant, R.M. et al. (2014) 'Uptake of pre-exposure prophylaxis, sexual practices, and HIV incidence in men and transgender women who have sex with men: A cohort study.' *The Lancet Infectious Diseases, 14,* 820–829.

Grant, R. et al. (2010) 'Preexposure chemoprophylaxis for HIV prevention in men who have sex with men.' *The New England Journal of Medicine, 363,* 2587–99.

Griffiths, C. (2015) 'The sexual health of young British Pakistanis in London: Social and cultural influences.' (Unpublished PhD dissertation). University College London.

Gross, R., Yip, B., Re, V.L III, Wood, E., et al. (2006) 'A simple, dynamic measure of antiretroviral therapy adherence predicts failure to maintain HIV-1 suppression.' *Journal of Infectious Diseases, 194,* 8, 1108–14.

Grov, C. et al. (2014). 'Gay and bisexual men's use of the Internet: research from the 1990s through 2013.' *Journal of Sex Research, 51,* 4, 390–409.

Grov, C., Parsons, J.T. and Bimbi, D.S. (2010) 'Sexual compulsivity and sexual risk in gay and bisexual men.' *Archives of Sexual Behavior, 39,* 4, 940–949.

Grupe, D.W. and Nitschke, J.B. (2013). 'Uncertainty and anticipation in anxiety: An integrated neurobiological and psychological perspective.' Nature Reviews. Neuroscience, 14, 488–501.

Halkitis, P.N. et al. (2005) 'Seroconcordant sexual partnerings of HIV-seropositive men who have sex with men.' AIDS, 19, S1, S77–86.

Halkitis, P.N., Parsons, J.T. and Wilton, L. (2003) 'Barebacking among gay and bisexual men in New York City: Explanations for the emergence of intentional unsafe behaviour.' Archives of Sexual Behaviour, 32, 351–57.

Halkitis, P.N. et al. (2014) 'Psychosocial burdens negatively impact HIV antiretroviral adherence in gay, bisexual, and other MSM ages 50 and older.' AIDS Care, 26, 11, 1426–34.

Henderson, S.W. and Martin, A. (2014) 'Case formulation and integration of information in child and adolescent mental health.' In Rey, J.M. (ed), IACAPAP e-Textbook of Child and Adolescent Mental Health. Geneva: International Association for Child and Adolescent Psychiatry and Allied Professions.

Hennelly, S. (2010) 'Public space, public morality: The media construction of sex in public places.' Liverpool Law Review, 31, 1, 69–91.

Hickson, F. et al. (2004) 'HIV, sexual risk, and ethnicity among men in England who have sex with men.' Sexually Transmitted Infections, 80, 6, 443–50.

Hubach, R.D. et al. (2015) 'Loneliness, HIV-related stigma and condom use among a predominantly rural sample of HIV-positive men who have sex with men (MSM).' AIDS Education and Prevention, 27, 1, 72–83.

Huebner, D.M., Binson, D., Pollack, L., Woods, W. (2012) 'Implementing bathhouse-based voluntary counselling and testing has no adverse effect on bathhouse patronage among men who have sex with men.' International Journal of STD and AIDS, 23, 3, 182–184.

Hunt, B. et al. (2003) 'Career concerns for people living with HIV/AIDS.' Journal of Counseling & Development, 81, 55–60.

INSIGHT START Study Group (2015) 'Initiation of antiretroviral therapy in early asymptomatic HIV infection.' New England Journal of Medicine, 373, 795–807.

Jaspal, R. (2012) 'Coping with religious and cultural homophobia: Emotion and narratives of identity threat from British Muslim gay men.' In Nynäs, P. and Yip, A.K.T. (eds), Religion, Gender and Sexuality in Everyday Life. Farnham: Ashgate.

Jaspal, R. (2014a) 'Arranged marriage, identity and psychological wellbeing among British Asian gay men.' Journal of GLBT Family Studies, 10, 5, 425–448.

Jaspal, R. (2014b) 'Social psychological debates about identity.' In Jaspal, R. and Breakwell, G.M. (eds), Identity Process Theory: Identity, Social Action and Social Change. Cambridge: Cambridge University Press.

Jaspal, R. (2015) 'The experience of relationship dissolution among British Asian gay men: Identity threat and protection.' Sexuality Research & Social Policy, 12, 1, 34–46.

Jaspal, R. (2017a) 'Coping with ethnic prejudice on the gay scene: British South Asian gay men.' Journal of LGBT Youth, 14, 2, 172–190

Jaspal, R. (2017b) 'Gay men's construction and management of identity on Grindr.' Sexuality & Culture, 21, 1, 187–204.

Jaspal, R. (2017c) 'Perceptions of HIV testing in three distinct contexts among MSM.' Poster presented at the Public Health England Annual Conference, University of Warwick, 12–13 September 2017.

Jaspal, R. and Breakwell, G.M. (eds) (2014) Identity Process Theory: Identity, Social Action and Social Change. Cambridge: Cambridge University Press.

Jaspal, R. and Cinnirella, M. (2010) 'Coping with potentially incompatible identities: Accounts of religious, ethnic and sexual identities from British Pakistani men who identify as Muslim and gay.' *British Journal of Social Psychology*, 49, 849–870.

Jaspal, R. and Cinnirella, M. (2012) 'Identity processes, threat and interpersonal relations: Accounts from British Muslim gay men.' *Journal of Homosexuality*, 59, 2, 215–40.

Jaspal, R. and Cinnirella, M. (2014) 'Hyper-affiliation to the religious ingroup among British Pakistani Muslim gay men.' *Journal of Community and Applied Social Psychology*, 24, 4, 265–277.

Jaspal, R. and Daramilas, C. (2016) 'Perceptions of pre-exposure prophylaxis (PrEP) among HIV-negative and HIV-positive men who have sex with men.' *Cogent Medicine. 3:* 1256850 DOI: 10.1080/2331205X.2016.1256850

Jaspal, R. and Dhairyawan, R. (2018) 'Sexual health, HIV & mental health in BAME communities in the UK.' In Raghavan, R. (ed), *Mental Health, Ethnicity and Cultural Diversity: Narratives for Transformative Services.* Bingley: Emerald Publishing Limited.

Jaspal, R. and Nerlich, B. (2017) 'Polarised reporting about HIV Prevention: Social representations of pre-exposure prophylaxis (PrEP) in the UK Press.' *Health: An Interdisciplinary Journal for the Social Study of Health, Illness and Medicine*, 21, 5, 478–497.

Jaspal, R. and Siraj, A. (2011) 'Perceptions of 'coming out' among British Muslim gay men.' *Psychology and Sexuality*, 2, 3, 183–197.

Jaspal, R. and Williamson, I. (2017). 'Identity management strategies among HIV-positive Colombian gay men in London.' *Culture, Health and Sexuality: An International Journal for Research, Intervention and Care*, 19, 2, 1374–88.

Jaspal, R, Jamal, Z., Paccoud, I. and Sekhon, P. (2016) 'P49 Sexual health knowledge, attitudes and practices among BAME MSM: A mixed methods study.' *HIV Medicine*, 17, S1, 30.

Jaspal, R. *et al.* (2018) 'Sexual abuse, psychological adversity and HIV risk among black and minority ethnic men who have sex with men in the UK.' *Mental Health, Religion and Culture*. DOI: 10.1080/13674676.2017.1414170.

Jaspal, R., Nerlich, B. and Cinnirella, M. (2014) 'Human responses to climate change: Social representation, identity and socio-psychological action.' *Environmental Communication: A Journal of Nature and Culture*, 8, 1, 110–130.

Jeffries, W.L. *et al.* (2015) 'HIV stigma experienced by young men who have sex with men (MSM) living with HIV infection.' *AIDS Education and Prevention*, 27, 1, 58–71.

Johnstone, L.C. (2011) *Psychological Formulation: A Radical Perspective.* University Research Repository. Accessed 4 January 2018 at http://eprints.mdx.ac.uk/9721

Kocet, M.M. (2014) 'The role of friendships in the lives of gay men, adolescents and boys.' In Kocet, M.M. (ed), *Counselling Gay Men, Adolescents and Boys: A Strengths-Based Guide for Helping Professionals and Educators.* London: Routledge.

Koester, K. *et al.* (2014) 'Sex on PrEP: Qualitative findings from the iPrEx Open Label Extension (OLE) in the United States.' Paper presented at 20th International AIDS Conference, Melbourne, 20–25 July 2014.

Kugle, S.S.A. (2010) *Homosexuality in Islam: Critical Reflection on Gay, Lesbian and Transgender Muslims.* Oxford: Oneworld.

Lee, M. *et al.* (2015) 'O11 Chemsex and the city: sexualised substance use in gay bisexual and other men who have sex with men.' *Sexually Transmitted Infections*, 91, A4.

Lee, R.S., Kochman, A. and Sikkema, K. (2002) 'Internalized stigma among people living with HIV/AIDS.' *AIDS and Behavior*, 6, 4, 309–319

LeGrand, S. *et al.* (2015) 'A review of recent literature on trauma among individuals living with HIV.' *Current HIV/AIDS Reports*, 12, 4, 397–405.

Linville, P.W. (1985) 'Self-complexity and affective extremity – don't put all of your eggs in one cognitive basket.' *Social Cognition*, 3, 1, 94–120.

Linville, P.W. (1987) 'Self-complexity as a cognitive buffer against stress-related illness and depression.' *Journal of Personality & Social Psychology*, 52, 4, 663–676.

Lloyd, S. and Operario, D. (2012) 'HIV risk among men who have sex with men who have experienced childhood sexual abuse: Systematic review and meta-analysis.' *AIDS Education and Prevention*, 24, 3, 228–41.

Martinez, S.M. *et al.* (2005) 'Body image in patients with HIV/AIDS: Assessment of a new psychometric measure and its medical correlates.' *AIDS Patient Care and STDs*, 19, 3, 150–56.

Maslow, A.H. (1943) 'A theory of human motivation.' *Psychological Review*, 50, 370–96.

McCormack, S. *et al.* (2016). 'Pre-exposure prophylaxis to prevent the acquisition of HIV-1 infection (PROUD): effectiveness results from the pilot phase of a pragmatic open-label randomised trial.' *The Lancet*, 387, 10013, 53–60.

McDavitt, B. and Mutchler, M.G. (2014) '"Dude, you're such a slut!" Barriers and facilitators of sexual communication among young gay men and their best friends.' *Journal of Adolescent Research*, 29, 464–498.

McKeown, E. *et al.* (2012) 'The experiences of ethnic minority MSM using NHS sexual health clinics in Britain.' *Sexually Transmitted Infections*, 88, 8, 595–600.

Meyer, I.H. (1995) 'Minority stress and mental health in gay men.' *Journal of Health and Social Behavior*, 36, 38–56.

Meyer, I.H. (2003) 'Prejudice, social stress, and mental health in lesbian, gay, and bisexual populations: Conceptual issues and research evidence.' *Psychological Bulletin*, 129, 674–697.

Meyer, I.H. and Dean, L. (1998) 'Internalized homophobia, intimacy, and sexual behavior among gay and bisexual men.' In G.M. Herek (ed.), *Stigma and Sexual Orientation: Understanding Prejudice against Lesbians, Gay Men and Bisexuals*. Thousand Oaks, CA: Sage.

Milam, J. (2006) 'Posttraumatic growth and HIV disease progression.' *Journal of Consulting and Clinical Psychology*, 74, 5, 817–827.

Miller, K., Wakefield, J.R.H. and Sani, F. (2017) 'On the reciprocal effects between multiple group identifications and mental health: A longitudinal study of Scottish adolescents.' *British Journal of Clinical Psychology*. DOI: 10.1111/bjc.12143

Millett, G.A. *et al.* (2012) 'Comparisons of disparities and risks of HIV infection in black and other men who have sex with men in Canada, UK, and USA: A meta-analysis.' *The Lancet*, 380, 9839, 341–348.

Mimiaga, M.J. *et al.* (2009) 'Childhood sexual abuse is highly associated with HIV risk-taking behavior and infection among MSM in the EXPLORE Study.' *Journal of Acquired Immune Deficiency Syndromes*, 51, 340–348.

Molina, J-M. *et al.* (2015) 'On-demand preexposure prophylaxis in men at high risk for HIV-1 infection.' *The New England Journal of Medicine*, 373, 2237–46.

Moscovici, S. (1988) 'Notes towards a description of social representations.' *European Journal of Social Psychology*, 18, 211–250.

Moscovici, S. (2000) *Social Representations: Explorations in Social Psychology*. Cambridge: Polity Press.

Moskowitz, J.T. *et al.* (2009) 'What works in coping with HIV? A meta-analysis with implications for coping with serious illness.' *Psychological Bulletin*, 135, 1, 121–141.

Murray, W. and Roscoe, S.O. (eds) (1997) *Islamic Homosexualities: Culture, History and Literature*. New York: New York University Press.

Nicholson, W.D. and Long B.C. (1990) 'Self-esteem, social support, internalized homophobia, and coping strategies of HIV+ gay men.' *Journal of Consulting and Clinical Psychology*, 58, 6, 873–876.

Nieuwkerk P.T. (2008) 'Lower perceived necessity of HAART predicts lower treatment adherence and worse virological response in the ATHENA cohort.' *Journal of Acquired Immune Deficiency Syndromes*, 49, 4, 460–2.

Nishina, A., Juvonen, J. and Witkow, M.R. (2005) 'Sticks and stones may break my bones, but names will make me feel sick: The psychosocial, somatic, and scholastic consequences of peer harassment.' *Journal of Clinical Child and Adolescent Psychology*, 34, 1, 37–48.

O'Leary, A. *et al.* (2003) 'Childhood sexual abuse and sexual transmission risk behavior among HIV-positive men who have sex with men.' *AIDS Care*, 15, 17–26.

Ogaz, D. *et al.* (2016) *HIV Testing in England: 2016 Report*. London: Public Health England.

Orlando, M., Burnam, A., Beckman, R., Morton, S.C. et al.. (2002) 'Re-estimating the prevalence of psychiatric disorders in a nationally representative sample of persons receiving care for HIV: Results from the HIV Cost and Services Utilization Study.' *International Journal of Methods in Psychiatric Research*, 11, 2, 75–82.

Overstreet, N.M. *et al.* (2013) 'Internalized stigma and HIV status disclosure among HIV-positive black men who have sex with men.' *AIDS Care*, 25, 4, 466–71.

Pachankis, J.E. *et al.* (2015) 'A minority stress-emotion regulation model of sexual compulsivity among highly sexually active gay and bisexual men.' *Health Psychology*, 34, 8, 829–40.

Pachankis, J.E. *et al.* (2014) 'The role of maladaptive cognitions in hypersexuality among highly sexually active gay and bisexual men.' *Archives of Sexual Behavior*, 43, 3, 669–83.

Parsons, J.T., Grov, C. and Golub, S.A. (2012) 'Sexual compulsivity, co-occurring psychosocial health problems, and HIV risk among gay and bisexual men: Further evidence of a syndemic.' *American Journal of Public Health*, 102, 1, 156–62.

Perera, S., Bourne, A.H. and Thomas, S. (2017) 'P198 Chemsex and antiretroviral therapy non-adherence in HIV-positive men who have sex with men: a systematic review.' *Sexually Transmitted Infections*, 93, A81.

Perlman, F. and Frankel, J. (2009) 'Relational psychoanalysis: A review.' *Psychoanalytic Social Work*, 16, 105–25.

Persons, E. *et al.* (2010) 'The impact of shame on health-related quality of life among HIV-positive adults with a history of childhood sexual abuse.' *AIDS Patient Care & STDs*, 29, 4, 571–80.

Peterson, S., Martins, C.R. and Cofrancesco, J. (2008) 'Lipodystrophy in the patient with HIV: Social, psychological, and treatment considerations.' *Aesthetic Surgery Journal*, 28, 4, 443–451.

Petrak, J.A. *et al.* (2001) 'Factors associated with self-disclosure of HIV serostatus to significant others.' *British Journal of Health Psychology*, 6, 1, 69–79.

Pollack, L.M., Woods, W.J, Blair, J. and Binson, D. (2014) 'Presence of an HIV testing program lowers the prevalence of unprotected insertive anal intercourse inside a gay bathhouse among HIV-negative and HIV-unknown patrons.' *Journal of HIV/AIDS and Social Services*, 13, 3, 306–323.

Pollard, A., Nadarzynski, T. and Llewellyn, C. (2017) 'O13 'I was struggling to feel intimate, the drugs just helped'. Chemsex and HIV-risk among men who have sex with men (MSM) in the uk: Syndemics of stigma, minority-stress, maladaptive coping and risk environments.' *Sexually Transmitted Infections*, 93, A5.

Prestage, G. et al. (2012) 'Is optimism enough? Gay men's beliefs about HIV and their perspectives on risk and pleasure.' *Sexually Transmitted Diseases*, 39, 167–172.

Protopopescu, C. et al. (2009) 'Factors associated with non-adherence to long-term highly active antiretroviral therapy: A 10 year follow-up analysis with correction for the bias induced by missing data.' *Journal of Antimicrobial Chemotherapy*, 64, 3, 599–606.

Public Health England (2015a) *HIV in the United Kingdom: 2014 Report*. Accessed 4 January 2018 at https://www.gov.uk/government/uploads/system/uploads/attachment_data/file/477702/HIV_in_the_UK_2015_report.pdf

Public Health England (2015b) National HIV surveillance data tables. Accessed 1 September 2017 at https://www.gov.uk/government/statistics/hiv-data-tables

Public Health England. (2017a) National HIV surveillance data tables. Accessed 15 September 2017 at https://www.gov.uk/government/statistics/hiv-annual-data-tables

Public Health England (2017b) *Sexually Transmitted Infections and Chlamydia Screening in England 2016*. Health Protection Report, 11, 20, 9 June 2017. Accessed 17 August 2017 at https://www.gov.uk/government/uploads/system/uploads/attachment_data/file/617025/Health_Protection_Report_STIs_NCSP_2017.pdf

Pufall, E. et al. (2016) 'Chemsex and high-risk sexual behaviours in HIV-positive men who have sex with men.' Poster presented at the Conference on Retroviruses and Opportunistic Infections Conference, Hynes Convention Center, Boston, Massachusetts, 4–7 March 2018. Accessed 13 August 2017 at www.croiconference.org/sessions/%C2%93chemsex%C2%94-and-high-risk-sexual-behaviours-hiv-positive-men-who-have-sex-men

Punyacharoensin, N. et al. (2016) 'Effect of pre-exposure prophylaxis and combination HIV prevention for men who have sex with men in the UK: A mathematical modelling study.' *Lancet HIV*, 3, e94–104.

Remien, R.H. et al. (2007) 'Medication adherence and sexual risk behavior among HIV-infected adults: Implications for transmission of resistant virus.' *AIDS and Behavior*, 11, 5, 663–75.

Rivers, I. (2000) 'Social exclusion, absenteeism and sexual minority youth.' *Support for Learning*, 15, 1, 13–18.

Rivers, I. (2001) 'Retrospective reports of school bullying: Stability of recall and its implications for research.' *British Journal of Developmental Psychology*, 19, 129–142.

Rivers, I. (2004) 'Recollection of bullying at school and their long-term implications for lesbians, gay men, and bisexuals.' *Crisis*, 25, 4, 169–174.

Rodger, A.J. et al. for the PARTNER study group (2016) 'Sexual activity without condoms and risk of HIV transmission in serodifferent couples when the HIV-positive partner is using suppressive antiretroviral therapy.' *JAMA*, 316, 2, 1–11.

Rogers, C.R. (1957) 'The necessity and sufficient conditions of therapeutic personality change.' *Journal of Consulting Psychology*, 21, 95–103.

Rohleder, P., McDermott, D.T. and Cook, R. (2017) 'Experience of sexual self-esteem among men living with HIV.' *Journal of Health Psychology*, 22, 2, 176–85.

Ross, M. and Rosser, B. (1996) 'Measurement and correlates of internalised homophobia: A factor analytic study.' *Journal of Clinical Psychology*, 52, 15–21.

Rosser, B.R.S. et al. and the Positive Connections Team (2008) 'Predictors of HIV disclosure to secondary partners and sexual risk behavior among a high-risk sample of HIV-positive MSM: Results from six epicenters in the US.' *AIDS Care*, 20, 8, 925–930.

Rowen, C.J. and Malcolm, J.P. (2002) 'Correlates of internalized homophobia and homosexual identity formation in a sample of gay men.' *Journal of Homosexuality*, 43, 2, 77–92.

Sachperoglou, E. and Bor, R. (2001) 'Disclosure of HIV seropositivity and social support: General patterns in Greece.' *European Journal of Psychotherapy, Counselling & Health*, 4, 1, 103–122.

Segerstrom, S.C. *et al.* (1996) 'Causal attributions predict rate of immune decline in HIV-seropositive gay men.' *Health Psychology*, 15, 6, 485–493.

Sewell, J. *et al.* (2017) 'Poly drug use, chemsex drug use, and associations with sexual risk behaviour in HIV-negative men who have sex with men attending sexual health clinics.' *International Journal of Drug Policy*, 43, 33–43.

Shernoff, M. (2006) *Without Condoms: Unprotected Sex, Gay Men and Barebacking*. New York: Routledge.

Shernoff, M. and Palacios-Jiminez, L. (1988) 'AIDS: Prevention is the only vaccine available.' *Journal of Social Work & Human Sexuality*, 6, 2, 135–50.

Sherr, L. (1990) 'Fear arousal and AIDS: Do shock tactics work?' *AIDS*, 4, 4, 361–4.

Sherr, L. *et al.* (2011a) 'HIV and Depression: a systematic review of interventions.' *Psychology, Health & Medicine*, 16, 5, 493–527.

Sherr, L. *et al.* (2011b) 'HIV infection associated post-traumatic stress disorder and post-traumatic growth: A systematic review.' *Psychology, Health & Medicine*, 16, 5, 612–629.

Sikkema, K.J. *et al.* (2011) 'The development and feasibility of a brief risk reduction intervention for newly HIV-diagnosed men who have sex with men.' *Journal of Community Psychology*, 39, 6, 717–732.

Simoni, J.M., Frick, P.A. and Huang, B. (2006) 'A longitudinal evaluation of a social support model of medication adherence among HIV-positive men and women on antiretroviral therapy.' *Health Psychology*, 25, 1, 74–81.

Skinner, B.F. (1938) *Behavior of Organisms*. New York: Appleton-Century-Crofts.

Smit, P.J. *et al.* (2012) 'HIV-related stigma within communities of gay men: A literature review.' *AIDS Care*, 24, 4, 405–412.

Smith, R.L. *et al.* (2012) 'Premature and accelerated aging: HIV or HAART?' *Frontiers in Genetics*, 3, 328.

Soni, S., Bond, K., Fox, E., Grieve, A.P., and Sethi, G. (2008) 'Black and minority ethnic men who have sex with men: A London genitourinary medicine clinic experience.' *International Journal of STD and AIDS*, 19, 9, 617–619.

Spieldenner, A. (2016) 'PrEP whores and HIV prevention: The queer communication of HIV pre-exposure prophylaxis (PrEP).' *Journal of Homosexuality*, 63, 1685–97.

Stonewall (2017) *School Report: The Experiences of Lesbian, Gay, Bi and Trans Young People in Britain's Schools in 2017*. London: Stonewall.

Tajfel, H. (1981) *Human Groups and Social Categories*. Cambridge: Cambridge University Press.

Tellegen, A. (1988) 'The analysis of consistency in personality assessment.' *Journal of Personality*, 56, 621–63.

Timotijevic, L. and Breakwell, G.M. (2000) 'Migration and threats to identity.' *Journal of Community and Social Psychology*, 10, 355–372.

Toppenberg, H. *et al.* (2015) 'HIV-related stigma in social interactions: Approach and avoidance behaviour in a virtual environment.' *European Journal of Social Psychology*, 45, 169–179.

UNAIDS (2017) *Ending AIDS: Progress towards the 90-90-90 Targets*. Joint United Nations Programme on HIV/AIDS (UNAIDS). Accessed 13 September 2017 at www.unaids.org/sites/default/files/media_asset/Global_AIDS_update_2017_en.pdf

Vignoles, V.L., Chryssochoou, X. and Breakwell, G.M. (2000) 'The distinctiveness principle: Motivation, identity and the bounds of cultural relativity.' *Personality and Social Psychology Review*, 4, 4, 337–354.

Vranceanu, S. et al. (2008) 'The relationship of post-traumatic stress disorder and depression to antiretroviral medication adherence in persons with HIV.' *AIDS Patient Care and STDs*, 22, 4, 313–21.

Wachtel, P.L. (2008) *Relational Theory and the Practice of Psychotherapy*. New York: The Guilford Press.

Wakimoto, R. (2008) 'Influence of level and instability of self-esteem on help-seeking orientation and help-seeking.' *The Japanese Journal of Experimental Social Psychology*, 47, 2, 160–168.

Wang, X. et al. (2017) 'InterPrEP: internet-based pre-exposure prophylaxis with generic tenofovir disoproxil fumarate/emtricitabine in London – analysis of pharmacokinetics, safety and outcomes.' *HIV Medicine*, 19, 1, 1–6.

Ware, N.C., Wyatt, M.A. and Tugenberg T. (2006) 'Social relationships, stigma, and adherence to antiretroviral therapy for HIV/AIDS.' *AIDS*, 18, 8, 904–910.

Weatherburn, P. et al. (2016) 'Motivations and values associated with combining sex and illicit drugs ('chemsex') among gay men in South London: Findings from a qualitative study.' *Sexually Transmitted Infections*. DOI: 10.1136/sextrans-2016-052695

Weaver, K.E. et al. (2005) 'A stress and coping model of medication adherence and viral load in HIV-positive men and women on highly active antiretroviral therapy (HAART).' *Health Psychology*, 24, 4, 385–392.

Welles, S.L. et al. (2009) 'History of childhood sexual abuse and unsafe anal intercourse in a 6–city study of HIV-positive men who have sex with men.' *AIDS Education and Prevention*, 24, 3, 228–41.

West, S.G. and Graziano, W.G. (1989) 'Long-term stability and change in personality: An introduction.' *Journal of Personality*, 57, 175–93.

Wilfong, J.D. (2006) 'Computer anxiety and anger: The impact of computer use, computer experience, and self-efficacy beliefs.' *Computers in Human Behavior*, 22, 6, 1001–11.

Wills, T.A. (1981) 'Downward comparison principles in social psychology.' *Psychological Bulletin*, 90, 245–271.

Wolf, M.S. et al. (2005) 'Relation between literacy and HIV treatment knowledge among patients on HAART regimens.' *AIDS Care*, 17, 863–873.

WHO (2006) *Defining Sexual Health. Report of a Technical Consultation on Sexual Health, 28–31 January 2002, Geneva*. Geneva: WHO Press. Accessed 17 May 2017 at www.who.int/reproductivehealth/publications/sexual_health/defining_sexual_health.pdf

Yip, A. and Khalid, A. (2010) 'Looking for Allah: Spiritual Quests of Queer Muslims.' In Browne, K., Munt, S.R. and Yip, A.K.T. (eds), *Queer Spiritual Spaces: Sexuality and Sacred Places*. Farnham: Ashgate.

Zervoulis, K., Lyons, E. and Dinos, S. (2015) 'Stigma and self-esteem across societies: Avoiding blanket psychological responses to gay men experiencing homophobia.' *BJPsych Bulletin*, 39, 167–173.

Subject Index

acceptance, by practitioner 73
AIDS, progression of 36
anchoring process 86–7
antibiotic resistance 36
anticipatory restructuring (coping strategy) 103
ART treatment
  adherence intervention 80–1
  early treatment with 36–7
  non-adherence 168–75
  treatment as prevention (TasP) 38
assessment, counselling 62–3
assimilation-accommodation 91
attachment theory 66

behaviour change models
  case study: Ahmed (British Muslim gay man) 75–6
  case study: Juan (gay man living with HIV) 80–1
  case study: Mark (HIV-negative gay man) 77–9
  overview of 73–4
  social cognitive theory 74–6
  theory of planned behaviour 76–9
  transtheoretical stages of change model 79–81

behavioural intentions 77
belonging (in IPT) 94
BME MSM Project 150–4
bullying, homonegative 42–4

case formulation 63
case study: Ahmed (British Muslim gay man)
  humanistic person-centred approach 68–9
  overview 21–3
  social cognitive theory 75–6
case study: Juan (gay man living with HIV)
  CBT 72
  denial as coping strategy 97–8
  overview 23–4
  relational psychoanalysis 66–7
  transtheoretical stages of change model 80–1
case study: Mark (HIV-negative gay man)
  overview 20–1
  theory of planned behaviour 77–9
  CBT 70–3
change *see* behaviour change models
chemsex 55–8
childhood sexual abuse 40–2
chlamydia 36
coherence 94, 120
'coming out' *see* disclosure

compartmentalisation (coping strategy) 101–2
compliance (coping strategy) 107–8
compulsivity, sexual 54–5
conditions of worth 68, 69
condomless sex
  negative attitudes towards condoms 50
  personality traits and 51–2
  reasons for 50–2
  serosorting and 50
congruence 68
continuity (in IPT) 93
coping strategies
  anticipatory restructuring 103
  compartmentalisation 101–2
  compliance 107–8
  definition of 29
  denial 97–8
  group action 112–3
  group support 111–2
  HIV-related stressors 130–1
  isolation 104–5
  multiple group membership 110
  negativism 105–6
  passing 106–7
  re-attribution 101
  re-construal 100–1
  real/unreal selves 99–100

coping strategies *cont.*
  salience of principles 102–3
  transient depersonalisation 98–9
core beliefs 70–1
counselling psychology
  acceptance from practitioner 73
  assessment 62–3
  case formulation 63
  case study: Ahmed (British Muslim gay man) 68–9
  case study: Juan (gay man living with HIV) 66–7, 72
  CBT 70–3
  facilitative approach of 61–2
  humanistic person-centred approach 67–70
  psychodynamic approaches 64–7
  relational psychoanalysis 65–7

decisional balance 80
defence mechanisms 64–5
denial (coping strategy) 97–8
depression 127, 153, 172
disclosure
  barriers to 42, 44–5, 48, 88
  Muslim MSM 121
  reciprocal 109
  to significant other 108–9
discourses of healthcare professionals 88
distinctiveness (in IPT) 93
drugs (chemsex) 55–8

empathy 68
epidemiology, of STIs and HIV 11, 35–9
evaluation process (in IPT) 91–2
'expert' voices 88

gay saunas
  HIV testing in 140
  SOAP (Sauna Online Assessment Project) 141–8
  as venue for health interventions 140
geospatial gay social networking 52–4
gonorrhoea 11, 36
Grindr 52–4
group action (coping strategy) 112–3
group support (coping strategy) 111–2

health promotion
  psychosocial factors and 30–1
  see also sexual health interventions
hepatitis A 11
hierarchy of needs 67
HIV
  and mental health 127–8
  positive coping 130–1
  PrEP 38–9, 161–8
  prevalence in UK 37
  progression of 36
  stigma 47–9, 124–7, 129–30
  see also ART treatment; testing for HIV
homonegativity, across the life course 42–5
humanistic person-centred approach 67–70

identity, definitions of 27–8
identity process theory
  anticipatory restructuring (coping strategy) 103
  assimilation-accommodation 91
  belonging 94
  coherence 94
  compartmentalisation (coping strategy) 101–2
  compliance (coping strategy) 107–8
  continuity 93
  denial (coping strategy) 97–8
  distinctiveness 93
  enhancement and threat of identity 94–6
  evaluation 91–2
  group action (coping strategy) 112–3
  group support (coping strategy) 111–2
  identity principles 92–4, 95, 102–3
  interpersonal coping strategies 104–9
  intrapsychic coping strategies 97–104
  isolation (coping strategy) 104–5
  multiple group membership (coping strategy) 110
  negativism (coping strategy) 105–6
  overview of 8, 89–90
  passing (coping strategy) 106–7
  re-attribution (coping strategy) 101
  re-construal (coping strategy) 100–1
  real/unreal selves (coping strategy) 99–100
  salience of principles (coping strategy) 102–3
  self-efficacy 92–3
  self-esteem 92
  transient depersonalisation (coping strategy) 98–9
incongruence 68
integrative framework approach 188–9
internalised HIV stigma 49
internalised homophobia 45–7, 120–1
intrapsychic conflicts 65
Islam *see* Muslim MSM
isolation (coping strategy) 104–5

Subject Index

location-aware applications 52–4

mental health 127–8, 172–3
metaphor use 87
MSM (men who have sex with men), definition of 28
multiple group membership (coping strategy) 110
Muslim MSM
  attitude towards homosexuality in Islam 118–20
  coming out 121
  family honour issues 122
  group membership management 123–4
  'hyper-affiliation' to Islam 122–3
  internalised homophobia 120–1
  threats to social relationships 122–3
  see also case study: Ahmed (British Muslim gay man)

needs, hierarchy of 67
negative automatic thoughts 70–3
negativism (coping strategy) 105–6
norms, and social context 78

objectification process 87

paranoia 44–5
passing (coping strategy) 106–7
person-centred approach 67–70
personality traits 51–2, 192–3
positive self-conception 128–30
post-traumatic stress disorder 126, 172
practitioners
  acceptance from 73

definition of 29
discourses of 88
implications from ART adherence studies 175–81
implications from PrEP use studies 175–81
implications from sexual health interventions 154–9
implications from theory and research 131–6, 193–6
integrative framework approach for 188–9
variation in approach to wellbeing 29–30
PrEP treatment 38–9, 161–8
psychodynamic approaches 64–7

racism 123
re-attribution (coping strategy) 101
re-construal (coping strategy) 100–1
real/unreal selves (coping strategy) 99–100
reinforcements, social 75
relational psychoanalysis 65–7
risk assessment 62–3

salience of principles (coping strategy) 102–3
self-actualisation 67, 68, 69
self-concept 68, 99–100, 128–30
self-efficacy 75, 80, 92–3, 125
self-esteem 92, 128
self-identity
  definition of 28
  self-identification differences 27
Selfie intervention 150–4
selves, real/unreal 99–100
serosorting 50
sexual compulsivity 54–5

sexual health, definition of 28
sexual health interventions
  BME MSM Project 150–4
  gay saunas 140–8
  implications for practitioners 154–9
shame 42, 64
Shigella 11, 36
sinister attribution error 44–5
'slut shaming' 49
SOAP (Sauna Online Assessment Project) 141–8
social cognitive theory 74–6
social learning theory 74
social networking, geospatial 52–4
social psychology
  and benefits for practice 29–32
  overview of 26–7
  see also behaviour change models
social reinforcements 75
social representations 87–9
social representations theory 86–9
  see also identity process theory
social support 173–5
stigma
  and ART adherence 173–4
  HIV 47–9, 124–7, 129–30
  PrEP 166–8
STIs
  chlamydia 36
  epidemiology of 11, 35–6
  gonorrhoea 11, 36
  hepatitis A 11
  Shigella 11, 36
  syphilis 11, 36
  see also HIV
substance use (chemsex) 55–8
syphilis 11, 36

TasP (treatment as prevention) *see* ART treatment
testing for HIV
  in gay saunas 140
  rates of 37–8
  stigma around 37–8
theory of planned behaviour 76–9

transient depersonalisation (coping strategy) 98–9
transtheoretical stages of change model 79–81
treatment as prevention (TasP) *see* ART treatment
Truvada (for PrEP) 38–9, 161–8

'Truvada Whore' 165, 167–8

'U=U' message 11
unconditional positive regard 68

wellbeing, definition of 28–9

Author Index

Ajzen, I. 76
Anderson, P.L. 39
Arreola, S.G. 41
Arseniou, S. 124, 127
Arvaniti, A. 127
Azar, M.M. 171

Baeten, J.M. 39
Bager-Charleson, S. 62
Bancroft, J. 54
Bandura, A. 74
Bardi, A. 95, 190
Beck, A.T. 70
Bennett, D.S. 126, 191
Bernier, A. 126
Bérubé, A. 52
BHIVA 38
Bimbi, D.S. 54
Binns, H.J. 105
Binson, D. 140
Birnholtz, J. 53
Blackwell, C. 53
Blais, M. 45
Boarts, J.M. 172
Bogart, L.M. 170
Bor, R. 126, 129
Boroughs, M.S. 40
Bourne, A. 56, 57, 126, 167
Braun, V. 118
Breakwell, G.M. 26, 89, 91, 92, 96, 188
Brooks, R.A. 164
Brown, A.E. 38
Brown, D.W. 40
Buckley, E.J. 140
Burns-Wortham, C.M. 54

Cambiano, V. 168
Carlisle, N. 44
Carrico, A.W. 127
Cass, V. 121

Cassidy, J. 66
Castrighini, C. 128
Catz, S.L. 174
Centers for Disease Control and Prevention 50
Chaney, M.P. 54
Chaudoir, S.R. 49
Chen, W. 125
Chryssochoou, X. 89
Cinnirella, M. 31, 89, 94, 102, 110, 117, 118, 122
Clark, A. 63, 69
Clark, V. 118
Clearwater, K. 42
Cloete, A. 49
Clucas, C. 131
Cofrancesco, J. 170
Cole, S.W. 129
Coleman, E. 54
Cook, R. 92
Corrigan, P. 121
Courtenay-Quirk, C. 125
Crocker, J. 47, 129

Daramilas, C. 30, 145, 162, 179
de Bruin, M. 168
Dean, L. 45
Debattista, J. 140
Desai, S. 149
Dhairyawan, R. 47, 127, 168, 172
Dhar, J. 149
Diaz, R. 41
DiIorio, C. 174
DiMatteo, M.R. 168
Dinos, S. 130
Dirks, H. 171
Dodge, R. 29
Dolling, D.I. 56

Dorahy, M.J. 42
Dowshen, N. 105
Duncan, D.T. 52, 53

Earnshaw, V.A. 49
Easton, S.D. 42
Emlet, C.A. 49
Eysenck, H. 70

Fekete, E.M. 49
Fish, J. 31, 132, 187
Flowers, P. 52, 126, 128
Frankel, J. 66
Freud, S. 64
Frick, P.A. 174
Friedman, M.S. 40
Frost, D.M. 47

Garofalo, R. 105
Genoway, S. 140
Gervais, J. 45
Gifford, A.L. 169
Gini, G. 44
Goedel, W.C. 52, 53
Gold, S.D. 46
Golub, S.A. 54
Goodwin, R. 193
Grant, R.M. 39, 163, 164
Graziano, W.G. 193
Griffiths, C. 149
Gross, R. 168
Grov, C. 53, 54
Grupe, D.W. 162

Halkitis, P.N. 51, 52, 172
Hébert, M. 45
Henderson, S.W. 63
Hennelly, S. 53
Hickson, F. 149
Huang, B. 174
Hubach, R.D. 49
Huebner, D.M. 140
Hunt, B. 126

INSIGHT START Study Group 38

Jaspal, R. 26, 30, 31, 37, 41, 44, 45, 47, 51, 54, 87, 88, 89, 92, 94, 95, 102, 104, 110, 117, 118, 121, 122, 124, 127, 140, 145, 149, 152, 155, 162, 163, 168, 171, 172, 177, 179, 187, 190
Jeffries, W.L. 49
Johnstone, L.C. 63

Khalid, A. 117
Kocet, M.M. 133, 190
Kochman, A. 128
Koester, K. 163, 164
Kugle, S.S.A. 118

Lee, M. 56, 57
Lee, R.S. 128
LeGrand, S. 126
Linville, P.W. 89
Llewellyn, C. 57
Lloyd, S. 40, 41
Long B.C. 130
Lyons, E. 130

McCormack, S. 39
McDavitt, B. 49, 165
McDermott, D.T. 92
McKeown, E. 149
Major, B. 47, 129
Malcolm, J.P. 46
Martin, A. 63
Martinez, S.M. 170
Martins, C.R. 170
Maslow, A.H. 67
Matthews, A. 121
Meyer, I.H. 43, 45, 47
Milam, J. 130
Miller, K. 104
Millett, G.A. 149
Millward, L.J. 95
Mimiaga, M.J. 41
Molina, J-M. 39
Moscovici, S. 86
Moskowitz, J.T. 127, 131
Murray, W. 91
Mutchler, M.G. 49, 165

Nadarzynski, T. 57
Neilands, T.B. 41
Nerlich, B. 31, 87, 163, 177
Nicholson, W.D. 130
Nieuwkerk P.T. 170
Nishina, A. 44
Nitschke, J.B. 162

Ogaz, D. 37
O'Leary, A. 41, 42
Operario, D. 40, 41
Orlando, M. 172
Overstreet, N.M. 48

Pachankis, J.E. 55
Palacios-Jiminez, L. 51
Parsons, J.T. 54
Perera, S. 57
Perlman, F. 66
Persons, E. 42, 49
Peterson, S. 170
Petrak, J.A. 129
Pollack, L.M. 140
Pollard, A. 57
Pozzoli, T. 44
Prestage, G. 162
Protopopescu, C. 172
Public Health England 35, 36, 37, 141, 148
Pufall, E. 56, 57
Punyacharoensin, N. 39

Remien, R.H. 171
Rivers, I. 44
Rodger, A.J. 38
Rofes, E. 44
Rogers, C.R. 67
Rohleder, P. 92
Roscoe, S.O. 91
Ross, M. 46
Rosser, B. 46, 54
Rowen, C.J. 46

Sachperoglou, E. 126, 129
Saltzman, L.Y. 42
Samakouri, M. 127
Sani, F. 104
Segerstrom, S.C. 128, 129
Sewell, J. 56
Shaver, P.R. 66

Shernoff, M. 51, 164, 165, 166
Sherr, L. 50, 126, 127
Sikkema, K. 128, 131
Simoni, J.M. 174
Siraj, A. 44, 92, 121
Skinner, B.F. 70
Skinta, M.D. 49
Smit, P.J. 48
Smith, R.L. 37
Soni, S. 148
Spieldenner, A. 165
Steele, C. 47
Stonewall 43

Tajfel, H. 123
Tellegen, A. 193
Thomas, S. 57
Timotijevic, L. 89
Toppenberg, H. 129
Tugenberg T. 173

UNAIDS 36

van Rijn, B. 62
Vignoles, V.L. 89
Vranceanu, S. 172

Wachtel, P.L. 65
Wakefield, J.R.H. 104
Wakimoto, R. 128
Wang, X. 39
Ware, N.C. 173
Weatherburn, P. 57
Weaver, K.E. 131
Welles, S.L. 40, 41
West, S.G. 193
WHO 28
Wilfong, J.D. 191
Williams, S.L. 49
Williamson, I. 104
Willis, D.G. 42
Wills, T.A. 167
Wolf, M.S. 174
Wyatt, M.A. 173

Yip, A. 117

Zervoulis, K. 130

About the Author

Rusi Jaspal is Professor of Psychology and Sexual Health and Associate Pro Vice-Chancellor for Research at De Montfort University Leicester, UK. He is also an Adjunct Professor of Minority Research at Åbo Akademi University in Turku, Finland. He is a Chartered Psychologist and a Fellow of the British Psychological Society, a Fellow of the Royal Society of Public Health, and a Fellow of the Royal Society of Medicine. His research cuts across the fields of public health and psychology, focusing particularly on HIV. It examines (1) the social, psychological and behavioural correlates of sexual risk-taking, and (2) the social, psychological and behavioural aspects of living with HIV, particularly among men who have sex with men. In addition to his research role, Professor Jaspal sits on the Advisory Board of the Terrence Higgins Trust and on the editorial board of *HIV Medicine*. He is a member of the British HIV Association, the British Association for Sexual Health & HIV, and the British Psychological Society's Division of Clinical Psychology Faculty for HIV & Sexual Health. Rusi Jaspal is the co-editor (with Dame Glynis Breakwell) of *Identity Process Theory: Identity, Social Action and Social Change* (Cambridge University Press, 2014).